AF361480

WHAT'S IN
A NAME

The Olamot Series in the Humanities and Social Sciences translates
recent and innovative books by Israeli scholars with the goal of making
them more widely available to English-speaking audiences.
The series aims to reflect the originality and diversity of Israeli scholarship
by publishing books on a range of topics in Israel and Jewish Studies from
antiquity to today. The series encourages scholarship that broadens
its particular field from perspectives that have not been sufficiently
explored or brought into dialogue heretofore.

SERIES EDITORS:

Irit Dekel
Assistant Professor, Germanic Studies and
Borns Jewish Studies Program, Indiana University, and
Director of the Olamot Center for Scholarly and
Cultural Exchange with Israel

Jason Mokhtarian
Associate Professor and Herbert and Stephanie Neuman Chair
in Hebrew and Jewish Literature, Department of Near
Eastern Studies, Cornell University

Noam Zadoff
Assistant Professor in Israel Studies, Department of
Contemporary History, University of Innsbruck

WHAT'S IN A NAME

Stories behind Arabic-Palestinian Place-Names in Israel

—⚬—

AMER DAHAMSHE
TRANSLATED BY LEIGH CHIPMAN

OLAMOT SERIES IN THE HUMANITIES AND SOCIAL SCIENCES
IN ASSOCIATION WITH INDIANA UNIVERSITY PRESS
BLOOMINGTON

This book is a publication of

Indiana University Press
Herman B Wells Library
1320 East 10th Street
Bloomington, Indiana 47405 USA

iupress.org

First printing 2026

Library of Congress Cataloging-in-Publication Data
Names: Dahamshe, Amer, author | Chipman, Leigh translator
Title: What's in a name : stories behind Arabic-Palestinian place-names in
  Israel / Amer Dahamshe ; translated by Leigh Chipman.
Other titles: Maḳom la-dur bo ṿe-shem lo. English
Description: Bloomington, Indiana : Indiana University Press, [2026] |
  Series: Olamot series in the humanities and social sciences |
  Translation of: Maḳom la-dur bo ṿe-shem lo : ḳeri'ah sifrutit
  Ṿe-tarbutit ba-shemot ha-'Arviyim shel ha-arets = A local habitation and
  a name : a literary and cultural reading of the Arabic geographical
  names of the land. | Includes bibliographical references and index.
Identifiers: LCCN 2025033214 (print) | LCCN 2025033215 (ebook) | ISBN
  9780253075178 hardback | ISBN 9780253075185 paperback | ISBN
  9780253075208 ebook | ISBN 9780253075192 adobe pdf
Subjects: LCSH: Names, Geographical—Arabic | Names,
  Geographical—Israel—Galilee | Names, Geographical—Israel—Etymology
Classification: LCC DS103.5 .D3413 2026 (print) | LCC DS103.5 (ebook)
LC record available at https://lccn.loc.gov/2025033214
LC ebook record available at https://lccn.loc.gov/2025033215

CONTENTS

WHAT'S IN
A NAME

INTRODUCTION

Methodology, the Problem of Terminology, and the Theoretical Framework

ONE SPRING DAY IN THE 1980s, my family and I woke up to the sight of bulldozers, accompanied by Israeli policemen, ascending the hill called Jabal Sīkh in Kafr Kannā. At the time, I was a pupil in elementary school, and we could clearly see the hill from the school. My teacher explained to the class that the Jewish National Fund workers were leveling the hill and planting pine and cypress trees that would provide shade for us in the play areas that would be erected between the trees. Years passed, playgrounds were not erected, and the hill was partly settled by immigrants from the former Soviet Union and given a biblical name: Mount Yonah. My friends and I continued to call the hill by the name we heard from the elders of Kafr Kannā.[1]

This anecdote combines two motifs that characterize the practice of constructing space in Israel: on the one hand, the way the Palestinian minority, despite constituting one-fifth of the citizens of the state, is dispossessed of its language and lands and the way this is marketed by the Israeli education system; on the other hand, how the Palestinian minority continues to animate the land through its traditions and memories.

After the 1948 war, more than half of the Arab Palestinian population was deported by Zionist forces, and its lands were allocated to Jewish settlements (Kadman 2015). Most of the streams and fields that had belonged to Palestinian villages were cut off from their surroundings and enclosed by the boundaries of nature reserve fencing, hiking paths, kibbutzim, or paved roads. In addition to giving Hebrew names to newly founded settlements, Zionism erased the existing Palestinian terminology for towns and natural features by translating and Hebraizing it.

In Israel, Palestinian geographical names, including those of populated localities, sites, and natural features (like inanimate objects and plants), have an impressively long history, with a multitude of local stories that explain their formulation, whose many motifs arouse awe in those who learn about or study them.[2] These Arabic names are used colloquially by the population but have not received official status and have not served to establish political facts. They are, however, intracultural expressions, laden with social and ethnographic sediments, that encapsulate the affinity between Palestinian society and its environment. In some cases, they represent this society's mental map,[3] with different versions having accumulated based on the locality's periods of settlement, just like strata in an ancient archaeological mound. They are an expression of many layers of national, communal, and personal memories. Furthermore, they preserve Hebrew and Aramaic words and roots. The cultural and linguistic grace that the Palestinians expressed by preserving these place-names is worthy of reward. But what occurred in practice is the opposite of reward: linguistic expropriation (Dahamshe 2010), or the elimination of Arab and Palestinian identity from the landscape by erasing thousands of Palestinian place-names, distorting the forms of thousands of others, and limiting Palestinians' ability to be involved in the design of public space (Sorek 2017, 6). Edward Said argues that the conceptual system of early Zionism derived from colonialism: Zionism saw Palestine in the same way that imperialism viewed the colonies—as empty territories (Said 1978, 3–15, 83–114).

The origins of Palestinian geographical names, which were used when the Palestinian people were still an agricultural and seminomadic society, are largely hidden in the mists of the past. Most of these names were not recorded anywhere but were passed on by word of mouth, and some have been included in geographical maps only recently. For example, Abu-Sitta's *Atlas of Palestine in 1948* was published in London only in 2004. This atlas documents about thirty-six thousand names and is considered the first comprehensive geographical map of Palestinian names (Abu-Sitta 2004). Although these names live on in the memories of the society that uses them, their existence is tenuous; they have been overwritten by new names given to those places and have been ignored by Israeli institutions. Most of them do not form part of the linguistic landscape of the public sphere in Israel (Landry and Bourhis 1997, 25).[4] As a result, they are absent from research and academic discourse. The prevailing tendency to exclude names anchored in Palestinian tradition from research means a vital layer of the map of Israel/Palestine is ignored, to the detriment of both research and the historical political-cultural map of this land (Wild 1988, 106–11). This omission leads to an exclusive commemoration of names associated with the agents of official history and Jewish Israeli historiography while knowledge disseminated from social and popular history, as well as personal stories, is forgotten and deemed inconsistent with the hegemonic narrative (Levine and Shafir 2012). However, ignoring the popular tradition of place-names tends to result in partial and flawed research (Nicolaisen 1979, 164–68).

To confirm my remarks, I survey a number of studies that recognize the importance of sourcing spatial definitions from locals. The anthropologist Riva Berleant-Shiller (1991, 92–93, 100), who studied geographical names on the island of Bermuda in the Lesser Antilles, notes that field research and interviews with locals are important sources of ethnographic information, enabling the researcher to become familiar with names not represented on maps that, in turn, can illuminate and enrich theories and hypotheses in the field of toponymy. Linguistic anthropologists regard the geographical names and language by which people describe their environment as cultural documentation that provides vital information. This information pertains not only to the morphology of the physical environment and its contents but also to how humans perceive it and how the land is conceived (Basso 1988a, 103; 1988b, 48–51). Keith H. Basso (1990, 144) even goes so far as to claim that names are among "the most highly charged and richly evocative of all linguistic symbols," as they may "summon forth an enormous range of mental and emotional associations," including those related to history and social activities. The study of how natives of a place name their surroundings provides information that contributes to a comprehensive understanding of how a place is perceived and interpreted according to the cultural principles and values of the naming society.

Scholars from humanistic disciplines believe that name-givers and the use of names should be at the center of the study of toponymy (Thornton 1997). Locals are in constant contact with the sites where they live, and therefore their familiarity with these sites' names exceeds that of outsiders, however expert (Miller 2000, 138). Geographical-historical studies have also emphasized the importance of integrating society's perceptions of the environment. Geographical-historical reconstruction restores not only the facts of a bygone time but also the ways of life, the spirit, and the atmosphere of that time (Ben-Arieh 1974, 17). Since the 1980s, the importance of memories and oral sources as tools to fill information gaps and create meaning has increasingly been accepted among researchers of history, literature, and culture. Scholar of literature and oral history Alessandro Portelli points out the importance of oral history and the power of facts and reconstructing events and memories from the past to create existential meaning, through which researchers learn how the past is used to reflect collective consciousness (Thompson 2009, 28) and through which they can understand the culture under scrutiny as told by voices excluded from the canonical discourse (Yassif 2011, 12, 15).

In light of this, the purpose of this book is to present, classify, and, above all, analyze name legends in order to offer a causal explanation for the various categories of toponyms in current use by Palestinians in Israel while discussing the perception of name legends as a genre with specific content and poetic characteristics.[5] The study of place-names used by Palestinians is an interesting case, since the history of these names is very long. Complex historical, political, cultural, religious, and linguistic charges are preserved within these names, and therefore, they arouse controversy and tension. These names include Palestinian and extra-Palestinian traditions and linguistic elements from Arabic and other languages. Most of the names came into being before 1948—that is, before the establishment of the State of Israel—but after 1948, they underwent a process of colonization and Hebraization by Israeli name committees. In this respect, and in the spirit of the postcolonial approach, my research deals with the development of theoretical and analytical structures concerning cultural representations that have been pushed out of Western and Israeli research. Given that most studies in critical toponymy have focused more on European and North American street names and their political significance and less on those of other regions of the world, including Latin America, Africa, and Asia (Bigon 2016, 4–5), this book fills a lacuna by exploring another geographical region: Israel/Palestine. I believe that studying the place-names created and used by the Palestinian minority living in Israel can enrich the study of place-names in general.

This book on Palestinian geographical names examines their pronunciation in local dialects, how they came into being, the motifs and themes underlying their bestowal, how they are perceived, and the cultural message that emerges from them. Its analysis provides an etiological explanation for the bestowal of these names, whose origin is explained in the local stories of the Palestinian minority as well as in popular explanations and their communal and autobiographical memories—as reflected in the ethnographic interviews I conducted with Palestinians, the users of these names.

The book demonstrates how Palestinians perceive themselves as the inheritors of various cultures despite the disruption of their culture and the erasure of important parts of it caused by the State of Israel upon its founding in 1948. The Palestinian names are not necessarily definitive or essential representations but rather partly influenced by historical and political variables and the conflict between the Hebrew and Arabic languages, which is part of the struggle over the identity of places in Israel.

The first step in this journey of discovery was locating the names and their origin stories. In Israel, one of the main purposes of the Dov Noy Israel Folk Story Archive (IFSA), founded in 1955, is to "rescue from oblivion the folk stories passed down by word of mouth . . . among the various ethnic groups *who immigrated to Israel or live in it,* and this by collecting them" (my emphasis).[6] But this goal has not been met when it comes to Arab folktales: the number of stories in the IFSA is 25,000, of which 2,200 stories are in Arabic (8.8%) and of which no more than 0.2 percent are Palestinian stories about the names of places.[7] The status of the names used by Palestinian society in Israeli academic institutions is an expression of Israeli academia's complex political attitude toward the spatial and linguistic heritage of Palestinian society and possibly a reflection of the State of Israel's attitude regarding the heritage of its Palestinian citizens.

Faced with this reality, I went to Arab-populated localities to record and write down the local communities' explanations for the names of settlements and natural features. The basis of this book is hundreds of oral narrative traditions and popular explanations for the names of various places, collected during fieldwork in Palestinian communities within the Green Line—Muslim, Christian, Bedouin, and Druze.[8] The common factor for choosing the names that are at the center of the analysis is thematic: they all have a causal explanation. Thus, the etiological story that repeats throughout the book links its chapters.

The process of learning the stories of place-names began with an appeal to acquaintances and intermediaries (contact persons) from the investigated localities, who recommended potential informants, but thereafter, the task of locating "effective" informants was not easy. After an initial meeting, the most suitable informants were selected, according to their ability to serve my research needs and according to the quality of their performance of narrative storytelling. When concern arose that a certain informant was concealing an explanation of a particular name—because of its association with a religious sect of which the informant was not a member, because the content of the name might arouse intersocial tension (such as a name that dishonored a family), or because it sounded dubious—I looked for additional stories from other informants.

The selected informants were residents local to the places whose names I wished to investigate. The population of informants is diverse in terms of age, sex, religious affiliation, and education level.[9] The meetings took place in the informants' houses, usually in private, but sometimes other people were present who also took part in the storytelling process by adding a comment or reference.

As mentioned, the informants transmitted etiological stories related to the naming of places. The stories were recorded with a tape recorder, and I transcribed and translated the recordings. Since the emphasis is on the etiology of the place-name—that is, the meaning of the name in the narrative medium—the informants were requested to tell the reasons for the name being given, within the framework of the tale. My presence during the storytelling and my direction of the informants were central factors in the creation of the monographs about the names.

During my visits to the villages, I heard quite a few informants complain about the Judaization and alienation of Palestinian territory—either by physical expropriation or by the systematic replacement of Arabic with Hebrew. The informants' evaluation of historical-folk sources and local tales is ambivalent. It is divided between a minority who saw the folk-historical legends as fictional inventions and a majority who viewed them as historical, reliable, and authentic sources. Casting doubt on the stories about the places' names can indicate a lack of awareness or sensitivity on the part of Palestinian society about how vital these stories are in creating feelings of belonging and ownership. It was easy to see the extent of the ignorance regarding local toponyms among the members of this culture. When I asked potential informants about the causal explanation for a place-name, more than once I received the answer: "How should we know! These are names we inherited from our ancestors." The situation is especially serious among the young, who constantly memorize Israeli names, to which they are exposed through Israeli media and the signage system that the State of Israel places on the roads. In effect, forgetting Palestinian heritage—not least of all Palestinian place-names—as a cultural and historical phenomenon has occurred and is occurring in parallel projects, among both Jewish Israelis and Palestinian Arabs. A similar situation happened to the Palestinian cities (Ḥasan 2017), which were forgotten by the Zionist movement and by the Palestinians after 1948, although this forgetfulness of both the names and the cities stems from different processes in each of the two societies, the Palestinian and the Israeli.

THE QUESTION OF TERMINOLOGY: ISRAEL/ PALESTINE AND OTHER TERMS

To be aware of the political significance of academic knowledge means to accept that the language of research is also politically loaded (Feige 2002, 15–16). Some of the concepts I use have an ideological charge and are themselves a product of the Israeli-Palestinian political conflict related to space and the

Israeli and Palestinian national narratives—I mean the use made in this book of language and terminology, such as Israel/Palestine, Palestinians / Israeli Arabs, *Palestinian names,* or *Israeli names.* The area I am discussing has undergone political upheavals, as a result of which different names have been attached to it. During the British Mandate, the official name of the region was Palestine. From 1921 to 1947, this name refers to the territory included today in the area of the State of Israel, the West Bank, and the Gaza Strip, and not merely to the territory that today is under the control of the Palestinian Authority. With the end of the mandate period in 1948, the State of Israel was established as part of the 1947 United Nations partition plan for Palestine. In the aftermath of the war that immediately broke out, Israel's borders, shaped by its achievements in the war, were wider than those recognized by the partition plan (Shenhav 2010, 10–12). Most Palestinians were exiled and became refugees outside the State of Israel. The minority that remained in the territory of the Jewish state received citizenship but did not enjoy full equality. As a direct result of the establishment of the State of Israel, the institutions of the state call the territory it controls "Israel" and converted thousands of Palestinian place-names from Arabic to Hebrew as part of a process of creating political capital. These place-names are very ancient and were used by the native population for hundreds of years before the foundation of the State of Israel (Clermont-Ganneau 1876). Given this situation, the use of the term *Palestinian names* and its derivatives—for example, "the names of the Arab Palestinian community"—is more appropriate than the term *Israeli names* and fits the identity of the indigenous names and of those who created them. In contrast to the Israeli viewpoint, in the Palestinian historical perspective, the territory on which Israel was established is Palestine and its place-names are Palestinian.

Using certain terms and preferring them over others may cause biased research. For example, the use of the name Palestine betrays the notion that the space is the property of the Palestinians and that the Jews have no claim to it. The use of the name Israel or Land of Israel is problematic for the same reason; it establishes a sense of ownership between the place and its Jewish residents while potentially implying that Palestinians lack a connection to this land. How do we deal with the nomenclature?

In this book, I considered it appropriate to use the emic and etic approaches common in ethnographic research. The emic approach utilizes internal cultural terms characteristic of the members of the culture being studied, while the etic approach employs the scientific language necessary for researchers to engage in discussion and analysis (Berry 1999, 166–68).[10] Therefore, this research is based on scientific-professional terms, without abandoning the integration of significant terms from the point of view of the members of the studied culture. Some of the informants identified themselves, directly or indirectly, as Palestinians, while others identified themselves as Israeli Arabs. Hence, I used both terms, Palestinians and Arabs, depending on the narrative context and the informants' perspectives. The use of the terms Palestine, the State of Israel, and the Land of Israel is also in accordance with these considerations, as is the use of the terms *Palestinian names, the names of the Arab Palestinian community,* and *Israeli names.*

Another matter that requires clarification is the proximity of the concepts "Arab society" and "Bedouin society," or the use of the terms Bedouins and Arabs. As we know, these are two distinct ways of life, and using the two terms and their derivatives to indicate Arab culture that is common to both is sometimes misleading. However, traditional Arab society and its basic values resembled the values of Bedouin society in certain aspects—for example, the status of the leader and women's roles. These two social forms drew from the substrate of the general Arab culture that they share (Ginat 2000, 44–45). In this spirit, my use of the two terms—*Arab society* and *Bedouin society*—in analyses of certain etiologies indicates the cultural foundations common to both.

In research, distinction is made between habitat names or place-names to specify the names of settlements and populated localities, on the one hand, and geographical names, or names of natural features, to specify the names of geographical formations such as caves, streams, trees, plots of land, and so on, on the other. Typically, research focuses on the names of settlements and their documentation, while the study of the names of natural features is often overlooked. This book seeks to fill this void, and therefore, it focuses on the motifs of both the names of populated localities and the names of natural features. As part of a critical discussion of the research conducted so far in this field, the book aims to disrupt the unity of the concept of "geographical names," in our case Palestinian names, and will highlight the potential inherent in separate categories of analysis for names of populated localities and names of natural features. Thus, this book shifts the study of names from the geographical and linguistic field to the cultural and ethnographic realms.

THE GENRE CONTEXT OF PLACE-NAME STORIES

Examining the explanations of names in the stories also necessitates clarification of the literary genre to which the narratives about place-names in this book belong. The criteria concerning the origins of place-names and their interpretation, as well as the factors that influenced the formation of these expressions, are the thematic elements that characterize the place-name stories in this book and enable an interpretive connection between them. The literary genre to which the corpus of stories belongs had a decisive influence on my research approach and on my understanding of the meaning and function of these texts. Classification of folktales by types is a basic tool for creating a common language among researchers of folk literature (Toelken 1979, 152–53).

The place-name stories in the book belong to the legend genre, known in German as *Sage*, and to the following subgenres: foundation legend, historical legend, and local legend or local story. Legends usually express social matters and expected rules of conduct and are concerned with everyday life and some kind of belief. The individual legend is anchored in historical time and in the geographical space of the narrator. The characters that inhabit it may be historical characters identified by name, or supernatural figures, such as demons and spirits, which according to the narrating society exist alongside humans. The legend genre enlists the listeners' trust in the narrative and establishes itself as a significant element in the collective memory (Alexander-Frizer 2008, 169; Hasan-Rokem 2000, 39–43, 146–52; Yassif 1999b, 15–23; Tangherlini 1990, 371–80).

A foundation legend is a story of an etiological nature that explains the origin of place-names and the natural features they reference. Foundation legends seek to explain a way of life in the past or in the present, and they refer to the foundation of a community in a new place (Bar-Itzhak 2001, 14–17). A historical legend is a tale in which a connection to historical events and a well-known figure is revealed. Some of its main functions are to shape the audience's consciousness of the past and increase trust in the narrator by using truthlike details. These details remind the listeners of details that are familiar to them (or have verisimilitude) from reality and from their society's collective memory (Hasan-Rokem 2000, 148). Local legends or local stories are foundation stories—etiological stories that explain the origin of a place-name or of unusual features in the environment, such as an oddly shaped stream, a strange rock, and even man-made objects (Yassif 2005, vi; Shenhar 2001, 165). Sometimes the origins of the names in the examined corpus are shaped in relation to a historical event or a historical figure, while others are attributed to natural features of the place. Some names are connected to events in local society or are derived from a foreign language.

Another matter relating to nomenclature is my use of the terms *place, space, nature,* and *landscape.* By these terms, I intend the physical surroundings of the environment represented in the narrative text and the array of natural features that inhabit this text, such as mountains, streams, trees and vegetation, cliffs, and more.

Another terminological question concerns the use of the word *story* in the study of folk literature. Some of the texts collected as part of this study do clearly maintain the classic story structure, which includes an opening, a plot, and an ending. However, in some texts this structure is violated. In this context, I decided not to employ the analytical categories used to define the term *story* by the linguist William Labov (Labov and Waletsky 1967, 12–13). As an alternative, I adopted the suggestions of the folklore researcher Dan Ben-Amos, who suggests applying the ethnic categories of the genre to the narrative expression and its literary forms, that is, applying the terms used by the speakers of the language to define their culture. These terms and the explanations transmitted by members of the culture are essential for understanding folk sayings and the value position of the genre as a whole in the culture in question (Ben-Amos 1975, 141–42). According to Ben-Amos, texts that lack a solid and analytically complete structure can also be considered stories because the narrators perceive them to be so.

This book does not explore the historical and linguistic evolution of names over time but rather the historical and linguistic significance of place-names and their stories as artistic-cultural expressions whose literary, cognitive, and cultural aspects are relevant to the speakers in a synchronic and contextual dimension. However, the book's discussion is linked to the general context of historical and local events in the area and to social and geopolitical processes. The book seeks to reveal the interpretation and significance of the place-names in the local inhabitants' cultural space. Engagement with names as a cultural practice that depicts a worldview deep within the linguistic forms of names is one of this book's purposes. The prevailing trends in international studies of place-names, in general, and with reference to the Arab world in particular, involve obvious issues: the meaning of the names, their linguistic development, and their identification with the locale. The topic of place-names has been addressed in historical (e.g., Room 1997, 17–419; Stewart 1975, 371–76), geographical-topographical (e.g., Zinkin 1984, 252–57), and linguistic (e.g., Abū Muṣliḥ 1989, 75–452) contexts, and recently attention has been paid to political and national aspects and to social power relations, mainly in the context of naming urban streets (e.g., Yeoh 1996, 298–305). A notable advantage of this book is its study of names through the literary traditions of the local society, in our case Palestinian society, and through the local lenses, that is, looking at the names and their uses among this community.

To the best of my knowledge, previous studies seldom addressed place-names in the context of the literary unit of the folk tale and its emic (internal cultural) interpretation.[11] This lack and, of course, the complexity of the research subject motivated me to devote myself to the subject of this book. Palestinian place-names have hardly been examined as a corpus with distinct taxonomic characteristics. In these respects, the book fills several gaps. This is the first time that the Palestinian names of places are discussed as semiotic expressions, as well as works of spatial significance, that go beyond the sounds of the names, the material structure of the space, and the places themselves.

A MODEL FOR ANALYZING PLACE-NAME STORIES

The stories of the place-names connect the etiological legends and the space (the place). The study of place-name stories is interpretive and phenomenological, occurring at the intersection of various fields: folk traditions, literature, toponymy, language contact, semiotics, geography, historical events, and communication.

According to the literary method, the analysis of a literary work should involve intraliterary tools and focus solely on elements within the text (Amir 2016). The interpretive point of departure in this book tends to be based on the text, but at the same time, it makes use of extraliterary contexts: cultural, historical, and ideological questions, parallel texts, and more. Combining intraliterary and extraliterary tools is one of the principles of interpretative-scientific research among folklore researchers, who perceive folk creation as having inherent characteristics and being situated in a cultural-social context (Sims and Stephens 2005, 19–20, 63).

The methods of analysis presented here are applicable to various literary texts. However, legends about geographical names possess distinct characteristics. The fundamental aspect of these legends is the principle of causality, which helps explain the name's meaning, the process of its formation, and the reason for assigning it to a specific place. In order to exhaust the elements of language and content that apply to the onomastic aspects of the names in the stories, I propose a five-layered model, as follows:

1. The linguistic-stylistic layer: This layer focuses on the textual fabric—the way the name is pronounced, its formation, and its narrative meaning—as well as on the stylistic-poetic elements (symbol, metaphor, etc.) woven into the place-name. In this layer, the intratextual connections between the name (an excerpt

from the text) and the story that explains it (the text) must be examined as a linguistic sequence.

2. The content layer: This layer is concerned with the content present in the story of the place-name, such as characters, events, locales, times, and more.

3. The traditional-semiotic layer: Sometimes the rationale of the name or the thematic elements that establish it are drawn from the traditional-semiotic pool of ancient traditions, beliefs, assumptions, and sources.

4. The interpretive layer: This connects the various elements constructed in reference to the first two layers, and its goal is to reach abstraction and formulate an idea that seeks to say something about the reality outside the text.

5. The referential layer (spatial representation): This layer concerns the way space is presented and depicted.[12]

Completing the study of etiological stories about place-names requires formulating the internal conventions of these works as a type and as a cultural phenomenon with the help of several theoretical approaches. The structuralist approach associated with the anthropologist Claude Lévi-Strauss (1963a) and, similarly, the hermeneutic method diverted researchers' attention from the description of relations in society and the description of visible cultural values to studying the meanings inherent in them. Texts must be understood as symbols that, from the start, express more than their literal and primary meaning. The direct initial meaning signifies and hints at another, indirect meaning. The structuralist approach distinguishes between visible structures and hidden ones, and it is the researcher's task to uncover the latter. This approach emphasizes binary contrasts as crucial for the production of hidden meanings in culture (Lévi-Strauss 1966, 93–95; Levy 1976, 76–95). Lévi-Strauss (1969) examined the names of people and places in totemic tribal cultures as hidden structures, as ciphers that interact with the belief system and rules of behavior of the society that bestowed the names.

The materials examined in this book are oral literary forms that are part of what the historian Fernand Braudel (1980, 25–54) called the *longue durée* of life. That is, they refer to long-lasting social phenomena and human activities that have continued for hundreds and even thousands of years. The possibility of chronologically determining the time of creation of the narrative traditions under study is limited, and therefore, Lévi-Strauss's approach is suitable as a theoretical framework for discussion. However, Lévi-Strauss's conclusions concerning the hierarchical relations between humans ("culture"—in our case, the givers of names) and the ecological environment ("nature"—in our case, the space given names) cannot be accepted unquestioningly, since the significances of the relationship between humans and nature can be complex. Linguistic anthropology and folklore emphasize the importance of field studies (Foley 1977, 1–5). They examine how native modes of geographical naming organize space according to ethnographic principles and cultural beliefs (Lévi-Strauss 1969).

The semiotic approach, according to Deborah Cameron and Thomas Markus (2002, 8–9, 32–33) and others, examines the relationship between sign systems, as a process of communication that can clarify meanings and messages and is related to social processes, following the linguist Ferdinand de Saussure (1974, 32–33). The existence of the message is conditioned, among other things, on the existence of an addressee, a recipient, a social context, and an intention. Apart from their primary role as spatial markers, place-names are a kind of text that bears a message and has a hidden symbolic meaning. The message is expressed in the spatial identity place-names create, through their morphology or in their grammatical form and gender.

A cultural interpretation aimed at discovering the meaning and message of place-names is at the foundation of these approaches. Literary critic and semiotician Roland Barthes used the semiotic approach to investigate myth. He sees a kind of myth, in the sense of ideology and the creation of meaning, in speech and other cultural products. Semiology assumes the existence of a relationship between the signifier, the signified, and the sign, which is the product of the first two terms combined. "Myth is a peculiar system in that it is constructed from a semiological chain which existed before it: it is a *second-order semiological system*" (Barthes 1977, 114–15; emphasis in the original).

As a whole, place-names form a signifying system on two levels (compare Darzie 1993, 50). The system marks, on the immediate level, the inhabited locality itself and, on the second level, the history, culture, and ideology, that is, the message and meaning encoded in the names. An example of duality expressed in the nature of a place is the city of Tel Aviv. At the immediate level, the reference to Tel Aviv is as a city founded by Jews on the coast of the Mediterranean Sea next to the city of Jaffa, which was mostly inhabited by Arabs. On the second level, the mythical level, it articulates the essence of the city in terms of the Zionist idea that it was meant to embody—the first Hebrew city established as part of the Zionist settlement project.[13]

Place-names are signifiers, and their signifieds are the places identified by them. The relationship between the signifier and the signified is fundamentally a cultural act, and like language itself, according to de Saussure, it is arbitrary.

This means that there is no necessary connection between the name of the place—that is, the signifier—and the place marked by it. In structuralist terms, the myth produces the cultural logic according to which the connection can be considered not as arbitrary but rather as bridging the contrast between nature and culture (Hasan-Rokem 2012, 277–82).

The "critical turn" in the study of place-names began after the 1990s. Critical approaches, such as postmodernism, postcolonialism, and critical toponymy, occupy a central place in the study of the naming of places and emphasize the process of "production" of names and examining them in broad contexts. The use of critical tools to examine the categories that geographical names create and blur allows us to comprehend the symbolism of naming, the control of the landscape by political forces, and how the history and cultural image of the space are presented. Geographic naming is regarded as a practice related to creating and replicating power relations in space and sociopolitical dynamics (Garth 2009, 237; Rose-Redwood, Alderman, and Azaryahu 2010, 455).

The analysis of place-names is part of a discussion of the relations between society and space. The concept that dominates research nowadays is the "production of space," per the phrase coined by the philosopher Henri Lefebvre (1991, 73–80), where space is an object of ideological and social activity. In cultural and modern geography, the concept of the landscape as a combination of a physical-material layer and a cultural layer is widespread. The cultural and literary construction of the landscape turns it into a resource that is also ideological, social, economic, and symbolic (Cosgrove 1984, 13; Lefebvre 1991, 36–39). Places and landscapes in literature and culture are loaded with symbolic value. The place or the sense of place—that is, the type of attachment that people have to their physical environment, their awareness of it, and the meaning they attribute to it as expressed in their culture (Shamai 1991, 347–49)—is a cultural construction, just as it is an existential-physical experience (Lefebvre 1991, 7–30). The toponymic practices and the names that people give to their surroundings are an expression of the perception of the place and its cultural and ideological design (Dahamshe 2021a). The anthropologist Edmond Leach (1976, 33–34) describes humans as creating their world through linguistic and symbolic construction. Giving names to natural features is a symbolic action that means defining them through language and turning nature itself into a usable resource. Based on Leach, Daniella Arieli (1997, 199–203) regards naming as a three-step process: (a) isolating the object, naming that distinguishes it from its surroundings; (b) imparting some meaning to the object by the observer, for example, through traditional verses of poetry that relate to it; and (c) turning the object into a symbolic resource for the collective—that is, the object becomes a link between the people, their heritage, and the place. Place-names are an expression of cultural and political relics and landscapes (Kliot 1994, 113–14; Berg and Kearns 1996, 105). The geographer Christopher Tilley examines the identity of places as depicted by their names. Assigning a name to a topographic landmark is of vital importance for constructing the landmark's identity and ensuring its enduring significance. An empty and meaningless piece of land gains life and a unique character through the name given to it by humans (Tilley 1994, 18). Toponymic addresses (name signs, accurate city maps) do not always appear in the city. The study of landscapes and places assumes that the space shows evidence of the culture and worldview of the people who live or lived in that landscape. This approach calls for deciphering the terminology of the space as a "text" even if there is no written text there, thus promoting a view of the landscape as a text instead of looking for a text in the landscape (Duncan and Duncan 1988, 117–26).

The viewpoints and approaches described here are reflected in the research method used in this book: On one level, it requires examining textual elements that describe the names' origins and their meanings. On another level, it involves uncovering the semiotic aspects related to the idea arising from the names and the spatial significance hidden within these expressions. This is achieved through phenomenological-interpretive tools, particularly by investigating the interpretation and meanings given to the geographical environment by the namers and the symbolic dimensions they attribute to the space. In essence, the book examines the link between modernity and the impact of social and ideological power relations on the landscape's design and the presentation of the space's history. In practice, I wish to take the study of names from the level of analyzing individual texts and demonstrating themes through investigation and interpretation—while selecting additional names and fragments from other name stories whose themes are related to these texts—to a description of the poetic characteristics of Palestinian toponymy.

A common principle in the study of geographical names is categorizing them with reference to current research. Therefore, the first chapter deals with the generic terms represented in the names and the classification of their sources and the surrounding data. It also provides a review and critical discussion of the state of research on place-names in Israel. In the second chapter, the main legends linking the arrival of Muslim warriors to Palestine and the adoption of names of populated localities are discussed, as are the influence of local leaders on the formation of Palestinian names of this type. The reflection of the natural environment, especially its fauna, in the names of populated localities, and the images of the Jews and people from other cultural traditions in these names, are also discussed.

The third chapter deals with the influence of ethnographic and local identities on the formation of names of natural features, under the subheadings of the marks left by the common people and peasants, the Palestinian woman, and figures from the British Mandate period. In addition, this chapter deals with the figurative language of the names of natural features and with agriculture in names of this type.

As a result of the distinct themes between the names of populated localities and those of natural features, the fourth chapter examines how society's symbolic perception of the geographical surroundings structures the environment in a dichotomous and hierarchical manner. I show how the practice of distinguishing the contents of the names and their spatial location is a semiotic expression of the perception of a place's name and its status, as well as of gender and class differentiation. In the fifth chapter, the different angles of observation, which dictated separate discussions, come together at the end of the research process to present the essence of Arab Palestinian toponymy and its various layers as a whole.

The five chapters converge to form an ethnopoetic discussion of place-name legends. The etiological foundations and the ethnolinguistic and sociolinguistic aspects, which are at the base of the toponymic discourse of this culture, make—so I hope—the book as a whole greater than the sum of its parts.

ONE

—∿—

THE STUDY OF PALESTINIAN PLACE-NAMES

Between Theory and Ideology

THE PLACE-NAMES OF PALESTINE/ISRAEL FORM an interesting case study in toponymy not only because they have been examined by parties, both foreign and local, with orientations of various kinds but also because the results of this examination show how researchers perceive the Other and their culture. Additionally, it reveals how theoretical and methodological starting points affect the way toponymic knowledge is produced and how the history and identity of a place are represented. Scholars writing from the postcolonial perspective have shown how Western researchers' epistemological perception of Eastern peoples in general, and of the Palestinians in particular, as groups devoid of history and culture caused their research to be biased (Rabinowitz 1998, 35–36; Young 2003, 2–3). Another point that has affected the representation of linguistic identity and the way research developed is the European—and following it, the Zionist—hierarchical conceptualization that placed Europeans and Zionist founders at the center and top and non-Western peoples and the Palestinians at the margins (Young 2003, 2). This hierarchy was also expressed in geographical names, with Hebrew names seen as the standard and Palestinian names as an illegitimate Other. Accordingly, knowledge about place-names in Israel/Palestine has been managed along the axis of center versus periphery (Dahamshe 2021a).

Evidence of initial scholarly interest in Arabic names of the region known today as Palestine/Israel can be found in the writings of medieval Arab and Jewish travelers. Western explorers who came to the region in the late nineteenth and early twentieth centuries evinced particular interest in the Arabic forms of place-names in Israel/Palestine.[1] After the establishment of the State of Israel in 1948, first Jewish Israeli writers and later Palestinian Arab authors published

17

books and articles on the names of places in Israel/Palestine. The perusal of publications on Israeli and Palestinian names reveals that the topic of names in this territory was largely discussed under three main aspects: identifying the locations and meanings of toponyms, linguistic phenomena in toponyms, and toponyms in political contexts.

STUDIES THAT IDENTIFY THE LOCATIONS OF TOPONYMS, THEIR MEANINGS, AND THEIR INTERPRETATIONS

In the fourth century CE, Eusebius, bishop of Caesarea, published the *Onomasticon of the Land of Israel*. The *Onomasticon* included the names of the places mentioned in the Bible (except for the books of Writings) and in the New Testament (Eusebius 2003).

The medieval Arab geographers treated Palestinian toponyms both as a subject in themselves and as an integral part of the Arabic names of the lands of al-Shām (Greater Syria) during the period of Muslim rule.[2] In their research, they relied on passages from Arabic poetry and manuscripts. These geographers presented the written form of the name based on identical and unchanging rules of grammar and phonetics and only rarely noted the spoken form of the name as pronounced by locals.[3]

In the fourteenth century, Ashtori ha-Parḥi examined 180 ancient names of settlements, rivers, locations, and so on and compared them to the contemporary Arabic names. Ha-Parḥi acted on religious motives and subordinated the Arabic forms of the names to the Hebrew forms of place-names mentioned in the scriptures: "And I will inform you that the names of the towns and rivers written in the holy Written and Oral Scriptures have been but little changed by the Ishmaelites" (Ha-Parḥi 1897, 245). Ha-Parḥi viewed the Arabic forms of the names as a means to reconstruct names of places mentioned in the Holy Scriptures.

In the nineteenth century, travelers from Western countries began to explore the Holy Land. The most important were Edward Robinson, a minister and biblical scholar, and Eli Smith, a missionary and scholar. Their approach was also motivated by religion; in their opinion, the Arabic place-names contained the ancient Hebrew names and therefore these names were mobilized to "redeem" the biblical sites and their names (Robinson [1856] 1970). Arabic names were written in Robinson and Smith's maps and indexes in a consistent transliteration into Latin letters that, while being mostly faithful to the dictionary form, rarely reflects the local pronunciation. The Orientalist Western travelers of this time aimed to discover the land of the Bible and were deaf to the voice of local society. This is evidenced by the words of Charles Simon Clermont-Ganneau, who warned European researchers not to omit the point of view of the Palestinian Arabs (Clermont-Ganneau 1876, 199). Clermont-Ganneau's ideas found a response in the detailed Arabic and English name lists in the *Survey of Western Palestine* (Conder and Kitchener 1881). In this book, published in 1881 on behalf of the Palestine Exploration Fund, the names of inhabited localities and natural features were collected. The Arabic entry is written in Arabic letters next to its English transliteration and dictionary interpretation.[4]

Beginning in the second half of the twentieth century, members of the Israeli Names Committees published a number of essays dealing with Hebrew toponymy in Israel, within which framework they included references to Arabic toponymy. Among the members of these committees were Isaiah Press, Ze'ev Vilnai, Naftali Kadmon (who did not deal with Arabic toponymy), and Yehuda Ziv. Press was one of the most prominent scholars in this field, and in his 1951 encyclopedia, he related the names of inhabited localities and topographical forms. The linguistic form of each name is provided in Hebrew and Arabic. In Vilnai's (1955) book, the names of inhabited localities were given according to their types and origins. Vilnai's words imply that the Hebrew form "did a favor" to the Arabic name because the latter apparently only took on meaning after Hebraization (Vilnai 1982a).

Naftali Kadmon (2004) included in his book the names listed in the card catalog of place-names at the Center for Mapping in Israel. The names approved by the Governmental Names Committee from 1951 onward are collected in this book. In practice, this meant that most Arabic names were not included in this lexicon, because the relevant Israeli authority granted legal status to the Hebrew names but refused to recognize Arabic ones. In Ziv's book (2005), only Hebrew entries were presented, with each entry indicating its geographical location, the meaning of the name, and the history of the Hebrew settlement there. Here, too, the author ignored the Arabic forms of the names: the number of those even mentioned is very small.

According to Vilnai, Ziv, and Kadmon, the Arabic names are linguistic forms that preserve biblical, Mishnaic, and Talmudic names with slight distortions. In most of the essays published by Israeli scholars serving on the name committees, we find a widespread phenomenon of Judaization of Arabic toponyms. Hebraization of these toponyms became a formal expression on the basis of whose sounds the Hebrew name is "redeemed" and Hebrew names for new settlements are determined.

Generally, the researchers serving on the Israeli name committees did not provide evidence to prove that it was the Arabs who borrowed the Hebrew names and not the other way around. The assertion that the original names are Hebrew ones that have been corrupted may stem from the assumption that the Arabs, and especially the Bedouins, are the descendants of the ancient Jews, who abandoned their religion but not their country.[5] Perhaps this assumption also arises because Hebrew written sources appear earlier than Arabic ones, in particular regarding the Land of Israel.

In addition to the publications presented here, there are Israeli publications that deal with Arabic naming in its geohistorical and linguistic sense without tying it to the issue of the precedence of the Hebrew Jewish presence in historical Palestine. An example of this is the *Mappa Encyclopedia*, which includes a prominent and broad quantitative representation of Palestinian toponymy. Here, the names of the settlements and of natural features in Hebrew and Arabic (including "what has disappeared," as defined by the editors) appear according to their types, locations, and origins (*Mappa Encyclopedia* 2000).

As for place-names in Arabic books, the first Palestinian reference work is the encyclopedia *Our Land Palestine* (Bilādunā Filasṭīn), written by the Palestinian exile Muṣṭafā al-Dabbāgh in 1967. This encyclopedia covered a wide range of topics: place-names, history, flora and fauna, and geography until 1948 (al-Dabbāgh [1967] 2003). In 1988, al-Dabbāgh published an essay dealing with the reflection of local flora and fauna in Arabic place-names (al-Dabbāgh 1988). In 1980, Constantine Khammār published a book listing the names of inhabited localities, natural landscapes, and man-made sites in Palestine until 1948. Along with the dictionary Arabic form of the name and its location on the map, he cited the Hebrew name given to each place after 1948 (Khammār 1980). In 2000, a dictionary was published that includes interpretations of the names of Palestinian cities and villages (Sharrāb 2000). In 2001, another book was published that includes a geographical listing of the Palestinian names presented as Hebrew ones in maps, atlases, and geographical records written in Israel ('Abd al-Karīm 2001). In 2004, a lexicon was published that includes the names of Palestinian cities and villages, together with their literal meanings (Lubbānī 2004).

Most of the Arab scholars listed here propose interpretations for the names of inhabited localities based on the dictionary definitions, and when the Arabic language fails to serve these writers, the names are identified as Canaanite, Phoenician, Syriac, and Aramaic, according to phonetic similarity. These researchers considered the place-names of Palestine to be Palestinian and Arab.

In 2004, Shukrī 'Arrāf compiled a list of geographical locations in Palestine/Israel. The emphasis there is on identifying the locations of the Arab Palestinian names of villages, cities, and natural features. Next to the name in Arabic, the name appears in phonetic transcription and in Hebrew, as determined by the Israeli names committees.

A perusal of the introductions to the Arabic works reviewed here shows that one of the authors' goals is to perpetuate the Palestinian names and preserve them in the face of Zionist elements working to erase and Judaize the landscapes of Arab Palestine. The publication of Palestinian works beginning in the 1960s—that is, twelve years after the 1948 war and about a decade after the publication of the first Israeli works—indicates that the Arabic books are a reaction to Zionist political activity and publications. Prior to the 1960s, Palestinian activity concerning place-names did not hold symbolic significance in the balance of power between Israelis and Palestinians. A similar idea emerges from the words of Meron Benvenisti (1988, 138): "The drawing of their maps is the answer to our maps. By the power of their subjective will, they try to preserve the old reality, the reality we have erased."

STUDIES OF LINGUISTIC PHENOMENA CHARACTERISTIC OF TOPONYMS

In the handful of studies published by Western researchers starting in the second half of the nineteenth century, there was a focus on purely linguistic phenomena. The work of Georg Kampffmeyer, who mobilized the Arabic form as a means to study linguistic processes that occurred in the biblical form, is frequently cited. Wilhelm Borée (1968) also focuses on a linguistic analysis of geographical names in the Land of Israel against the background of biblical names.

In the last two decades of the twentieth century, three studies were published that dealt with place-names in the linguistic and grammatical context. The first is a doctoral thesis on the history of sixty names preserved by the Arabs from the *Onomasticon* of the aforementioned church father Eusebius (Elitzur 1993), which was later published as a book (Elitzur 2004). Next to each name is an analysis of the grammatical phenomena that appear in the changes the name underwent. The second work discusses the Arabic place-names of Palestine as part of the place-names of Greater Syria. The entries in this study were taken from medieval Arab geographical writings. Next to each entry is its geographical location and usually also its lexical meaning as well as the identification of its historical-linguistic roots and their development (al-Ḥilw 1999). The third essay deals with place-names in the tannaitic literature from the linguistic point of view, identifying the names' locations (Greenzweig 2000).

STUDIES OF TOPONYMS IN POLITICAL CONTEXTS

The toponymy of the "Hebrew map" has played a distinct political and national role in shaping the landscape identity of Israel and in how the land's history has been presented. Studies published by Israeli geographers from the end of the twentieth century onward examine Israeli name-giving in its political and diplomatic context.[6]

The geographers Soul Cohen and Nurit Kliot focused on the names given to settlements in the Occupied Territories. In their research, the two examine the process of naming as a practice that reflects the influence of political-national power relations on the design of the map of place-names in these territories (Cohen and Kliot 1992, 658–76). The geographer Yossi Katz (1998, 108–14) discusses the struggle of the Jewish community against the British and the Arabs regarding the representation of Hebrew names on the maps of the British Mandate government in Palestine. The geographer Maoz Azaryahu and his colleagues focus their research on Hebraization and the construction of Zionist geography and its political symbolism (Golan and Azaryahu 2004, 264–65; Azaryahu and Kellerman 1999, 111–19). An exception in terms of self-criticism and familiarity with the Palestinian side is the writing of Meron Benvenisti (2000, 5–54), in which a comparison between the map of Israel's Department of Surveys and the map printed by the Palestinians in 1983 is drawn, highlighting the destruction that Zionism brought on Palestinian toponymy.

What does the examination of essays and studies on Palestinian names reveal? In general terms, it can be said that the a priori theoretical starting points of the authors and the methodology they employed had far-reaching results on the body of toponymic knowledge about Israel/Palestine. The theoretical assumption of most Western travelers and Israeli researchers is that the existing Arabic names mask the real identity of the place and its Jewish history. Restoring the pre-Palestinian layer is possible through new research on the place. The discourse of Western travelers and Israeli researchers is positivistic and participates in the reproduction of national power relations. It is based on Jewish religious writings and the maps and archives of Zionist bodies, thus removing from history and forgetting the Other—that is, the Palestinian or Arabic—names that are not represented in these documents. The study and recovery of place-names were mobilized as a story within the frame of Jewish ownership of the place. The documentation and investigation of the land's nomenclature became part of the struggle between Christian travelers and Palestinians over the land of the Bible/Palestine and then between Jews and Palestinians over Israel/Palestine. Western travelers, and likewise Israeli scholars, ignored the names used by the Palestinians as a research object in their own right. They regarded them as mere linguistic-phonetic references and an epistemological link to names from the Bible, the Talmud, and the Mishnah and applied a process of alienation that disconnected these names from their Arabness in order to emphasize the legitimization of European religious concepts and the Jewish ownership of the place.

The researchers working for the Israeli name committees examined Israeli names as part of the Zionist process of constructing the Israeli national identity and as an integral part of the Zionist metanarrative. Israeli researchers' sparse references to Arab Palestinian names were performed under this conceptual mechanism while relying on Israeli maps without any observation of the field or knowledge of Arabic and, of course, without examining the Palestinian reaction (Garth 2009, 238). The Arab and Palestinian reaction, recording Arab/Palestinian names, was part of a move to preserve the memory of lost Palestine. Research into place-names in Israel/Palestine has become part of a national political campaign of rewriting and erasure and part of the "game" of historical property, under the guise of a discussion of place-names. Politicization has increased since the second half of the twentieth century—that is, after the establishment of the State of Israel—and it continues to this day. In fact, since the 1960s, in the shadow of the Israeli-Palestinian conflict, "oppositional toponymy" has come into being in Israel: each side attributes the origin of place-names to its own language, as confirmation of its political claim to the land.[7]

The dismissive approach of Western and Israeli researchers has also affected the production and presentation of the body of toponymic knowledge and its scrutiny. This approach viewed Palestinian names as garbled and meaningless forms; according to it, Arabic place-names are biblical Jewish forms that have been distorted by Arabic speakers. In this manner, the linguistic landscape was reconstructed and cut off from its native Arabic identity. Against this background, those advocating this view attacked researchers who did not align with it. Elitzur (2018), for example, sees my research as hostile to Israel and Zionism. His reaction, and that of his friends from the Israeli naming committees, shows how colonial writing practices attempt to silence the presence and the representations of subaltern cultures—in our case, Palestinian culture—to hide the complex history of Israel/Palestine while dismissing the value of the Palestinian past in understanding the change in the dominant linguistic landscape in this place in the present.

Methodologically, almost no Western and Israeli researchers regarded the Arab name-giver as a subject who influenced the linguistic identity of the environment. Thus, the place of Palestinian society in research does not reflect the role that this community played in history. The approach of these researchers expresses the Orientalist view, in which the Western study of the East is characterized as alienated from native influences on the design of the space (Said 1978, 226–54). Another methodological shortcoming is that Western and Israeli researchers treated place legends and biblical name traditions as historical facts, not as religious legends or fictional stories (Whitelam 1996). Yet another is the registration of names according to the grammatical rules of lexical and literary Arabic rather than registering the names as pronounced by the locals, ignoring the various dialectical changes in Palestinian society.[8]

In addition to these dismissals, previous Western researchers relied on dictionaries and maps as their sources, and their main work was typological— namely, sorting names into categories and specifying their dictionary definitions. In these studies, no field research was conducted "from below" to learn about the traditions and origins of the names as perceived by Palestinians, the users of the names. The researchers had no interest in "society," in the sense of the people who lived in the places and their culture; they did not communicate with the locals and did not learn about place-names from them. In addition, European explorers and travelers often focused on the names of sacred and blessed sites, prominent spots and locales in the environment. But the names of the small and peripheral places, whose "signified" is limited and modest, such as hills, paths, and plots of land, are usually absent from these compositions (with the exception of Conder's study). These travelers did not know the local language very well, which explains the incorrect spelling of many of these names.

Analysis of the Jewish Arab toponymic discourse in Israeli geographical thought indicates that like the Europeans before them, these researchers (except for Benvenisti) probably do not speak Arabic and did not perform fieldwork to learn about toponymy and its uses in the lives of the locals. Furthermore, the methodology of research on the subject is quite reminiscent of the hands-off policy of British colonialism, which preferred absolute reliance on maps and dictionaries as sources. An example of this is an article by Kliot that deals with the meanings of names of Arab-inhabited localities according to their definitions in Hebrew dictionaries. The following sentence from her article also raises questions: "The largest group among the Arab settlements are settlements the origins of whose names could not be determined, and this is because the various lexicons could not provide an explanation for the origin of the name" (Kliot 1990, 71–72). These examples show that relying on dictionaries instead of utilizing ethnographic knowledge based on the language of the fellaheen as a research tool has resulted in defective lexical toponymic knowledge.

FIELD RESEARCH DATA AND ITS SIGNIFICANCE

In the Galilee, there are eighty-one recognized Arab-inhabited localities. The fieldwork I conducted on the origins of their names revealed that they are explained in 158 stories. Half of these place-names have more than one etiological explanation.[9] I also collected 221 name legends about natural features. Some of the lands and natural features in this category were expropriated from the Arab-inhabited localities and annexed to a Jewish municipal domain or for the benefit of the state authorities and received a new name and status.

The number of locality names and names of natural features is 302, and the number of stories explaining the names is 379. This last number is significant and enables the conclusions of the study to be generalized to the entire research area.

Informants

The 175 informants are divided on a religious-sectarian basis into Muslims, Christians, and Druze.[10] They were interviewed to document the place-names and their etiological stories. The religious-denominational distribution of the informants is as follows:

126 Muslims
25 Druze
24 Christians

The distribution of informants in percentages is shown in figure 1.1. In localities whose population is religiously mixed, the informants were selected not according to the religious criterion but in accordance with the needs of the study. It may be assumed that the paucity of stories that explain place-names using Christian motifs is due to Muslim informants making up the majority of all those interviewed to collect information on the origins of place-names in the Galilee.

Generic Components of Toponyms: Topographic Terms, Family Members, Relationships, and Body Parts

In a two-part name, there are two components: a generic one and a specific one. The generic component describes the geographical essence of the place. It is a type of general name, like *kfar/kafr*, "village" (e.g., Kfar Yehezkel [Ezekiel's village], Kafr Qara' [Qara' village]), and its meaning is often explained in the dictionary (Kadmon 2000, 314, 321). The specific element is the essence of the place-name, distinguishing it from the other names belonging to the same division, like *asad* (lion) in the place-name 'Ayn al-Asad (the spring of the lion). The studies that have dealt with generic terms in Arabic toponymy are

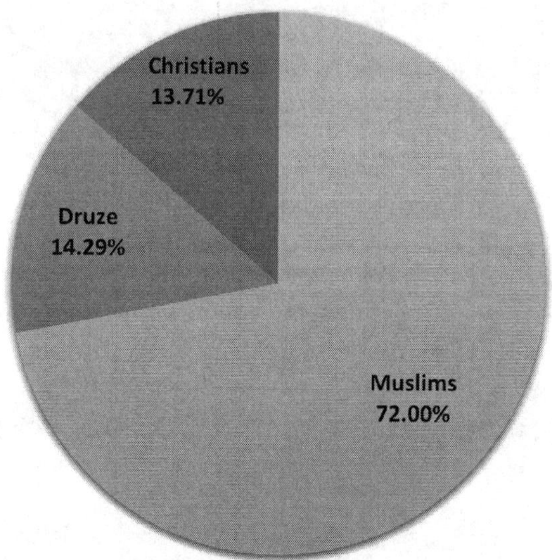

Figure 1.1 The religious distribution of the informants

limited to the linguistic field and to specifying the features visible on the land's surface. The majority of these studies is devoted exclusively to generic terms in the names of inhabited localities, and in fact, the shortcomings of these studies mainly stem from the neglect of generic terms in the names of natural features (e.g., al-Ḥilw 1999, 105–14).

The list of generic terms in Arabic is long, about fifty topographical terms "from the field," not all of which are recognized in dictionaries. But when it comes to the names of settlements, it turns out that apart from a certain division of words, in practice there are very few two-part names—mainly, they are ones that start with the six words *kafr*, *ʿayn*, *dayr*, *bayt*, *shaykh*, and *abū*. Many names were originally a single word, and they became two-word phrases in the locals' speech by adding an identifier to distinguish them from other places with the same name (Elitzur 1989, 21). An example of this is the addition of the word *ʿarab* to the name of an inhabited locality, which in Palestinian usage is typical of Bedouin settlements. In some cases, it precedes the identifying element, such as ʿArab al-Hayb. The word *ʿarab* is a kind of declaration of intrasectarian and cultural identity. By calling themselves *ʿarab* and by applying this term to the names of their settlements, the Bedouins seek to emphasize their authentic Arabness as the original Arab tribes.

The list of generic terms in the names of natural features is very diverse. A small piece of land that has prominent geomorphological-topographical features may receive names that indicate the differences between the parts that make it up. Notable in number are the names that begin with these words: *abū* (father), *umm/imm* (mother), *bi'r* (well), *jabal* (mountain), *wādī* (riverbed), *khalla*,[11] *maghāra* (cave), and *'ayn* (spring).

Examining the general names given by the Palestinians to identify their surroundings reveals some of the features of the map of the Arab village. The list of terms given by the locals to plots of land and natural formations in their surroundings is detailed and long; both large, prominent geographical objects and small, modest ones received specific identifying names: a stone, a path, and the like. Palestinian toponymy is sensitive to the variety of forms of the land surface—mountains, valleys, streams, cliffs, and every fold of land were all differentiated from each other: *ra's* (head) is the area around the hill; *ru'aysa* (the diminutive form of *ra's*) is the land around the somewhat low hills; *ẓāhir* (back) is the area of a nearby hill range; *ṣadr* (chest) is the land that is slightly elevated from its flat surroundings. The topographic forms of the plots of land and their various colors, sizes, and appearances are also each given a term that distinguishes them from each other or their surroundings: *ṭārūg* is a flat and elongated piece of land; *khānūg* is a plot of land between two hills; *rbā'* is a terraced slope; *jalāla* is a narrow piece of land located behind a *rbā'*. Some of these terms serve as a key to understanding the forms of economic organization of the land and denote units of area: a *shakāra* is a small plot sown mainly with vegetables that barely provides enough yield for one family; a *māris* or *ḥakl*, on the other hand, is a large plot sown with various kinds of grain and gourds; *ma'āna*, in the sense of "furrow," is a plot of land with an area of half a dunam; *al-ḥabl* (the rope) is an area of three to four dunams in some regions and six dunams in others ('Arrāf 1996, 105–14).

Another prominent aspect of the nomenclature is naming the environment after family members, that is, the use of the parental terms *abū* (father) and *imm* (mother)[12] and terms for other relatives. *Abū* and *imm* (e.g., Ṣalīb Abū 'Adwān, which is the name of a piece of land adjacent to a crossroads, literally "Abū 'Adwān's crossroads") tend to mark spaces as indicating an individual's private ownership of the place, but this meaning is not exclusive. The terms *abū* and *imm*—which, by the way, are absent as generic elements from Hebrew place-names[13]—have additional meanings: not a place named after a man or a woman but a place with an immediately recognizable sign and a geographical-topographic entity with a certain characteristic. In certain cases, *abū* and *imm* indicate places where a plant, tree, or animal is found in abundance. These terms are repeated in the names of the inhabited localities researched for this book,[14] but their presence is more pronounced in natural features. The main types of natural feature names are as follows:

- *Abū* in conjunction with the name of a plant or tree indicates a place that is associated with a type of plant or with a specific type of tree that grows there. For example, Abū al-Bilān, which means "the father of the prickly burnet" (in the village of Buqīʿa), refers to prickly burnet (*Sarcopoterium spinosum*) that grows thickly in the area. Sometimes a single tree will grow in a certain area, and this area is then called by the name of that tree with the addition of *abū/imm*: for example, Abū Kharrūba, "the father of the carob tree" (in the town of Dabūriyya).
- *Abū/imm* in conjunction with an animal or a group of animals indicates a place that is associated with the animals present there. For example, Imm al-Ḥayāya, "the mother of snakes" (in the village of Haṣīniyya).
- *Abū/imm* in combination with a word indicating a rare natural phenomenon designates a place where that phenomenon occurs. For example, Maghārat Imm Bābayn (in the villages Kamāna, Iksāl, and Yāfat-ʿAnāṣira) refers to a cave with two entrances.

Besides *abū/imm*, other family members also appear in the names of natural features: for example, *banāt*, "girls, daughters," in the name Ghadīr al-Banāt (the tributary of the girls) comes from the fact that only girls and women used to swim there, while *ʿazība* (unmarried woman) refers to a plot of land that is not suitable for cultivation because of the stones and thorny plants massed there.

Similes and metaphors taken from bodily organs (mainly to indicate plots of land) hold a place of honor among names for surface features. A study of the terms for natural features shows that the names of body parts, from head to foot, make up a significant part of the inventory of toponyms given by the Palestinian natives to their natural environment. Table 1.1 presents body-related terms almost in the order of their appearance in the body from top to bottom and shows that nearly all the names of the external and peripheral organs of the body are present in the terms used to indicate units of land and natural features. The elements that repeat with high frequency in names of natural features are *raʾs*, *ẓāhir*, *dhīl*, *dhirāʿ*, and *bāṭin*. The names of the body parts embedded in the natural features may shed light on the shape of the land and its organization in the local culture, and they present space as a pictorial iconographic text. These

Table 1.1 The names of body parts within the names of natural features

Name	Comments	Name	Comments
ra's, head		*kū'*, elbow	
raqaba, neck	*raqabat* in the genitive	*dhirā'*, arm	pl. *dhir'ān*
lisān, tongue		*baṭīn*, belly	
sinn, tooth		*ẓāhir*, back	
kitaf, shoulder		*rijlīn*, legs	
baṭṭ, armpit		*dhīl*, tail	
ṣadr, chest		*kaff*, hand/foot	

markers are like spectacles through which the ground's surface and appearance are visible. In other cases, the names of the body parts indicate the spatial location of a piece of land, such as *dhīl*, tail, indicating a piece of land located at the edge of an inhabited locality.

Why did the Palestinians give places signifiers that are used to indicate family members and body parts? In a semiotic reading, it can be assumed that the preference for these signifiers (names) for naming natural landscapes is derived from the perception of space in the studied society. According to the anthropologist Haim Hazan, groups of people tend to use terms that denote kinship relationships (uncle, sister, mother, etc.), even if there is no blood or marriage relationship between the members of these groups. The purpose of the usage is to symbolize the strength of social relations (Hazan 1992, 44–50). The use of Arabic as a familial language—that is, the application of the terms *abū/imm*, *banāt* (daughters), and *'azība* (unmarried woman) to the geographical surroundings—is a type of metaphorical use that indicates emotional closeness between Palestinian society and the land. The members of this society expressed their intimate closeness to the land in terms commonly used to express respect, closeness, and great value for the recipient. This is even if in rare cases the identifying name after the initial *abū/imm* contains a tone of sarcasm, such as the name Imm al-Barāghīth, "mother of fleas" (in Ṭūbā).

It is worth paying attention to the sexual identity expressed in the words *imm*, *banāt*, and *'azība*. These words are assigned to the feminine semantic field. On the other hand, the word *abū* is specific to the male and is the only generic term that references male family members.[15] The numerical ratio (1:3) between the terms denoting family relationships when they appear in place-names indicates a preference for feminine words and reveals a gendered or romantic perception of the land, its cultivation, fertility, and yield. This manner of conceptualization links the land with the feminine. At the same time, this conceptualization serves as a reminder of how the land is perceived in Palestinian culture—that is, of the Palestinians' great dependence on the land as a source of livelihood.

As for the use of terms for body parts to identify the territory, world language and literature are replete with comparisons of the human body to natural landscapes and buildings. The world becomes comprehensible to humans when it is conveyed analogically with the help of concepts that are used to name the human body (Lutwack 1984, 77–79).[16] This usage presents the territory as part of the living world and anthropomorphizes it while expressing, on a metaphorical level, a kind of anatomical kinship between the territory and the name-givers. Under the influence of the organs of the body, the place-names create an identity between the animate and the inanimate. Naming landscape forms (geomorphology) after body parts also has a practical value: to make the names of the environment tangible and catchy.

TOPONYM ORIGINS AND CLASSIFYING THEIR SOURCES AGAINST THE BACKGROUND OF PLACE-NAME STORIES

Classifying the origins of place-names according to types is one of the starting points in toponymic research (Randall 2001, 1–35). There are many approaches to the subject of names and their classification, according to various principles. Each principle has its own rationale. However, two main trends can be distinguished in the classification of names: (1) classification derived mainly from the nature of the research material and (2) classification based on the three basic categories of content motif, linguistic-historical axis, and time scale.

Many studies have stopped at these category starting points, while I propose a different classification method that fills in the gaps by being derived from the local society's point of view. The order in which the categories of name sources appear in my book reflects the general picture and is based on the number of names in each category, starting with the highest number and ending with the lowest.

Origins of the Names of Inhabited Localities

As for the names that have a single source, the largest category quantitatively is of inhabited localities named after people and figures. The second-largest category is of names originating from nature, the landscape, and agriculture. The number of inhabited localities whose names are related to a plot element or to animals is relatively low. The number of names related to historical periods and Quranic traditions is quite marginal. The categories are as follows:

1. Historical personages: Three main divisions can be distinguished here. The first category is of names influenced by Muslim heroes and warriors from the time of Muḥammad, the first caliphs, and heroes from the time of Saladin.[17] These are Muslim soldiers who came to Palestine to "liberate" it from Roman, Byzantine, or Crusader rule. The second category comprises names influenced by local Arab figures, including in inhabited localities named in relation to local leaders, founding fathers, tribes, and other communal figures. In addition, there are names commemorating the activity of biblical figures and figures from the period of the Mishnah and the Talmud (otherwise known as the period of Roman and Byzantine rule in Palestine). Some inhabited localities are named after Roman, Byzantine, and Crusader figures and warriors as well as European military men from the nineteenth century.

2. Names influenced by nature and agriculture: These names are divided into three subgroups: flora and agriculture, smaller topographic features, and larger geographical-physical features.

3. Names connected to an event or action: After classifying the place-names, it became clear to me that there are names that do not meet one specific definition, and therefore, it is difficult to place them in a specific category. The common denominator of these names is the unique way in which they are explained and not necessarily the conceptual motifs. The names of inhabited localities are connected to an event or the actions of human or other figures, yet the place-names do not include the figure's name but are derived from their actions, their way of thinking, or a message they uttered. For example, Mashhad is so called because a resident of the village testified (Ar.: *shahida*) to Jesus's prophethood when he passed from Mashhad to Kafr Kannā.

4. Names connected to the animal kingdom: Some places have names that include animals. For example, Imm al-Aghnām, which means "mother of sheep."

5. Names that originate in Hebrew, Greek, or Latin: Some place-names have a folk or real etymology deriving them from other languages. For example, the locals believe that ʿIlabūn is derived from the Hebrew word *ʿelbon* (insult), while Naḥif is derived

from the Greek word *nif*, which means a church or the entrance to a church.

These five categories that I have proposed so far are a primary classification. In chapter 2, which deals with the analysis of place-names, a secondary division is possible. Moreover, despite distinguishing among various categories, pointing to an unequivocal and rigid division between them is impossible. For example, names related to an event or action are also names referring to characters, because an action is performed by a character.

Origins of the Names of Natural Features

The names of natural features are divided into five main categories, with the latter categories having only a small number of examples.

1. Names influenced by Arab and Palestinian men and women of low socioeconomic status: In this category, there are two main divisions of characters in terms of their gender identity. The first category includes names of natural features that refer to local male figures of low socioeconomic status—ordinary people and the inhabitants of the villages. The second division includes names of natural features that refer to local female figures and their actions: women accused of dishonoring the family, traditional activities of peasant women, and stations in the bride's processional journey, for example.

2. Metaphorical names: Names of this type are not used in their literal meaning but instead take on a borrowed significance, ascribing certain attributes and characters from another semantic field to illustrate the place's identity. The names in this group aim to indicate topographic features, soil quality, and natural phenomena.

3. Names influenced by the nature and agriculture of the Palestinian village: The names in this category are divided into three subgroups. The names in the first subgroup describe the physical qualities and properties of the natural features, such as taste, climatic phenomena, and color. The second subgroup comprises topographical names referring to the feature's appearance and shape. The third subgroup comprises place-names of a rural nature, relating to agriculture and vegetation.

4. Names connected to animals: Names of this type are divided into two subgroups. In the first, animals that fit into a short name story without having played a role or having played a simple and

typical one. In the second kind, the animals are shown in a special and symbolic light, either by the unusual role they play or by the plot's development.

5. Names indicating a particular time: Some natural features received their names from a particular time or season, for example, *al-tajādīd*, which means the renewed plots. These plots were fallow lands that were recently plowed, and cultivation resumed there.

Like the names of the inhabited localities, this is the main and primary classification of the names of natural features that serves as a basis for further divisions. Again, difficulty in dividing place-names among the various categories not only is a property of the names of inhabited locations but is also characteristic of some of the names of natural features. For example, Bi'r al-Ṣafā (the well of limpidity) was called by that name not because of its clear waters but because it was dug in a time of peace and tranquility in the lives of the local residents. Therefore, the well was given a metaphorical name. However, in the story explaining the name's origin, there are references that hint that the days of calm that pleased the locals chronologically preceded the arrivals of the British and the Zionist movement in Palestine, and for that reason, the name cannot be completely disconnected from the group of markers that suggest a period.

The conclusion is that in some cases, it is difficult to classify Arabic names according to their origins and to indicate a single exclusive source for a particular name. This is for the following reasons: (a) the foundations of the Arabic forms of place-names are rooted in folklore, folktales, and imaginary stories and (b) some place-names can be explained in different ways. Their sources are rich and are used indiscriminately. How, for example, can the names Wādī al-ʿAfan (the river of trash) or Wādī al-Aʿwar (the river of the one-eyed man) be classified?

Indeed, the foundation of Arab culture, its values and customs, the historical memories of the Arab and Muslim *umma*, and Palestinian society's spatial memories in Palestine—all these elements serve as sources from which place-names largely derive their causal explanations. Furthermore, characters, people, and personalities as a source of place-names have primacy in both divisions. The explanation for the dominance of these figures may have a hermeneutic basis—that is, it may originate from the fact that in the field research, the informants were asked to tell me stories about the meanings and origins of place-names. Since the character is one of the basic elements in the story genre, this may be the reason why it stands out over other sources of place-names in this book.

Differences between the Names of Inhabited Localities and the Names of Natural Features

Half of the names of inhabited localities are given more than one etiological explanation. In other words, the multitude of explanations provided for the origin of a single name is one of the distinguishing characteristics of inhabited localities, whereas one of the hallmarks of the names of natural features is the marginality of this motif. Most signifiers of uninhabited locations have a single explanation. Another disparity is the frequency of the Jewish motif in the category of inhabited locality names compared to its marginality in the names of natural features.

Another difference pertains to the categories of the sources: in the names of natural features a category of metaphorical names is found, which does not exist in the names of inhabited localities. The presence of spirits and demons in the names of inhabited localities is also minimal, but it is very prominent in the names of natural features.

A further distinction relates to gender, as reflected in the names of localities and natural features. The use of feminine references in inhabited locality names is almost zero. This trend is reversed in the names of natural features; the names of inhabited localities exhibit a distinct patriarchal element, whereas the names of natural features encompass both matriarchal and patriarchal elements. The gender division of the space through its names is based on gender relations and social power dynamics. There is also a division here between public space (inhabited localities) and private space (natural features).

In light of the findings presented, and since the conceptual bases for the origins of the names of inhabited localities differ from those attributed to the names of natural features, it is possible to indicate the existence of two separate onomastic systems in the same geographical-cultural context: names of inhabited localities and names of natural features.

Place-Names That Hint at a Historical Period— Why Is the Time of Saladin Preferred?

Attributing the origins of place-names to figures and events associated with distinct historical periods forms one of the hallmarks of the names of inhabited localities, whereas there is almost no mention of distinct historical periods in the explanation of names of natural features. Scrutiny of the names of inhabited localities reveals that many were attributed to people and events dating from Saladin's wars. This is the age of victories over the Crusaders. It is likely that the leaders and events that characterized the period evoke enthusiasm, admiration, and nostalgia for the glorious past. Another important time period is that of Ottoman rule over Israel/Palestine. Ottoman rule lasted for nearly four hundred years, and it is natural that it left its mark on place-names. The periods of the Mishnah and the Talmud in the first centuries CE are also prominent in the explanations of place-names, and this indicates the depth of penetration of the Hebrew version into the Arabs' consciousness.

An interesting point that requires examination is the marginality of stories that attribute the origins of place-names to the period of the first Muslim caliphs (632–61 CE). Wars in this territory were initiated by the first caliphs with the purpose of liberating Filasṭīn/al-Shām from the Byzantines.[18] The liberation of Palestine from the Crusaders also was one of the motives for the wars of Saladin and the Ayyubids. The marginal influence of Arab and Islamic rule in Israel/Palestine in late antiquity on the formation of place-names, compared to the significant influence of Saladin and his commanders, can be explained on two levels. The first level is related to time. The first caliphs' wars against the Byzantine emperors lasted for at most seven years (633–40 CE), while the Crusades lasted for nearly two hundred years (1096–1277 CE). Saladin fought the Crusaders for nearly twenty years (1170–93 CE). It can be assumed that the ongoing battles between the Muslims and the Crusaders, particularly those involving Saladin and his soldiers, left a deeper imprint on the collective memory than the relatively short period of the first caliphs.

The second level pertains to the political-cultural activity in the Ayyubid era. Saladin and other Ayyubid rulers (including the Mamluks who followed the Ayyubids) emphasized the centrality of pilgrimage to martyrs' graves—*maqāmāt*. These sites achieved fame and sanctity in the Ayyubid era among rulers and locals alike. Forgotten or destroyed sites were renovated by means of sanctifying pilgrimage, and others were founded near these strategic centers (al-ʿĀrif 1961, 176–77; Benvenisti 2000, 285). The motivations behind focusing on the cult of the martyrs and their tombs were ideological, and the trend was to concentrate the greatest number of villagers and soldiers around these sites and strategic points for potential future Crusader attack. The renewal of sites of worship was also a reaction, countering the visits of European pilgrims to the Holy Land. By defining the customs of pilgrimage, the Muslim commanders sought to instill a sense of belonging and strengthen the bond between the population and the land. This thought, I believe, has infiltrated another cultural field that emphasizes humans' connection to the land, that of geographical names.

To end this chapter, let us reiterate that Arabic geographical names are divided into two systems: the names of inhabited localities and the names of natural features. I discuss each of these systems in its own chapter.

TWO

ARAB HISTORICAL MEMORIES AND LINGUISTIC SHADES OF OTHER LANGUAGES

THIS CHAPTER DEALS WITH FOUNDATION legends and place legends rooted in historic details that reveal how Muslim warriors' arrival in Palestine led to Arab names being adopted for inhabited localities. The legends show the influence of local leaders and role models of Jewish, Byzantine, and other backgrounds on the formation of names. The legends also reflect the connection between the natural environment and the names of Palestinian inhabited localities.[1] Due to the abundance of material, I present it only in part and usually discuss a single legend from each category.[2] I mention other legends briefly.

Eponyms are historical or legendary figures from whose names geographical terms are derived. Geographical and linguistic sources indicate that the Arabic map of Israel/Palestine is covered with many personal names. The names of personalities and generals from Islamic history, among them companions of Muḥammad, are common in this map (Vilnai 1982a, 671–72; Rainey 1982, 23–24, 73). These sources identify, in general terms, figures on the Palestinian map, but the following issues need to be expanded: What is the background to the character's activity? What is their relationship with other characters? What are the characteristics, actions, and notions that arise from imprinting such names in space? These issues become more prominent and more vital when it comes to local figures and leaders, whose traits and deeds cannot be reconstructed from canonical books of history and religion. Folk literature, in which framework I examine Palestinian names, contains antihierarchical and antiauthoritarian elements (Hasan-Rokem 2000, 96). I chose to discuss Palestinian names in the folk genre because doing so reveals the voices of popular and local figures as well as gender issues. Analysis of characters' traits is facilitated by the distinctions made by Shlomit Rimmon-Kenan (1983, 29–42), who presents two basic types of textual means of constructing literary characters: direct definition and indirect presentation.

THE MEMORIALIZING OF MUSLIM WARRIORS AGAINST THE BYZANTINES

The protagonists of name legends about Muslims' battles in Palestine are legendary Muslim warriors, whose names, in many cases, were imprinted on the land because of their skill or success in fighting for the Muslim umma, their religious faith, and the liberation of Palestine from the Byzantines and Crusaders.[3] In other words, the circumstances of name formation are anchored in Muslims' past battles and in the Islamic conception of Palestine's history, as the following example demonstrates:

al-Daḥī (الدّحي)[4]

When the Prophet (peace be upon him) was born, his mother died. He was cared for by a woman named Ḥalīma al-Saʿdiyya, who was also the mother of the boy named Duḥaya.

At the outbreak of the war, *al-ṣaḥāba* came to Palestine.[5] Duḥaya was killed near al-Lajjūn, and the enemies dismembered his body with a sword. He had a she-dog, who carried his flesh and put it in a cave. People came, buried him, and erected a shrine with a tombstone and called it [the tomb of] Duḥay, which is Duḥaya al-Kalbī—the suckling brother of the Prophet Muḥammad.

[And what did the people do near this tomb?]

Whoever's son was sick would slaughter a lamb, two lambs, invite people from the neighboring villages, hold horse races, and hold a celebratory feast after the son recovered. Whoever's son was sick would also take him and cut his hair near the cave, because there is a blessing, because Daḥī is holy, a follower of Allah.[6]

This legend derives the name of the inhabited locality of al-Daḥī from a connection to the warrior Duḥaya, who fought in battles between Muslims and Byzantines in seventh-century Palestine. The context of the name's origin highlights figures and events from the distant past that are meaningful for the collective religious identity of Muslims. The protagonist Duḥaya is, in addition to being one of his companions,[7] the suckling brother of the Prophet Muḥammad (i.e., they were nursed by the same woman), a trait that seems to be attributed to

Duḥaya to endear him to listeners. He is depicted as a warrior who came to Palestine to liberate it from the Byzantines, as hinted through the story's events and characters. He bravely confronted the enemy and ultimately gave his life for the sake of religious ideas. His body was dismembered by the enemy and transferred by his dog to a cave.[8]

From that moment on, the warrior Duḥaya became a battlefield martyr, and this new status required a new attitude on the part of members of his group. They rewarded the hero by naming the village after him and by turning his burial place into a center of pilgrimage. The act of naming the village is an immediate response to an interreligious military confrontation. Duḥaya, the hero faithful to the commandments of Islam calling for the liberation of Palestine, came from afar and sacrificed his life for his religion. As befits such a hero, his people memorialized him in the name of their village: Duḥaya, with a slight formal change, became Daḥī. Naming the village after him glorifies his actions and expresses an ideological and collective commitment to those acting for the sake of religion and the umma.

In terms of its subgenre, this is a historical legend that has become a saintly legend, a folk tale centered on the charismatic figure of a righteous saint, and the purpose of the legend is to instill belief among its audience. Be that as it may, the cave, the martyr's burial place, became a site of pilgrimage, and he himself became a mediator between the inhabitants and God. People believed in his power to heal the sick, thanked him at banquet ceremonies, and held horse races in his memory near the site.

The legend of Daḥī does not exist in a vacuum. Its tangible and spiritual expressions continue among the locals to this day, as evidenced by the fact that the mountain above the village is called Jabal Duḥaya (جبل دُحَيَه) and the holy site at the top of the mountain throughout the year attracts locals seeking healing or fertility. The site served as a place of worship until a mosque was built on the site in 1970.

Another case that memorializes Muslim warriors in Arab place-names is that of Shafā'amr (شَفاعَمِرو).

Shafā'amr—Many people think, and most of their explanation is correct, that the name Shafā 'Amr consists of two words: *shafā* and *'Amr* ('Amr's recovery). 'Amr is 'Amr b. al-'Āṣ. And historically it is known that 'Amr b. al-'Āṣ, on his way to liberate Egypt from the Byzantines, passed through our village and seems to have felt unwell. It is said that after drinking from one of the springs, he recovered (Ar.: *shufiya*) from his illness. Therefore, to this day the spring is called *'ayn al-'āfiyya* (the spring of health), because 'Amr b. al-'Āṣ recovered thanks to its waters.[9]

In explaining the name's meaning and origin, the legend takes the linguistic-literary step of dismantling the name Shafā'amr into two elements: *shafā* and *'Amr*, meaning the recovery (from illness) of 'Amr. The figure referenced is 'Amr b. al-'Āṣ, a Muslim general during the period of the first caliphs. This general was entrusted with the liberation of Egypt and Greater Syria from the Byzantines. During his campaign he felt ill, went to the local spring,[10] drank from its waters, and *shufiya*—recovered. Thus, the combination *shufiya 'Amr* ('Amr was healed) became Shafā'amr.

To establish the name of the inhabited locality in the heroic-religious context, three elements are combined. One is a symbolic figure, the figure of 'Amr b. al-'Āṣ, who acts in the name of the Islamic values that call for war with the Byzantines. The second is the period associated with the dawn of Islam and the Muslim umma. The third is the place, the spring of water that cures the commander's illness. The story of the inhabited locality's name connects the three elements and thus connects the locality's history with the religious history of Muslims in Palestine, embodied by the figure of the commander. The story is unique in its focus on two episodes in the protagonist's life and their combination: the illness and the war. The clash between his physical distress and his desire to liberate Palestine and its environs was resolved by the spatial contribution: the spring of water, blessed with the virtue of healing. The healing opens a door to the hero's name being incarnated in that of the inhabited locality, and thanks to the healing, the hero goes out to complete his mission. This mission is perceived as a sublime value by the locals; therefore, the hero who fulfilled his mission and honored the place and its inhabitants by drinking from the spring was glorified, and his name became identified with the village.

In the Talmud, the linguistic form Shefar'am appears rather than the current Arabic name Shafā'amr.[11] The Talmudic form appears with a very slight distortion in medieval Arab sources. There is reason to believe that the form Shefar'am became Shafā'amr in the locals' speech. In its current linguistic form, only the first name of the commander is present in the name of the inhabited locality rather than his full name—that is, 'Amr, not 'Amr b. al-'Āṣ—although in the legend the name of the commander is mentioned in full.[12]

Saladin and the Crusaders

At the center of the legends we are interested in, stand Saladin (Ṣalāḥ al-Dīn, 1139–93) and his commanders. The historical nucleus around which the legends arose is the campaigns fought by Saladin and his generals (and their successors) against the Christian Crusaders between 1174 and 1277.

al-Ṭayyiba (الطَّيِّبه)[13]

> Ṭayyiba, according to what we heard, was initially called ʿOfrah and not
> Ṭayyiba. Saladin, accompanied by his army, passed on his way to al-Quds
> [Jerusalem] from here and drank from the spring. And he said: "For some
> reason it was called ʿOfrah! Its water is good (*Ṭayyiba*), and it is appropriate
> that it be called Ṭayyiba." From that day to this, its name is Ṭayyiba. And
> Ṭayyiba is ancient, very ancient.[14]

The name's origin is anchored in Saladin's activities and speech. The legendary
commander drank from the waters of the local spring on his way to liberate
al-Quds (Jerusalem) and enjoyed their pleasant taste, as shown by the word
ṭayyiba, which means good and pleasant. The word was imprinted as the name
of the village, and thus, by merging Saladin's words with the place's uniqueness,
the name was created and given its meaning. In folk history, which is interwoven with the plot, the village is called by two names in two periods. Before the
Muslim wars against the Crusaders, the village was called ʿOfrah, signifying
a demon and evil spirit in Arabic; it is recorded as such in the Bible, where it
is identified as the locality from which Gideon came to fight the Midianites
(Judges 6:11). According to local tradition, the village got its name because evil
spirits (*ʿifrīt*, pl. *ʿafārīt*) used to buzz around it. This name gives the place and
its inhabitants a negative image. The name Ṭayibba appeared when the Muslims came to the place; it emerged against the background of a semantically
opposite linguistic form. It is possible that the folk etymology, connecting the
name to the *ʿifrīt*, sought to give meaning to the Hebrew form ʿOfrah, which is
meaningless to Arabic speakers.

Changing the place's name from ʿOfrah to Ṭayyiba is an emotional and
conceptual action that gives it a new status. The story emphasizes the locals'
beneficent power through mobilizing the space and its secret to their point of
view—to the side of their commander. Thus, the place is no longer frightening
and harmful, as previously believed by the villagers. Moreover, if the place is
desirable for their leader, it is surely also desirable for them.

The term "euphemism," coined by Richard Hartman in the nineteenth century, means substituting a pleasant element for an unpleasant one (Rainey
1982, 22). The change of name from ʿOfrah to Ṭayyiba is a kind of scholarly
testimony, from the informant and the character in the story, to the principle
of euphemism and to the belief that a name has power over a place's identity.
The Finnish folklore researcher Lauri Honko (1981, 23–26) regards this type of
change as an adaptation in the morphology of tradition, one of whose manifestations is the replacement of elements foreign to a culture by familiar ones.

The change to Ṭayyiba reconstructs the place's identity and gives it a favorable sense of belonging, by both eliminating the existing cultural dissonance and creating a positive association for Arabic speakers.

Another legend that connects a name's origin with the founding of the village and locates both in the Muslim-Crusader battles is the legend of the name Kawkab Abū al-Hījā (كَوْكَبْ أبو الهِيجا):

> Saladin was the commander of the Muslim forces and with him were other commanders, such as Abū al-Hījā, who was a company commander, and the like.
>
> Our master, Abū al-Hījā, was one of the commanders of Saladin al-Ayyūbī during the conquest of Acre. After conquering Acre, they headed for the area of Kawkab. And where was the great campaign of Saladin? Adjacent to the ʿarab an-Najīdāt-Buʿīna (عرب النَّجِيدات- بْعِينة), in an area called Imm al-ʿAmad (إم العَمَد). In this decisive battle, Abū al-Hījā was killed: many cavalrymen attacked him and he *hāja*, assaulted. And what does *hāja* mean? It means began to snort, like the stormy camel, and foam dripped [from his mouth], and he punched right and left until the Creator killed him and he was buried there. Because of the large number of horses and people killed—and the responsibility lies with the transmitter of the tale, as they say—both the horseman and the walker on the road encountered dead bodies.
>
> Abū al-Hījā was killed here, and here he was buried, and after his death the people and his friends, who are our ancestors, moved here and still live here to this day. The village was called Kawkab Abū al-Hījā. [And why *kawkab*, a star?] Because it is in a high place.[15]

The founding of the inhabited locality of Kawkab Abū al-Hījā and the origins of its name are the result of historical circumstances: the military conflict between the Muslims and the Crusaders. The name is composed of three words.[16] The meaning of the first word is "a star," and this word is based on the village's topographical uniqueness, being located in a high place. The second and third words form the name Abū al-Hījā, one of Saladin's commanders. The name legend is constructed on two levels: the first explains how the commander earned the nickname Abū al-Hījā, and the second, deriving from it, leads to the reason why the village was named after him. According to local tradition, the commander's original name was Ḥusām al-Dīn. This particular signifier was replaced by the nickname Abū al-Hījā, "the father of the assault," which was bestowed on him for his heroic behavior during the campaign against the Crusaders: he *hāja*, meaning "he assaulted [the enemies]." The commander's militant actions aroused the admiration of his interlocutors and motivated them to grant him a new status, summed up in his nickname. Using his personal nickname for the name of the village rewards the warrior for his bravery. Due to the esteemed qualities of the commander in the battle of Hattin as well as his heroism and devotion to the common good and jihad, his followers and relatives commemorated him by coming from afar to the place where he fell in battle and founding the village to perpetuate his memory.[17]

The locals' belief in the name legend is evident in two practices in the village. First, on the northern border of the village stands the site of the tomb attributed to Shaykh Abū al-Hījā, and many Muslims, seeking healing for their ailments, visit it. Second, Abū al-Hījā is the name of one of the clans in the village and of other clans in other places who trace their origin to this leader (Slyomovics 1998, 225–28).

In fact, such a foundation story connects the arrival of warriors from Islamic lands during the wars against the Byzantines and the Crusaders and is based on the same recurring ideological foundation that is expressed in a multitude of variations. We see before us a case of "multiple existences" of the same story, which is reshaped again and again using different formulas (Yassif 1999b, 5). The historical legend and the place legend play a central role in shaping the community's collective consciousness and identity (Yassif 1999b, 325). For a text to reflect the collective consciousness of a period, it must have parallels (Yassif 1999a, 194). Thus, the multiplicity of stories and versions of stories that link the names of inhabited localities to Muslim fighters and Islamic history is proof that the legends are part of the narrating society's collective memory and form a component of its collective identity.

The contemporary form of the place-name is explained in the context of the Muslim wars against the Byzantines and the Crusaders, a collective historical memory that is meaningful to Muslims. Setting the names in this context gives them a mythic status in the narrating society. Folklorists and historians note that communities choose from their past culture and history those traditions, events, and heroes who fit the present-day community members' preferred reading of their past (Ben-Amos 1984, 114–15; 'Abduh 1993, 35). The narrating group's interpretation of a space's identity and name is also subjective, often reading name legends to the groups' own benefit.

The protagonists of the stories express the historical conception and status of the place (Palestine) among Palestinian Muslims. The name of the village is far from being the story's singular source; its uniqueness is emphasized in an onomastic explanation deriving from historical stories and cosmological events. Thus, the place's linguistic identity is not discrete because many villages boast of Saladin's and other Muslim generals' contribution to their heritage.

Scholars have emphasized the role of the distant past in inventing traditions and in creating the illusion of historical continuity and persistence between the past and the national community in the present (Hobsbawm and Ranger 1983). The name legends adhere to an ancient historical kernel and to the names of Muslim warriors, to explain the name of the present place. They link the local village's history to Islamic history, which in turn undergoes a process of localization that gives the general narrative a unique local character. Thus, by means of the historical kernel, a historical sequence and connection between the past and the contemporary local community is also created. The period of victories and the spread of Islamic ideology continues in the present, even if its heyday is long over.

While the legends mention heroes and important leaders who appear in the chronicles, they also highlight commanders who were not at the head of the political hierarchy. Historians glorified the rulers who operated during the caliphate and lauded Saladin's victory, but they ignored the contribution of the junior commanders on the battlefield. The study of names in legends shows that these names reveal a hidden chronicle, even constituting another history—an oral, local Arab Palestinian social history.[18] The protagonists of this history have disappeared in part from the canonical history books or are mentioned only in passing.

Migrations and population movements are depicted in the background of the name legends. The figures immortalized in place-names, whether well-known heroes or junior army commanders, came to Palestine from distant lands and acted on behalf of their people. Following the warriors, many migrants established inhabited localities in Palestine. This is how the land was moved from chaos to cosmos. These motifs are reminiscent of Mircea Eliade's (1954, 9–10) statement: "All these wild, uncultivated regions and the like are assimilated to chaos; they still participate in the undifferenti- ated, formless modalities of pre-Creation. That is why when possession is taken of a territory . . . rites are performed that symbolically repeat the act of Creation . . . a territorial conquest does not become real until after—more precisely, through—the ritual of taking possession." The presence of the Byz- antines and the Crusaders is not explicit in the legends, but it is implied by the presence of the opposing factor—the Muslim warrior. Historians—includ- ing Muslim ones—have documented the Crusaders as worthy opponents (Ibn Munqidh 1999, 64). But in legends about the names of villages, there is no echo of the Crusaders' chivalry, and they are mentioned only in general and as those who were defeated by the Muslim forces, or vice versa: as those who subdue the Muslims. The presence of the geographical terms connected to Muslims and the disappearance of the terms of the Crusader side are an expression of the "deliberate silencing" of the Christian other and an expression of spatial power relations.

The military history of the Muslims in Palestine is the source of inspiration for name stories. The first Muslim period was characterized by operations of the Muslim Arabs against the Byzantine Empire. These wars are called *al-futūḥāt*, and they mark the beginning of the spread of Islam. The second period is that of the Crusades. Both the first caliphs and Saladin viewed their wars as fulfilling a religious commandment to fight the Christians and acted from religiopolitical motives. The Byzantines and the Franks were perceived in Muslim historiography as invaders and infidels, and it was the Muslims' duty to liberate Palestine (and other lands) from them.[19] Jihad (holy war) had a huge appeal throughout the entire Islamic world (Prawer 1971, 435–38). Thus, at the core of the names commemorating the early Muslim wars against Christians and Saladin's wars against the Crusaders are acts imbued with fighting spirit, pathos, and militancy. In the local consciousness, the Muslim victory on the battlefield also reflected the triumph of Arabic rhetoric in the spatial language. This victory spawned a development in the linguistic landscape and shaped the map of geographical space as speaking to the Muslim military heritage. Interweaving the memory of the Muslim commanders in the geographical landscape turns it into a memorial site and is a declaration of spatial autonomy and proof of Muslim territorial ownership.

One of the emphases of the structuralist method proposed by the anthropologist Claude Lévi-Strauss (1966, 85–89) is the search for binary contrasts between programmatic elements, contrasts that allow researchers to find a supercontrast within the whole from which its meaning can be deduced. Based on this approach, we can discern a recurring chain of contrasts in the name legends that deal with confrontations between Muslims and Byzantines or Crusaders. The scheme is demonstrated in figure 2.1. The binary contrasts in the figure are mediated by the story. The mediation process builds a model of Muslim-infidel relations and outlines their connection to the spaces of Muslims and of infidels. This model reflects the value norms of the narrating society and highlights the positive image of the Muslim collective in its living space. This is in contrast to the negative image of the "infidels," whose actions are mostly not related to the land and about whose origins the legends do not provide information.

The stories also highlight the contribution of the environment of each and every village to the story of the Muslim umma. The Palestinian village is presented as a staging post in the warrior's journey: natural features supposedly call on the Muslim general to enter their territory and use their advantages in

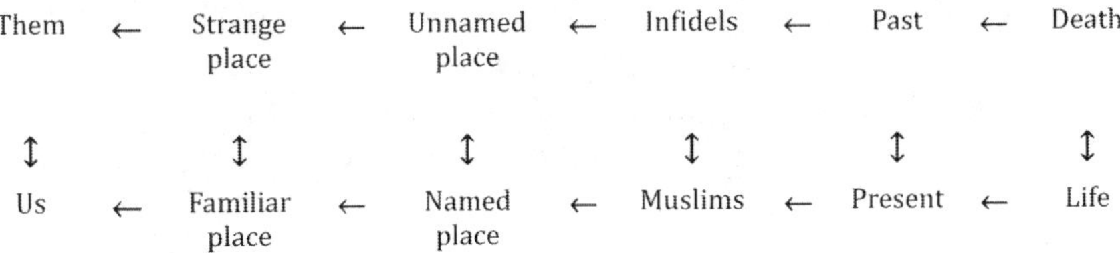

Figure 2.1 Schematic model of binary relations in name stories centered on Muslim warriors

his war with the enemy. In the end, either the Muslim general is killed in battle and is buried on the spot, or the place benefits him and is physically and morally beneficial to him: the Muslim commander enjoys the taste of the spring water or is even healed by it. He and his army enjoy a safe rest in the village. The shaping of the area of the village as a battlefield between "us" and "them" depicts it as a place charged with emotional qualities and as a source of pride for its residents. In the name stories, one can see foundation legends that play a role in territorial socialization. The role of the legends is to deal with external challenges (rival religious identities that claim the space) and internal ones to provide spiritual-religious justifications that root the Muslims' descendants in their homeland.

The stories of the names connect the place vertically to its historical past and horizontally to its local geographical identity. With the help of their names, the Palestinian villages skip over hundreds of years and shape a consciousness according to which "our living space" in the "small" place is an extension and continuation of the great ancient Islamic homeland.[20]

The Tribe and the Founding Fathers: Glory and Power, Forced Marriage, and Hospitality

Within Palestinian society, there are common etiologies that link the names of Arab-inhabited localities to local Palestinian figures and intrasocial values. These are the names of local leaders and residents, communal figures, and founding fathers and tribes.

Wādī Sallāma (وادي سَلَامه):
"In the name of God, the Merciful, the Compassionate. We asked the elders: What is the history of this ruin? Where did this name come from?" Most of the elders of the place were unanimous about one story, and this is its tale:
Sallāma was a Druze village that imposed its authority on the entire region. Shaykh Sallāma lived there. Shaykh Sallāma once passed through ʿArrāba—of course, its inhabitants are Sunni Muslims—and because he is an older and

noticeably strong shaykh, no one could stop him. He saw a Muslim maiden from ʿArrāba and said: "I want to take this young woman, to marry her."

He addressed her parents, the residents of ʿArrāba. The residents of ʿArrāba were afraid to reject him and embarrassed by this demand.

By God's will, a foreigner came to ʿArrāba—a Bedouin from the az-Zaydāna tribe. His name was ʿUmar az-Zaydānī. He saw that they were embarrassed and asked the villagers: "What is the story?"

They said: "We have a very difficult problem."

"What is the problem?"

"The problem is that the Druze Shaykh Sallāma has asked for the hand of one of our maidens and we cannot say no to him."

He told them, "Give me a day to think."

ʿUmar az-Zaydānī made his way to ʿArab aṣ-Ṣaqr. The Bedouin of aṣ-Ṣaqr lived between Tiberias and Beit Shean. He consulted with them.

He returned to ʿArrāba and said to them: "Tell him [the Druze Sallāma] that you agree, provided that the old and honorable Druze elders come to the Arabs and are received with dignity and great splendor. We will honor them, spend the evening together and have a party, provided they stay with us."

And so it was: the Druze residents of Sallāma came to ʿArrāba with their sheikh and spent the evening in ʿArrāba with songs, debka dances, and so on, until the end of the night. Each of the residents of ʿArrāba hosted a man from Sallāma, and Shaykh Sallāma, who was the groom, was the guest of ʿUmar az-Zaydānī.

The plot was that ʿUmar az-Zaydānī would kill Shaykh Sallāma by shooting him. And when the shots were fired, anyone with a Sallāma guest must kill him. And that's what happened. After the ʿArrāba residents murdered their guests from Sallāma they proceeded to the village itself, to Sallāma. It is said that they eliminated all the residents. And that was the end of the inhabited locality called Sallāma.

To this day Sallāma is a ruin. This is a history of three hundred years and no more; from 1700 until today, the story is spread by word of mouth among the residents of the area.[21]

This story, from the end of the seventeenth or the beginning of the eighteenth century, about the changes in the name of the Bedouin village of Wādī Sallāma, is widespread among the elders of the Galilee. It was even transcribed in one of the main works from Ẓāhir al-ʿUmar's reign in the Galilee (al-Muḥāmī 1996, 29). By way of the story, the incarnations of the name are explained: the original Khirbat Sallāma (خربة سَلَّامة) "the ruin of Sallāma," and the present-day Wādī Sallāma. This phenomenon is called "name migration" in toponymic research; sometimes a name becomes detached from the original site and continues to be used as a name for a place next to it (Rainey 1982, 22). In the context of the name in question, the first part, *khirba*, was replaced by the word *wādī*, while the person's name, Sallāma, remained the same.

The focus of the legend is the strained relationship between the communities. The plot emphasizes the heroism of the weak (Muslims) in their struggle against the strong (Druze) and the victory of the former by outwitting the latter. The main character is the Druze shaykh called Sallāma, who is known for his power. His authority is political and social: "Because he is an older and noticeably strong shaykh, no one could stop him." As narrated, he saw a Muslim maiden from ʿArrāba and said, "I want to take this young woman, to marry her." Shaykh Sallāma was a figure whom no one dared disobey. He could marry any girl he liked, without her and her parents' consent. The Druze shaykh's demand to marry the Muslim girl from ʿArrāba, whether the Muslims liked it or not, is perceived as a serious violation in traditional societies. The violation of a woman's honor is also a violation of the honor of her menfolk and their tribe (Epstein 1933, 40–41). This fact, as well as Islamic law's prohibition of marriage with the Druze, turned this event into an interethnic and interreligious conflict. This confrontation is shaped by collective and representative figures: the Druze Shaykh Sallāma, on the one hand, and ʿUmar az-Zaydānī, on the other (al-Muḥāmī 1996, 29–33).

In the legend, the Bedouin leader acted according to the ruse proposed to him by the members of the aṣ-Ṣaqr tribe after he approached them for advice, and at the end of the festive meal, he was the first to shoot the intended groom, Shaykh Sallāma. Following this, the residents of ʿArrāba murdered the rest of the guests. The Bedouin leader and his friends continued to the Druze village of Khirbat Sallāma, killed all its inhabitants, and destroyed it. The confrontation with a member of the Druze community reveals the Bedouin's personality. He is cunning, very zealous regarding his tradition and tribe, and not afraid of anyone. These qualities are highlighted against the background of the behavior of the Druze shaykh, who is presented as an oppressor who violates the rules of etiquette of Bedouin and Muslim society. The contrast between the leadership figures parallels the contrast between the Muslim-Bedouin community and the Druze one.

Why did the Bedouin Muslims find it appropriate to name their land after their Druze enemy, Sallāma, despite the bloody wars? The name and its story are intended not only for internal consumption but also for external needs in dealing with other groups, who should see this and beware. It is possible that the Bedouin mentality, glorifying courage, revenge, and honor, highlights these values against the background of the inferiority of the Druze leader Sallāma and the story of his defeat. The leader is perceived as a metonym of his society and his descendants, and therefore, the story that focuses on the character of a concrete shaykh is important because it is not a general story about interethnic struggle but one that, by commemorating Shaykh Sallāma, continues to be a living testimony to the heroism of the counterfigure of the Bedouin shaykh. Memorializing his name conveys a public message about the fate of a person who offends the values and dignity of the narrating society.

Among the names attributed to local figures appear the names of local collectives, who are often characterized by positive qualities. The following discussion focuses on one legend about al-Ṭayyiba and another about Sakhnīn, in whose names hospitality is the recurring conceptual element.

al-Ṭayyiba (الطَّيِّبه)

The name is given to the village not by the residents themselves but by the guests who would come to this locality. They would say of them: "The inhabitants of this village are *ṭayyibīn*, good people, and greet the others in *ṭīb*, with a warm welcome."

When a person was passing by and one of the residents was sitting on the doorstep of his house, he would greet him: *salām ʿalaykum*, and intend to continue on his way. But the villager would bring him into his house and treat him generously. He would pour him coffee and if it was time for lunch, dinner, or breakfast, he would treat him to a meal. Only then would he allow him to continue on his way.[22]

Sakhnīn (سخنين)

Sakhnīn was called by this name for several reasons. One of these reasons, according to people, was a clan that settled in the west of the village and stood out in their *ṣakhāʾ*—in their hospitality. That is why the people were called *as-sakhnāniyyūn*, the generous ones.

The name *as-sakhnāniyyūn* comes from the word *as-sakhāʾ*—hospitality. And throughout history and to this day Sakhnīn is famous for its hospitality.[23]

The name is given to localities by passersby, visitors, and people who came from nearby localities. The etiological legend derives the signifier al-Ṭayyiba from the adjective *ṭayyibīn* and the signifier Sakhnīn—from the adjectives *sakhnāniyyūn* or *sakhāʾ*. The adjectives, which signify hospitality, are nicknames for the locals. The storyteller's purpose is not only to explain the name but also to highlight the locals' identity. Al-Ṭayyiba and Sakhnīn were so called due to collective characteristics and positive behavior perceived as common to all the residents. The locals were characterized by their hospitality, and thanks to this virtue, the guests gave the hosts their nickname, which became a name for their village.

The hosts' generous behavior should be understood against the background of the customs of Arab society, in which hospitality is an ingrained trait.

Therefore, the generous behavior of the people of Sakhnīn and al-Ṭayyiba is a metonym for a cultural position rooted in their society's custom of hospitality (Barakāt 1986, 75–76).

Apart from al-Ṭayyiba and Sakhnīn, who received their names in connection with the local inhabitants, the names of the inhabited localities of Kafr Kannā (كفركَنّا) and ʿAkbara (عَكْبَره) are also attributed to figures of this type. Kafr Kannā arose as the location's name because its inhabitants were jealous (from the Hebrew root Q-N-ʾ, which became Kannā) of their honor and good name. The name ʿAkbara refers to the word *akābir* (honorable, rich [pl.]). The source of the village people's wealth was the natural resources of the village environment and its fields.

Some villages are named for the ancient tribes that settled there, including those from the following periods: the Canaanite period, early Islam, the Middle Ages, and approximately the seventeenth century. For example:

Al-Jishsh (الجِشّ)
Al-Jishsh was founded five or six thousand years ago. It was founded by a Canaanite tribe called Jisqāla, and in time the name was changed to Jishsh. This is the Arab point of view.[24]

To explain the origin of the name al-Jishsh, the popular understanding exploits the partial phonetic similarity between the name of the village and another word that the narrator attributes to the Arabic language, that is, Jisqāla, although this word is not of Arabic origin.[25] The first two letters of the name of the Jisqāla tribe are similar to the pronunciation of the name of the inhabited locality, which also consists of two letters.[26] The explanation borrows the first two letters of the tribe's name for its etiological purposes and creates the village's name from them. The tribe is of Canaanite descent, and the Arab Palestinians perceive themselves to be descendants of the Canaanites. It is possible that this explanation was intended to establish sovereignty over space by means of a historical justification. This version is the antithesis of another local tradition, according to which the origin of the name al-Jishsh is from Giscala, the Greek transliteration of the name Gush Ḥalav.[27]

Another type of name is based on the founding fathers, as demonstrated in the following legend:

Dayr al-Asad (دِير الأَسَد)
As I heard from our ancestors and elders, its original name was Dayr ar-Ruhhāb (دِير الرُّهاب), the monastery of the monks. The name was changed from Dayr ar-Ruhhāb to Dayr al-Asad.

As the previous generations reported centuries ago, there was a shaykh named Muḥammad al-Asad. He was a righteous man, who lived in Safed and wanted to leave the place and come to Dayr ar-Ruhhāb.

He had a beast of burden. He loaded his belongings and possessions in two sacks on either side and rode on his beast. On his way from Safed to Dayr ar-Ruhhāb, he passed by ʿAyn al-Asad—there is a village called ʿAyn al-Asad. He said to himself: "By Allah, there is a spring here and I want to stop and rest in the place" ([he was] tired, a long and tiring journey). "I want to give fodder to the beast and water it, and I, too, will drink some water, rest and then, with the help of Blessed Allah, I will continue to Dayr ar-Ruhhāb." And indeed, he stopped at the place and rested under a tall tree.

After a while, he fell asleep. Then this man, Muḥammad al-Asadī, got up. When the afternoon prayer came, he went down to the spring to purify himself for prayer. He purified himself and prayed. He finished and suddenly saw a lion (Ar.: *asad*) devouring his beast. He went to the lion, untied the reins from the beast and tied them to the lion's head and said to him: "Whoever eats the donkeys of the Arabs, will kneel under the waterskins." He took his belongings that were on the beast and loaded them on the lion. As is well known, a sated lion does not harm anyone. After the lion ate and was satiated, he rode on it until he reached Dayr ar-Ruhhāb.

When he arrived at the place, Shaykh Muḥammad al-Asad wanted to find out about the village and its residents. They said to him: "This is Dayr ar-Ruhhāb" [the monastery of the monks]. He asked that the name be changed from Dayr ar-Ruhhāb to Dayr al-Asad [the monastery of the lion], despite the monks' displeasure.

The people of the village, who saw him riding the lion, were filled with fear, and he informed them [the Christians]: "You must evacuate this place, we want to call it Dayr al-Asad instead of Dayr ar-Ruhhāb. Go to Baʿna, to the village next to us." The people saw that he was a righteous man, a *walī*,[28] and a powerful man, and they agreed to move to Baʿna [and agreed] that Dayr al-Asad would be reserved for the Muslims. Since then, the place has been called Dayr al-Asad.[29]

Dayr al-Asad's name legend is a frame story that describes the background of the changes made to the village's name. This story is familiar to the locals, from young to old. The name consists of two words: the first word, *dayr*, means monastery, and the meaning of the second word, *asad*, is a lion—"the monastery of the lion." The word *asad*, which signifies an animal, was changed to refer to the name of the village's founder, and in time, he became known as Muḥammad al-Asadī. This figure is presented in the written sources as someone who actually existed (al-Dabbāgh [1967] 2003, 7:394–96).

As mentioned in the story, Shaykh Muḥammad left Safed and migrated on his beast to the village that would later be named after him: Dayr al-Asad. An incident occurred during his journey: while resting near the ʿAyn al-Asad spring,[30] a lion preyed on his animal.[31] The shaykh took control of the lion, harnessed it, and led it to his destination. The predator surrendered and accepted the rider's control thanks to the latter's extraordinary piety. Following the shaykh's miraculous deed—taking control of the predator—his name was changed to Asad (lion). The lion's surrender to a leader or hero after preying on a donkey is an ancient and international theme. This motif is recorded in the miracle stories (*karāmāt*) of Muslim shaykhs recorded in the medieval composition by Ḍiyāʾ al-Dīn and in other legends (Talmon-Heller 2002, 122).

In cultural conceptions, the motif of the lion preying on a donkey symbolizes the supremacy of one ideology over another (Bonfil 1989, 110, 123–26). The name's justification shows how folk culture associates names with religious tensions that are resolved to the narrating group's benefit.[32] I think in the story of Dayr al-Asad, the narrators concealed an understanding that the lion symbolizes Islam and the donkey, Christianity. The lion that preys on the donkey implies the end of the donkey's faith and thus the victory of Islam over Christianity. In fact, this event foretells the continuation of the story, according to which the shaykh expelled the monks, the representatives of the Christian community, from the village. The shaykh's material act, founding a Muslim-inhabited locality from which the representatives of Christianity were exiled, is accompanied by a cultural and poetic action, establishing a value-laden linguistic expression bearing the imprint of the Muslim community in the inhabited locality and indicating al-Asad's achievements as a Muslim saint (*walī*). Shaykh al-Asad converted the second element in the inhabited locality's name: he established the name *al-asad* in place of *ar-ruhhāb* (the monks), while the first element, *dayr* (monastery), remained intact. The monastery is a relic of an earlier name and testifies to the existence of a Christian community in the village in the past. In today's demographic reality, the monastery component preserves the spatial identity of the Christian minority.

The explanation of the name by the locals aims to establish the etiological element by glorifying the saint's power. In Dayr al-Asad there are additional cultural modes that express the depth of belief in the saint. The shrine is located next to a mosque bearing his name—Jāmiʿ al-Shaykh Muḥammad al-Asadī. According to local belief, thanks to the intervention of the holy man, the villagers escaped the Zionist forces that besieged the village in 1948. *ʿAmud al-muʾmin* is the olive tree of the believer in God, of the saint al-Asad. The tree stands in its place to this day. Moreover, the largest family in the village is the al-Asadī family, who are descendants of Shaykh al-Asad. Thus, the thematic-ideological element at the base of the story of the name of the village of Dayr al-Asad is repeated in other modes of discourse.

—m—

The explanation of the names of inhabited localities called after Palestinian figures realizes the sonic potential in the linguistic patterns of the villages and connects patterns to the names of local figures with a similar sound with a slight phonetic change. In other cases, the story justifying the name tends to indicate authenticity and historical credibility, as in the cases of Wādī Sallāma and 'Arab al-Hajajra, which is named for the founding father al-Hajjār.

The names of Palestinian personalities and the founding fathers embedded in the names of villages are derived from the communal Arab culture. The names of inhabited localities are related to a variety of the customs and lifestyle of traditional Arab society: forced marriages, intercommunal and intertribal conflicts, mutual aid, hospitality, the honor of the tribe and its founding father, and the affluence and nobility of the locals.

The legends that explain the names' origins do not provide information about the time at which the names were given, but they may indicate the period in which the ideals on which they are based were dominant and flourished. The names of the localities whose foundation is associated with the glorification of intragroup values, express empathy, continuity, and connection with the Arab social tradition.

Scholars of Arabic nomenclature have issued shallow yet comprehensive statements regarding the Arab map that indicates the names of local leaders, founding fathers, and tribes. In contrast, the present study seeks to establish the folkloric map created in the local society's consciousness and drawn by means of its memories. This point of view, of the local society, sheds new light on the phenomenon of using personal names to mark localities. Examining the development of names, the contexts in which the personalities and people operated, and the meanings of their actions reveals cultural aspects of local society to which scholars of nomenclature have seldom paid attention. Names of a social nature (e.g., explanations of the names al-Ṭayyiba and Sakhnīn in connection with the motif of hospitality) such as those discussed in this book have received even less representation and elucidation in studies of names of inhabited localities than the names of individuals and personalities. The ideals expressed in the names of local personalities associated with the names of inhabited localities are ethnographic expressions of social history and local folklore. An analysis of the ethnographic elements intertwined with the names reveals the conventions, aspirations, and anxieties of the group under study as a society, not a nation.

JEWS IN THE MAP OF ARAB TOPONYMS

Language is one of the main means of emphasizing affinity to a nation. This affinity is achieved by means of linguistic policy. In the State of Israel, ideology drives linguistic policy, and the issue of language is highly charged and symbolic (Olsen 2012, 402). This is also reflected in the field of personal names, family names, and place-names.[33]

The naming or renaming of places can provide information about historical and political processes that have occurred in a space. Place-names are an essential part of the colonization process, and they reflect asymmetrical power relations between conquerors and conquered or rulers and subalterns. In cases of disagreement between groups speaking different languages and those of cultural friction between the majority group and an ethnic minority, place-names become a charged and symbolically powerful issue (Nicolaisen 1990, 95, 102–3; Cavallaro and Jing Yi 2020, 64).

In the following, I examine Palestinians' use of elements from the Jewish tradition to justify the origins of names of inhabited localities in which a Palestinian population lived. Also given here are examples of places (roads, mountains, springs, intersections, etc.) for which Hebrew names are used even though they have linguistic markers in Arabic.

The following discussion focuses on two main areas: The first is an analysis of literary, stylistic, and linguistic aspects of the pronunciation of the locality's name, its formation, and its meaning. The second focus deals with cognitive aspects of the extralinguistic reality associated with the Palestinian minority's use of Jewish name traditions and Hebrew toponyms in Israel.

In studies that examined political-national aspects of the names of localities and landmarks in Israel, a trend of historization is noticeable in the description of political circumstances and in the description of the differences in power relations that caused changes in the linguistic landscape of Israel/Palestine (Benvenisti 1997; Suleiman 2004, 159–75). These changes occurred already during the pre–Israeli state period, continued with the establishment of the State of Israel, and became stronger following the Six-Day War.

My discussion examines the Judaization of space from another angle, unrelated to the issue of Jewish national-territorial sovereignty over the land, even though Israeli institutions have erased the linguistic-geographical landscape of the Palestinian minority. I characterize the Palestinian minority's use of elements from Jewish narrative and linguistic traditions and analyze this in its quotidian cultural context. My study of this use moves from the national to the cultural and social arenas and includes the economic living conditions of this minority. This book thus also contributes to the understanding of the connection between names and ethnic conflicts in the context of the ongoing intercultural encounter between the majority Jewish population and the Palestinian minority without limiting the discussion to binary and conflictual terms.[34]

Postcolonial thinkers, including Franz Fanon, Edward Said, and Homi Bhabha, have dealt with questions of language and power, nationalism, race, and the cultural bias inherent in the modes of discourse and practices of Western cultures. These thinkers sought to articulate the consciousness and cultural identity of the conquered in the face of colonial reality. The postcolonial situation is not concerned only with questions of military repression. Its principles are evident in other aspects, such as linguistic and literary hierarchies (Young 2003, 140).

Fanon mainly described the practices used by the leaders of the French Republic, who sought to cause Blacks to internalize White domination codes and thus leave them in a state of the oppressed, imitating Whites (Fanon 1967, 17–40). Said revealed the dichotomous nature of the power relations between the "Orient," the submissive Oriental, and the dominant Western Orientalism. Orientalism as a discipline and as an institution is based on an ontological and epistemological distinction between the Orient and the West (Said 1978, 44, 66–67, 83–84). Bhabha objected to the binary position and spoke of the phenomenon of "imitation" and the concept of "hybridity," thus expressing reservations regarding the binary oppositions of Said and Fanon and challenging the apparently unequivocal distinction between the ruler and the subaltern (Bhabha 1990).

My scrutiny of the use made by Palestinians in Israel of elements from the Jewish tradition to justify the names of some Palestinian inhabited localities is divided into four main categories: (1) names inspired by Jewish figures from late antiquity; (2) names inspired by the remnants of Jewish culture; (3) names of places in Arabic with a pronunciation similar to Hebrew linguistic patterns; and (4) cognitive-cultural aspects of the use made by Arabs of Jewish traditions and names.

Toponyms Inspired by Jewish Figures from Late Antiquity

'Arrāba (عَرَّابِه):[35]
The very famous Jewish rabbi, Ḥanina ben Dosa, grew up in 'Arrāba, and whenever two people disagreed, they would go to him for mediation. Where are you going and where are you coming from? From the rabbi. Where are

you going? ʿa-rab (to the rabbi). They would say: ʿa-rab, ʿa-rab, ʿa-rab. The Jews hold that the rabbi has an affinity to the Divine, he is a pious man, like a prophet—later, so many said ʿa-rab, ʿa-rab, that the name became common.[36]

The name ʿArrāba is associated with the figure of Rabbi Ḥanina ben Dosa,[37] known by the locals as al-ṣaddīq, the righteous man. Rabbi Ḥanina was an arbitrator, and whenever the locals disagreed, they came to argue their cases before him. When asked about their destination on their way there, they used to say: ʿa-rab (to the rabbi). This was said so frequently, and then underwent linguistic change, to reach the form ʿArrāba. Another local tradition links the place's name to Rabbi Ḥanina's son, named ʿArav. Apart from stating that the son was the only one left alive, the Arab tradition does not provide details about him.[38] The name and its story are therefore taken from an ancient period in the joint Jewish and Arab history of the place. They are attributed to a well-known religious figure who mediated among the locals. This personality is glorified and shown in a positive light. His contribution to peace among local Arabs and Jews was admired and, therefore, commemorated in the place's name. The name of the inhabited locality of Sakhnīn, near ʿArrāba, is related, according to one version, to the figure of Rabbi Joshua de-Siknin, called by the locals al-nabī al-ṣaddīq, the righteous prophet.[39] According to the name legend, Rabbi Joshua was famous for his learning. His daughters were also known for their wisdom and knowledge, and Rabbi Joshua used to seek their advice on issues brought before him. The Arabs of the Galilee used to swear by the site of the tomb of Rabbi Joshua de-Siknin and ask for healing for themselves and their descendants (ʿArrāf 1993, 2:111).

Other Jewish names are related in the Arab folk tales about the origin of the names of the inhabited localities, including the figure of Issachar of Kfar Mandi—he is the sage after whom Kafr Mandā (كَفر مَنْدا) is named. The name Kafr Samīʿ (كَفر سْميع) originates from a man named Samā, who came to the village to heal Rabbi Eliezer from snakebite, but Rabbi Eliezer refused to receive treatment because Samā had converted to Christianity.[40]

In legends that explain name origins as inspired by a Jewish figure from late antiquity, the figure is usually flat in affect, with features that are limited and general. The figure does not change from the moment he or she appears in the text but has a dominant characteristic: for example, a religious sage who sometimes served as an arbitrator or healer. On the textual level, there is no direct connection between the Jewish sage and the space of the Arab village and its natural resources. In other words, the character is not described as coming into active contact with the Arab village's space and its natural environment or undergoing a transformation, conscious or physical, while in these places.

Toponyms Inspired by Remnants of Jewish Culture

Shafāʿamr (شَفَاعَمرو):

Some residents say that Shefarʿam was the center of the Sanhedrin. The Jews called it in Hebrew the *shofar ʿam*, meaning the *shofar* [trumpet] of the people, because the Sanhedrin, which is the religious council, lived in Shefarʿam, and in fact gave all the instructions to the people.[41]

This story clarifies the linguistic pattern Shafāʿamir by breaking it down into two Hebrew words with a similar pronunciation: *shofar ha-ʿam*. The Hebrew form is associated with the Sanhedrin—a major spiritual-governmental institution of the Jewish people, which established its seat in Shefarʿam in the second century CE (b. Rosh Hash. 31a–b).

The characterization of the place and its name actually testify to the role played by the Sanhedrin, which can be viewed as a kind of *shofar* (trumpet) that issued rulings and instructions to the Jewish people during the periods of the Second Temple and the Mishnah. In other words, the reason for the name's form according to the Arabs is a phonetic resemblance to the Hebrew expression, which indicates the role played by the Sanhedrin as the religious and spiritual leadership of the Jewish people in Palestine in the middle of the second century CE. Justifying the name in relation to a Jewish institution means acknowledging the existence of a Jewish community in the past in a place inhabited by Arabs in the present.

The name Mashhad (المشهَد) is another example of a locality whose inhabitants associate its name with the remnants of Jewish culture. According to local tradition, the inhabited locality is named after *mashhad al-nabī Yūnis*—the tombstone of Jonah the prophet. Local tradition says that when the first Palestinian settlers arrived, they found the tomb of Jonah ben Amitai near the *masjid al-nabī Yūnis*, the mosque of the prophet Jonah, and established their settlement next to it.[42]

Arabic Toponyms with a Pronunciation Similar to Hebrew Linguistic Patterns

Yāfa (يافه):[43]

About the giving of the name Yāfa, according to the story in the Bible and as it is told by the elderly men and women, Yāfa was named thus for two reasons: The name Yāfa comes from the word *yafah*. *Yafah* in Hebrew means "beautiful," and we are told of the beautiful girls and boys of Yāfa, a beauty that was expressed by the girls being tall, with beautiful hair and a beautiful face. And today the boys of Yāfat al-Nāṣira (يافِة النّاصره; Yāfa of Nazareth), with all due respect to the people living in Nazareth, are polite, do not look for problems, have no communalism, and there is no clan-based cohesion. It has never happened that two people from Yāfat al-Nāṣira argued in a court of law. This is how it was during my father's time and in my day.[44]

The folk legend explains the name Yāfa based on a phonetic resemblance to the Hebrew word *yafah*, beautiful. At the lexicographic level, the signifier of the locality is an adjective attributed to the girls of Yāfa in particular, but it attests to the residents of the locality in general. In the overt layer, the interpretation of the name in connection with the Hebrew adjective "beautiful" describes the beauty of the girls of Yāfa and attributes the origin of the inhabited locality's name to their fine appearance.[45] On the metaphorical level, the story proclaims the inner beauty of the residents and the character traits that set them apart. The story derives the external features of the locals from their character traits, thereby depicting the residents as perfect people, emphasizing their superiority, and distinguishing them from the neighboring population.

Another example is the name Jathth (جث), which is derived from the Hebrew word *gat* in the sense of a pit hewn in the rock where grapes are treaded into wine. Indeed, in the area of the village there are many winepresses hewn in the rocks for treading grapes.

In order to give meaning to the names in this group, the popular etymology connects linguistic patterns in the Hebrew language (roots, nouns, and adjectives) to the name of the inhabited locality used by the Palestinian residents. It thus appears that in terms of genre, the stories are etiological name legends that describe the origin and formation of the locality's name while preserving the affinity to the locality's uniqueness. From the literary-stylistic aspect, the main interest of the elements from the Jewish tradition through which the Arabic names are interpreted is not in the factual and historical realm but in that they are used to explain the origin of a name that is foreign to the Arab ear. The Arab popular narrator is familiar with Jewish cultural and linguistic elements and sees them as a supportive framework for explaining the origin of unfamiliar names.

The legend recruits the auditory-melodic element of the names of Jewish figures from late antiquity, of Jewish cultural traces, and of the Hebrew language, which are similar in their pronunciation to the names of Arab-inhabited localities. Based on this resemblance, it constructs the meaning of the names of inhabited localities, describing their origin and story while sometimes deviating, semantically and morphologically, from the Hebrew linguistic element and making present geographical elements and material cultural remains or hinting at their existence.

Similarities in pronunciation between linguistic forms in Hebrew and names of Arab-inhabited localities influenced the semantic content of the locality's name and served as a source of inspiration for its explanation and formation. It is also possible that we may be dealing with a centuries-old tradition, which relates to and preserves Jewish culture. The Palestinians gave expression to Jewish identity in the area and reflected the Jewish history of the place without coercion by the authorities. This toponymic behavior indicates that in these cases the Arabs, as name-givers, did not hide the cultural-linguistic traces of the Other but regarded them as an interpretive anchor.

Studies claim that the Arabic names reflect and distort Greco-Roman, biblical, and Talmudic sources (Rainey 1982, 20–23). A study of names in local traditions shows that quite a few of the traditions, along with the etiological element attributed to other traditions (in this case the Hebrew tradition) have an accompanying component in which the villagers or the topographic environment of the inhabited locality find expression. The name is illuminated twice over, by factors both external and internal to the place: on the one hand, referring to the Hebrew-speaking majority and to the language of this society and, on the other hand, allocating space to the topography of the Palestinian village. The etymological legend does not limit itself to borrowing the denotative meaning from the Hebrew tradition but adds its own connotative significance to the borrowed Hebrew element. In so doing, it gives the name a subjective meaning that emerges from the associations or experiences of the Arabic speakers.

Cultural-Consciousness Aspects of Palestinians'
Use of Jewish Names

The Arab Palestinian culture that has taken shape in Israel recognizes and makes present the complexity of a political situation in which it finds itself the national culture of a minority, and as a result, under certain circumstances it attempts to resemble the dominant culture and be part of it (Kimmerling 2004, 383, 402–4). The Palestinians in Israel, including the narrators of the name legends, live in a specific time and place. They are aware of the geopolitical changes and are exposed to the dominant language in Israel and the influence of Israeli-Jewish culture. Educated Palestinians in Israel read Hebrew books and newspapers, attend Hebrew plays, and sing Hebrew songs. Hebrew not only is used by Palestinians in Israel for media and practical purposes but has also permeated cultural and literary spaces, as evidenced by the phenomenon of literature written in Hebrew by Arab authors in Israel (Hever 1993, 27); of course, this book being originally written in Hebrew also testifies to this phenomenon. As noted, the adoption of elements from Hebrew culture by the Arab citizens of the country and their application to various areas of life did not eschew place-names and the narrative traditions associated with them.

The use of Hebrew names by Palestinians, and especially the use of elements from the Jewish tradition to justify the names of their inhabited localities by Arabs, is a symbolic cultural phenomenon that harbors a number of messages and seeks to expand the existing boundaries of discourse. The discussion of this phenomenon is part of a more comprehensive one, concerned with the interrelationships and power relations between the Jewish majority culture and the Palestinian minority culture, and refers to several areas.

The first area is mimicry. The Palestinian toponymic discourse, in that it tends to ignore the Arab and Palestinian past of the space and the spatial identity of the affiliation group, reveals its conscious or unconscious desire to integrate into majority culture in the hope of gaining fair treatment. This statement is in the spirit of postcolonial thinkers, who regard language and imitation as means of social mobility. According to Fanon (1967, 25), wearing European clothes, embellishing the local language with European expressions, and more, all "contribute to a feeling of equality with the European and his achievements." Homi Bhabha sees the mimicry of subalterns in colonial and quasi-colonial frameworks as an action aimed at two goals: abnegation before the objects of imitation and achieving better conditions, on the one hand, and subversion of the hierarchical and colonial order, based on a perception of binary separation between Europeans and natives, on the other (cited in Hever and Ophir 1994, 141–43).

Palestinians in Israel use Jewish traditions to justify the origin of Arab names, and when they use Hebrew names rather than Arab ones to indicate inhabited localities and identify landmarks (such as Ahihud [al-Birwa, البِرْوِه], Megiddo [al-Lajjūn, اللَجّون], Mount Yonah [Jabal Sīkh, جبل سيخ], Golani Junction [Miskana, مِسّكِه], Rosh Pina [Jāʿūna, جاعُونه], and Ramat Aviv [Shaykh Muʿnis, شِيخ مُؤْنِس]), the use they make of the spatial marking system of the majority not only is for information and communication purposes but is also teleologically aimed at achieving improvement in their living conditions.[46]

The Palestinians' desire for equality and their attempt to be included in the political and cultural identity of the state are reproduced by using elements from Jewish culture and the Hebrew language to mark the spatial identity of the territory in which a Palestinian population lives or lived. Erving Goffman (1959, 12–15) regards human relationships as a theatrical system in which people present themselves to others and control the impression they create. The Palestinians' use of Jewish traditions and Hebrew names is a practice of linguistic and verbal play, in which the Arabs seek to externalize their Israeli civic identity in the eyes of Jews and to shed their Arab Palestinian identity for a time. Preference for Hebrew names is an active attempt by the Palestinian minority to redefine the boundaries of Israeli society through the creation of an Israeli-local and hybrid culture.[47] In doing so, they hope to influence and change reality. As such, the Palestinian toponymic discourse serves as a kind of story within the narrative framework of Jewish-Arab relations.

The manner in which Israeli Arabs oppose Israeli rule is also reflected in the stories of the names. Following Bhabha's understanding, opposition to the existing hierarchical order is encapsulated in the process of the native imitating the hegemony (Hever 2002, 79–83). When Arabs in Israel identify places and landmarks by their Hebrew names, they seek, as subalterns, to participate in the process of the Israeli takeover of space and language. In doing so, they attempt to challenge the binary oppositions that organize Jewish Israeli discourse. The toponymic discourse established by Israeli Arabs symbolically disintegrates the cartographic and linguistic hierarchy and undermines the exclusivity and supremacy of the language of Israeli hegemony in space. The subalterns take an active part in the process of building the place's linguistic and conscious identity, thus blurring the boundaries of the unity that the hegemony sought to create by imposing a Hebrew typology and dispersing the Arabic one.[48] The abolition of the coercion of the language of the Jewish space and the striving against Zionist conventions occur alongside the Arabs' use of a bilingual map to identify their surroundings.

The representation of Jewish cultural elements in the Arab toponymic discourse shapes the space as a site of two ethnic-linguistic groups and of two semantic landscapes. To clarify this assumption, we will make use of the term *heterotopia*, coined by Foucault to indicate the existence of counterspatial locations. One of the meanings of the term is a form of spatial organization in which at least two different locales exist: the physical-tangible locale, which is in contact with all the space that surrounds it, and the conceptual-linguistic locale, that is, an intangible space.[49] Similarly, the use by Palestinians of Jewish name traditions and Hebrew linguistic markers alongside the use of Arabic names creates a bilingual imaginary map. Thus, in effect, the place is shaped as having a heterotopic status, being a place that willingly accepts two opposing spaces and two peoples living in it, one alongside the other. This design means the subaltern minority's acceptance of the spatial existence of the ruling Jewish majority. The toponymy spoken by Palestinians as a form of communication uniquely reflects both the historical map of the place in the past, within which Arabs and Jews lived, and the mental map that users of names today seek to present. Thus, the Palestinian toponymic discourse in the spatial context makes present its temporal dimension, in the form of the political and historical changes that Israel/Palestine has undergone over the years, yet also preserves the space of the Jewish people.

The use of Hebrew names, as mentioned, is a kind of linguistic tactic used by rejected societies in certain situations in the face of the hegemonic order. In his discussion on the power-language relationship, Yasser Suleiman notes that in a situation of unequal power relations between groups, mobilizing linguistic resources—in this case, the language of space—can achieve a kind of balance in certain circumstances.[50]

Another issue that emerges from the analysis of stories of place-names is the process of socialization that the minority, controlled by the majority, undergoes. The purpose of colonial discourse is to label the minority as an inferior population in order to justify its control by establishing systems of administration and teaching (Bhabha 1990, 75). According to Said, the Orientalist sets himself the goal of converting the East from one thing to another. This is a process that comes to fruition through written materials, traditions, and rhetoric (Said 1978, 48, 66–67, 94–95). Texts created by academies and governments can drive not only knowledge but also the reality they seek to understand and present it in a particular way. The Palestinian minority's use of Hebrew forms instead of Arab ones is also the result of the government's activity, through the education and media systems. This use is the result of Israeli language and media education as reflected in road signs and natural landmarks. Indirectly, the absence of Palestinian names from the linguistic landscape also promoted the domination of the ruling majority's narrative.

In my opinion, the use of Hebrew names by Palestinians can be attributed to the latter's lack of awareness and insensitivity to their own tradition and to the vitality of the geographical names handed down to them. But this argument is nullified if one considers that the Palestinian population has been weakened by the Zionist establishment, which entrusted "experts" working on its behalf with responsibility for the educational and scholastic content available to the Palestinian minority and for its cultural and media system. The language education policy for Palestinian Arabs and the curricula in Arab schools in Israel are aimed at educating learners in the values of Jewish society. These curricula present the Palestinians as lacking an affinity to the place and emphasize the deep affinity between the land and the Jewish people (Kimmerling 2004, 378). In such a reality, a state of camouflaged socialization is created, in which the subalterns internalize the message and images of the hegemony without being aware of the process that they have undergone.

Indeed, the territorial representation expressed in the name stories told by the Palestinians presents the reality, the intricate and multilayered identity of the place, without erasing the layers of memory that refer to the Jewish Other; rather, it interprets the memories of this figure. Palestinian popular narrators search for interpretations and sources for names that are incomprehensible to Arabic speakers and give them meaning through constructive use of elements from Hebrew culture and language. The narrators see these elements as interpretive "frames of reference" and use them to construct the names' meanings, sometimes with slight morphological and phonetic deviations from the Hebrew form and adapting it to the local pronunciation.

The Palestinian toponymic discourse that has emerged in Israel is a cultural key through which it is possible to try to understand the construction of the linguistic landscape of names, its image as a sociocultural process, and both of these as emerging and changing concepts within the social and political contexts in which they were created. The Palestinian minority living in Israel is aware that the homeland in which they live has metamorphosed in many ways. As a result, this minority has developed a toponymic discourse and a linguistic-spatial identity driven by pragmatic, social, and economic considerations.

TRACES OF GREEKS, BYZANTINES, AND CRUSADERS

Traces of Greek and Byzantine traditions are also found in the place-names used and interpreted by the Palestinians. In such cases, the Arabic place-name is usually derived from the name of a Greek, Roman/Byzantine, or Crusader commander or governor, with a slight change in form.

Dayr Ḥanā (دير حنا):
Dayr Ḥanā is named after the Crusader groups that conquered the country. The Crusaders used to build monasteries. The head of the monastery here was Mar Yoḥanan and this name was distorted in the transition to the Arabic language and became Dayr Ḥanā. After the Crusader war, the inhabited locality was destroyed, and it remained in ruins for a long time until the az-Zaydāna tribe arrived and renovated it almost 270 years ago—in the year 1731 of the Christian calendar.

Saʿd al-ʿUmar, who was the brother of Ẓāhir al-ʿUmar az-Zaydānī, is the one who founded the inhabited locality here, and thought of changing its name from Dayr Ḥanā and calling it by a different name. He suggested that the inhabited locality be named Dayr Suʿūd, but one of his escorts told him— maybe jokingly, maybe seriously—"Call it Dayr al-Qurūd [monastery of the apes]," but Saʿd al-ʿUmar said: "I prefer that it remain Dayr Ḥanā."

The name Dayr Ḥanā remained and was not changed.

The legend anchors the name in the Crusaders' wars against the Muslims and in their physical and cultural activity in the Holy Land. The name consists of two words: the first word, *dayr*, means monastery, and the second word is the proper noun Ḥanā. An ancient local monastery still exists in the village. The name Ḥanā is a distortion of John (Johannes), a Crusader religious leader. According to the story, he participated in the Crusader campaign that besieged the Muslim locality and built the monastery there.

This story is educational, providing firsthand testimony to Arabic speakers' tolerant attitude toward the linguistic heritage of other peoples, in our case the Crusaders. The local ruler Saʿd al-ʿUmar (brother of Ẓāhir al-ʿUmar az-Zaydānī, the eighteenth-century governor of the Galilee appointed by the Ottomans), refused to abolish the name Dayr Ḥanā and replace it with the name Dayr Suʿūd, after one of Ẓāhir al-ʿUmar's sons. He also rejected the proposal, possibly made in mockery, to call the place Dayr al-Qurūd, that is, the monastery of the apes. In today's demographic and political reality, both the "monastery" component and the "Ḥanā" component used by Arabic speakers preserve Christian religious identity and traces of the Byzantine and Crusader presence in the Holy Land.

Other examples attribute names to the Byzantines and Romans. The inhabited locality of Kisrā (كِسرى) received its name in connection with Julius Caesar, and so, too, Rummāna (رُمّانة) was called after the Romans who settled on the village hill that served as their fortress.

From a stylistic-literary point of view, like the figure of the Jew discussed previously, the figure of the Crusader and Roman Other embedded in the name of Palestinian villages is usually a flat one, with very few and very general features. The legends are content with noting the ethnic origin of the Other, which is characterized by a dominant trait. In most cases, the Other does not have a direct connection to the natural environment of the Arab village.

The village arena is described as a site where historical events occurred and as a place visited by Byzantine and Crusader historical figures whose traces are evident in the Arabic forms of the names. It is possible that in terms of historical facts, the story may be inaccurate, but this is not of great concern to our research since the legend's importance is not its historicity but rather the reasons for its formation and its contribution to the understanding of the historical awareness of the narrating society (Khurshīd 2002, 79). The popular narrator is aware of the historical figures and events and regards them as a supportive framework for the formation of the inhabited locality's name, even if they are not historical facts. However, the possibility of a centuries-old tradition, linked to the Byzantine and Jewish cultures and preserved by the

Palestinian Arabs whose identity and religion have undergone many incarnations, cannot be ruled out.

THE BOUNTIFUL AND PROTECTIVE LAND—FLORA AND AGRICULTURE, TOPOGRAPHY AND GEOGRAPHY

Nature, agriculture, and vegetation play a significant role in the names of Arab localities, from trees, shrubs, and vegetables to grains and herbs.[51]

> Ṣandala (صَنْدَلَة):
> It is said that this village dates from the Roman period. According to what the old people say, Ṣandala is named after a type of tree called *ṣandal*.[52] Anyone who looks at the village from the southeast side, sees that there are terraces on the plain. It is obvious that this is man's doing.
>
> The residents who lived here used ṣandal for healing: they would peel the bark and bandage wounds with it. Another use for ṣandal trees is the production of incense: after it is burned, the ṣandal spreads a fragrant scent.
>
> Ṣandal had other uses. According to the elders, they would place the trunks above the roof beam in the ceiling and cover them with a straw of sesame seeds, prickly burnet [*Sarcopoterium spinosum*], and above it clay. Another use is *ash-shabāra*: it is known that in our village they used to produce lime. The chalk was hewn from the mountains and brought to the village, a pit was dug in the ground, the stones were piled up and the *ṣandal* trees were burned until the chalk became limestone.[53]

To explain the name's origin, the legend connects the signifier of the tree and the name of the village: *ṣandal* becomes Ṣandala. The locals associated their village with the tree not only because of its abundance in the environs but also because of their direct dependence on it. The existential contribution of the ṣandal trees, and the medical and economic benefits that the villagers derived from them, influenced the naming of the inhabited locality. In addition to bodily matters, the villagers made their surroundings pleasant through the fragrance of the incense extracted from this plant. The villagers also used the trees to build their dwellings. The name legend gives the impression that the Palestinians are intimately connected with nature: "They would peel the bark and bandage wounds with it." The Palestinians' dependence on nature and plants is also evident in their homes, which are built of natural materials: trees, stones, and the plants sesame and prickly burnet. The exterior shape of the houses, hence the appearance of the whole village, are in harmonious conformity with the ṣandal terraces and the immediate surroundings.

As mentioned, the village's name is related to the immediate geographical area, the ṣandal trees. Thus, it marks the individual local identity of the rural space, its lands, and its houses. The description of the trees' benefits, from the perspective of the local society, reflects the subjective and unique meaning that the locals attributed to the vegetation of their geographical environment.

> Ṭamra (طمرة):[54]
> The location of the village is high like the *ṭamar* tree, the palm tree. The inhabited locality is located in a high and good place and is clean.
>
> The Bedouin would come from Syria and Jordan and from the valleys to the land of Ṭamra, especially to an area called al-Marāgha (المراغة), situated in a high place. It is higher than Jabal Sīkh.
>
> Whoever among them had a barren wife would settle here for a month, and his wife would fall pregnant thanks to the dew and the fresh, clean air, like that of Safed, of Hadassah.[55] In the land of the Maghāra in Ṭamra, there was fine grazing for the flocks; that is to say, the sheep that grazed in this land would yield twice as much as those in other villages.
>
> Ṭamra is also called Ṭamrat az-Zuʿabiyya after the az-Zuʿabiyya tribe who came from Baghdad to Syria and from Syria to Jordan and from there to Palestine, and this area is their property, it was recorded in the estate book during the Turkish period.[56]

The meaning attributed to this name is related to the climatic and geographical features of the place. Although there is a phonetic parallel between the name of the village Ṭamra and the signified *ṭamar* (palm tree), this parallel is invalid in the semantic layer of the text. The name legend indicates that the signifier Ṭamra originates from a palm tree, but it does not connect the name's origin concretely to the plant; rather, it uses the tree metaphorically to indicate the location's height. The repeated use of the adjective *high* in the text and the comparison to other points of known height in the immediate and further surroundings are intended to highlight the village's geographical elevation. The virtue of height is also further validated by the location of the Marāgha hill, whose prominent summit touches the horizon, within the village's area. The village's lands and its hill were blessed with fresh air, dew, and fine grass. The village environment was known for benefiting the flocks and the people. Thanks to the quality of the village's lands and pastures, ewes gave birth to twin lambs and barren women fell pregnant. This spatial essence spread the name of the village far and wide, and barren Bedouin women, together with their husbands, came there from distant regions to be blessed with fruitful wombs. This story expresses a belief in the fertile and healing power of the local space and its natural objects, which are presented as generators of revolutionary change that ensures the continued existence of the Bedouin nomads who come to the place.

The evidence for the great advantages that the place bestows on those who visit the area comes from outside, from the families who visited it. The fact that the reputation of the village's environment was spread by outsiders, not its residents, confirms the reliability and objectivity of the place's virtues among the narrating society. One can feel the displacement and migration of people at the base of the place's name. The direction of migration is toward it. This act glorifies the supremacy of "our place," thus implying the inferiority of the other places, mentioned only by name (Jordan, Syria, and the valleys) and nothing more.

In the language of the locals and according to the residents of the Galilee, the village is called Ṭamra az-Zuʿabiyya to distinguish it from Ṭamra in the western Lower Galilee. The second part of the construct appears to have been added in a later period due to political or social circumstances (or both). Az-Zuʿabiyya, which is the second element in the name, is the largest clan in the village, and therefore its name has become an element in the village's name. This last matter is evidence of the influence of social structure on the name over time, and also of the intrasocial role of the name as conferring power and glory. The addition of the "az-Zuʿabiyya" component gives that clan a sense of ownership toward the place and dwarfs the presence of other families.

> Buqīʿa (بْقِيعَه):
> The people lived in a ruin in the mountains in southern Lebanon, and they noticed that near them was a *buqʿat māʾi*, a small valley of water, and then they said: "Here is a *buqʿa*, there," and moved their place to the vicinity of this water source.[57]

According to the text, the name of the village Buqīʿa originates in the word *buqʿa*, a small valley: an area lower than its vicinity, surrounded by mountains, that during the winter fills with water and alluvium. This explanation is consistent with the village's topography, surrounded by mountains on all sides. The signifier is interpreted by the signified, the village's external features. In this case, too, a migration is the foundation for the name—immigrants from Lebanon abandoned their place of residence, a ruin, and came to settle in a place where there was a water source. It is enough to say that their previous place of residence was a ruin to characterize it as barren, and therefore, it was worthwhile to move to a place where there was water, one of the requirements for life. Although the name of the village is a general and visible term, the popular narrator tends to interpret it, linking the explanation to the benefits that the space provides to human beings.

Another example is found in the name Ḥaṣīniyya (حصينيه). The popular interpretation takes the word *muḥaṣṣana* (fortified) and, due to the phonetic similarity, derives the name of the locality Ḥaṣīniyya from it.[58] The inhabited locality is surrounded by mountains and hills and, until recently, the road leading to it was unpaved.

—⁓—

Interpretations that create an affinity between village names and the village's surrounding flora, agriculture, topography, and geographical features link the sources of the names to real physical elements. Names of this type are influenced by the immediate natural environment. They present nature as a vital factor and relieve it of its muteness. These names indicate special hallmarks of the inhabited localities, signs that distinguish them from their surroundings and other neighboring villages: the ṣandal tree (sandalwood), the fertility of the soil and its produce, grazing areas, a comfortable climate, and the like. Orly Derzie (1993, 68–73) regards the names of Israeli localities that connect to the immediate natural environment as creating a space of private significance. In this spirit, one can consider the names of Arab villages that connect to immediate natural features (or, alternatively, to the individual names of the natural features) as names related to the place's local identity.

Folk etymologies outline the naming process and shed light on how the interrelationship between nature and humans gives rise to the place-name. One of the revelations of this interrelationship is that some of the names based on affinity to nature arise from immigrants' former spatial experience in their homelands. Immigrants became acquainted with the natural environment of the new village area or the natural features in its surroundings (a spring, a hill, a crop) or benefited from and enjoyed the area's ecological potential and subsequently determined the name of the inhabited locality in direct relation to its qualities.

In order to sort and analyze the space domains as expressed in names that refer to nature, I use Heda Jason's (1972, 153–67) spatial model. According to this model, the narrators and their community stand in the center, and around them, in expanding circles, are the other spaces. Following Jason, it can be stated that the first area present in Palestinian place-names referring to nature is "our village," the second domain is "our region," and the third domain is "the human world beyond our land." The relationship between the areas of space is centripetal (moving toward the center). The "named" village ("our village") is the main focus and the center.[59] The direction of movement of immigrants and wanderers is toward the village, designated as a magnet thanks to its beneficial qualities for those who enter its field. Avoiding characterization of the "other" space (the space from which the wanderers came) is a narrative means, a metaphor for glorifying the superiority of the local space.

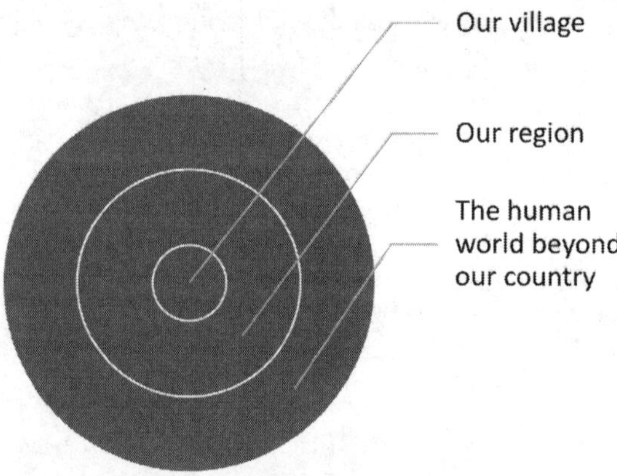

Figure 2.2 The areas of space in the names of the
localities attributed to nature and the direction of
movement of the characters in the name legends

Names of this type distinguish spatial elements and usually present them
in a positive light. The natural images emphasize the pleasant feeling that the
place instills in its residents and those who came to it, and they proclaim the
physical, material and health benefits of natural features to the local inhabitants, the Palestinians, and their guests.

Studying the names, the forms of inflection, and the list of titles and images
that accompany natural features in folk etymologies of place-names makes
it clear that many of them end in a morpheme indicating the grammatical
feminine: Jūlis is derived from *jālisa*, Ḥaṣīniyya is derived from *muḥaṣṣana*,
Ṭayyiba is a feminine adjective, Ṭamra is interpreted as "tall," *ʿāliyya*, and the
like.[60] Grammatical structures express the way in which language speakers
act and think and how they view the world (Whorf 1964, 173–204, esp. 173,
201–2). I believe that the tendency to use feminine grammatical structures
to indicate place-names depicts the village, its lands, and its resources as female, maternal figures and hints at the users' gendered spatial perception of
these names within Palestinian society.[61] Given the positive language images
related to the names of the inhabited localities and the natural environment,
images related to traits perceived in this culture as feminine, such as fertility, benevolence, and beauty, it may be said that this discourse reinforces the
status of the Palestinian village as a place that has everything, in contrast to
the desolation of the Other space, from which people came to the village.
The construction is twofold: glorification of "our village," on the one hand,

and estrangement from "their village," on the other. The values attributed to places in name stories create a subgenre committed to the ideals and ideas of the narrating society.

The names of the localities that refer to nature and space can be divided into two main categories: (1) names indicating geographical, topographical, and climatic features (and more), in relation to the spatial experience of the name-givers, and (2) names describing the geographical-topographic status of the locality. Unlike geographical and topographical works that merely indicated the influence of these physical phenomena on the creation of names (Vilnai 1982a, 9, 673; Stewart 1975, 89–97), this book presents name-givers' spatial experience and affinity for the natural features that engendered the localities' topographical- or environmental-origin names.

TOPONYMS CONNECTED TO NARRATIVE ELEMENTS

The names of inhabited localities in Arabic can also be related to events, acts performed by humans, or their sayings and words. The conceptual elements present in the names in this section are varied. The main elements concern conflicts among Bedouin tribes and conflicts between Bedouins and others.

Ṭūbā (طوبا):[62]
An uneducated crowd of people from the al-Hayb tribe, some of them highwaymen, would raid convoys and loot them. When the Turkish police arrived to catch them, the men would flee and only the women remained in the tents. Their deeds abounded, and the Turkish government sentenced them to death, but they rebelled against it and did not return to their homes. Once, the [Turkish] police came and arrested their wives and daughters—they said: "Maybe we can get something from them."

When they were arrested, it was hard for the men whose wives and daughters were in prison. They consulted among themselves and said: "O people, honor is above all. [Rather] death—and not a life of disgrace, what shall we do?"

They said, "We will go and give ourselves up and free our wives."

They rode their mares to Acre, to Aḥmad al-Jazzār.

They entered and found the slave there. They said to him: "Where is the governor Aḥmad al-Jazzār, we have come to the governor."

He told them, "I will let him know immediately, come in."

He went to him and said: "Sir, ten horsemen have come, and want to meet you."

He said to him, "Well! Go down to them and ask them where they are from, and I will come after you immediately. Let me know before I get to them."

The slave came down to them and said, "O people, what are you asking of al-Jazzār?"

They said: "We are from the tribe of al-Hayb. We have come to give ourselves up."

The slave told al-Jazzār their story.

Al-Jazzār came to them, they stood up to greet him.

He said to them, "What is your problem? What do you want? Why did you come?"

They told him: "We have been tried, and the government has arrested our wives and daughters. We are coming to give ourselves up, so that you will free our wives."

He said to them, "Very well! Sit down." He looked and noticed that the youngest of them was a boy, and said to him: "You, come." He handed him over to his servants and told them, "Slaughter him, cook him, and serve him on a large platter of rice, and place him on top. Put his head in the middle and serve this to them so they can eat it. We'll see what happens."

The servants performed this task. They brought the platter and al-Jazzār came with them.

He said them, "Please, eat your lunch now."

As told, the father of the slaughtered boy was a hero. He looked around and said to them, "O men, this is the flesh of my son Jiʿdān, and if you do not eat it, they will throw it to the dogs. Instead of the dogs eating him, we will eat him."

He crushed the meat and began to eat, followed by everything else.

Meanwhile, al-Jazzār lost consciousness, then his condition improved slightly, and he said to them: "Why are you like this? And why did you do it?"

They began to excuse themselves to him: "The government is persecuting us. We have no place. We have no land. What shall we do?"

He said to them: "If I settle you in a location, in a permanent place, will you stop your deeds and troubles against the government?"

"If only [you would], sir."

He said to them, "What place do you want?"

They said: "We want a place on the bank of the river, close to *al-Sharīʿa*."[63]

Al-Jazzār issued an order: "*Ṭawbuhā, ṭūbuhā*, write the land in their name." And they called it Ṭūbā, because al-Jazzār said: "*Ṭawbuhā*, write the land in their name."[64]

The legend connects the name of the inhabited locality and its meaning to a word with a similar sound in the Arabic language. The name Ṭūbā is formed from the word *ṭawbuhā*, in the instruction to register a plot of land in the name of the local tribe. The background to the name was a confrontation between Bedouin nomads and the Ottoman authorities. The conflict was resolved by the surrender of the eighteenth-century Ottoman governor, the pasha Aḥmad al-Jazzār, to the nomads' demands for their own plot of land. He ordered his soldiers and men to register the bulk of the land that would later become their permanent seat in the nomads' name. The name is associated with the history of the al-Hayb tribe in the Upper Galilee region—its living conditions, its memories associated with the place, and its hostile relations with travelers and especially with the Ottoman government. Al-Jazzār is also a representative figure by virtue of his status as governor. The Bedouin way of life, which was characterized by raids and robbing travelers, was seen as defying Ottoman rule and its representatives, who failed to restrain the tribe by force of arms. The recurrence of the tribe's robbery and flight to the mountains from al-Jazzār's soldiers intensified the tensions and polarity between the nomads and the powerful governor, who sought to use a ploy to secure his rule: "Once, the [Turkish] police came and arrested their wives and daughters." The trick of arresting the women worked nicely, as the Bedouins gave themselves up; in doing so, they revealed another of their traits: sensitivity and jealousy toward the honor of their women.

From here on, the plot changes direction and becomes balanced in terms of power relations: al-Jazzār has laid his hands on the wanted men who undermined his authority. The next step he took evokes his nickname of al-Jazzār, the butcher: He commands his servants to slaughter the son of one of the tribesmen and to serve his head and flesh as a meal. This act is fitting of the governor's nickname, who was famous for his cruelty and tyranny (Schur 1984, 14–15).

The balance seemingly achieved was disturbed, and the Bedouins were once again found to be fearless heroes. Led by the father, the members of the tribe, despite recognizing the flesh of the son served to them, did not refrain from eating it. At the sight of this tragic scene, the governor fainted, and thus, the father and tribe defeated al-Jazzār "on his own ground." A father and his relatives eating a son's flesh is of course perceived as cruelty and a violation of taboo. The explanation for this violation is given as the preservation of the son's dignity; otherwise, the son's flesh would have been thrown to the dogs, which are considered unclean animals in Islamic law. One can also see in the tribe's action a reinforcement of their uniqueness and heroism, an act designed to prove to the governor that the Bedouin's heroism is always available. The governor's loss of consciousness is a statement of weakness and lack of control, and it symbolizes the governor's admission of the Bedouins' victory.

The naming of the inhabited locality is not the only motive for the birth of the legend; personal names and nicknames also receive clarification and elucidation. We have already discussed the connection between al-Jazzār's name and its meaning that emerges from the character's behavior in the legend, but in the story, there is also a reference to the nicknames of the son and the tribespeople. The son's name is Jidʿān ("sturdy camel"), and when eating his flesh, the members of the tribe call themselves *judʿān*, meaning brave heroes. Thus the resemblance between the son's name and his tribe's nickname is both phonetic and semantic, expressing ideals of heroism.

From the beginning, the plot seems to lead the readers along a path of contrast between the characters to the climax, which glorifies both Bedouin heroism and the surrender of the antagonist, al-Jazzār. Al-Jazzār closes the story with the word *ṭawbuhā*—that is, "register this plot of land in the name of the Bedouin"—and thus, he recognizes the Bedouins' entitlement to their own plot of land. This word appears with a slight change in the name of the inhabited locality, which is a kind of poetic expression of the Bedouins' connection to the place, on the one hand, and their connection with the governor, on the other. In other words, at the end of the story, the singular historical event connects to a broader conceptual and existential meaning. The name, as explained in the legend, is a metonym for processes in the tribe's history and in Bedouin values. The legend that justifies the name is meant to characterize the Bedouin and elevate their heroism and, simultaneously, is intended to link their story with the specific place.

The background elements of the story (time, character, and place) also exist in another version, called "the Aḥmad al-Jazzār Pasha administration" (Ashkenazi 2000, 307–8). In this version, which does not explain the name of the inhabited locality, there is a reversal in the image of the Bedouin; here they are shown as soft-spoken figures at al-Jazzār's mercy. Such a change is consistent with Honko's distinction, which concerns the levels of adaptation of the folk tale to its geographical-cultural environment. One of the four levels is the functional adaptation that emphasizes, among other things, the influence of the narrator's personality, the composition of the audience and the listeners' areas of interest, on the creation of the tradition, its action, and the responses it evokes (Honko 1981, 27).

Carl Brockelmann (2017, 48–49) notes that the experience of tribal wars left its mark on the contents of Bedouin literary works. An echo of this experience can be found in the story of Ṭūbā, as relayed here, and ʿArab al-Hayb (عرب الهيب), whose name is attributed to Bedouin soldiers who participated in Saladin's wars against the Crusaders, among other Bedouin-inhabited localities. These soldiers' task was to scan the battlefield and light beacons while calling aloud the slogan *ilhib*, meaning, "Light the beacon!" The inhabited locality of ʿArab an-Nujaydat was also named after the participation of Bedouin soldiers from Najd in the Arabian Peninsula in Saladin's wars.

The Christian tradition of Jesus and the Gospels can also be found in folk etymologies of place-names associated with plot elements, as in the following story.

> Nīn (نِيْن):
> Nīn is one of the ancient inhabited localities. The reasons for the name and its history are related to the coming of the Messiah. The Messiah, when he came to our land, came to the borders of Nazareth, jumped from Jabal al-Qafza (جبل القفزه), the Mount of Beatitudes, in Nazareth and came to our region, here.
>
> There was there a widowed woman with an only son, who fell ill and died. [Jesus] went to her and she was *bitān*—sobbing. He asked how she was: "What is the matter, why are you in such a situation?"
>
> And she replied: "My only son, the Creator took him from me, and this makes me heartbroken."
>
> On the spot, a miracle of God, the Messiah breathed life into him. Later, a small room was built on the site, which eventually became a church. And of course, this woman believed in Him—she believed that He was, indeed, the Messiah who was longed for in this land.
>
> Following this incident, the name of the village came about: Nīn from the word *anīn*, the woman's sobbing.[65]

This legend is common among the villagers, young and old, and is drawn from Luke 7:11–17 (New International Version translation).

> Soon afterward, Jesus went to a town called Nain, and his disciples and a large crowd went along with him. As he approached the town gate, a dead person was being carried out—the only son of his mother, and she was a widow. And a large crowd from the town was with her. When the Lord saw her, his heart went out to her and he said, "Don't cry." Then he went up and touched the bier they were carrying him on, and the bearers stood still. He said, "Young man, I say to you, get up!" The dead man sat up and began to talk, and Jesus gave him back to his mother. They were all filled with awe and praised God. "A great prophet has appeared among us," they said. "God has come to help his people." This news about Jesus spread throughout Judea and the surrounding country.

The name of the inhabited locality in the New Testament is Nain, which was a city in those days. According to the apocryphal book of John, the name of the widow's son (in Arabic) is Yunan (Degani 1989–90, 39). The popular narrator borrowed this story from the apocryphal book, adding the detail of the widow sobbing (*anīn* in Arabic) and using the similarity between that word and the name Nīn to explain the village's name.[66]

In Eusebius's third-century *Onomasticon*, the locality is mentioned as Naʿīn. This form also appears in nineteenth-century sources (Twain 1871, 542). The popular interpretation gives the inhabited locality a name that is meaningful in the Arabic language through the use of phonetic proximity and alliteration, although the story gives no hint of the mother and her son being Arabs. The significance attributed to the name gives local Christianity an Arab identity and also links a local event to one of cosmic and theological significance, since—in addition to his divine status for Christians—Jesus is considered a prophet by Muslims and is perceived as an entity connecting the Great Place (God) and the small place (the land). The story gives the name a symbolic quality and the place a status of holiness. The story creates the site as a place that is not homogeneous in relation to its environment but distinct from it: the place where the miracle of the resurrection of the dead took place.

TOPONYMS INFLUENCED BY ANIMALS—ZOOLOGICAL REALITY OR HINT AT GEOPOLITICAL CHANGES?

The number of names associated with animals is small. In the stories surveyed, the animals mentioned are birds, sheep, a lion, and a mare.

> Wādī al-Ḥamām (وادي الحَمَم):
> It was called Wādī al-Ḥamām because this area is isolated, special. Tens of thousands of *ḥamām*—pigeons—millions, could not spend the winter season anywhere except in these mountains. There were many caves in the mountains, and the pigeons and vultures used to live in them.
> During the sowing season, the kibbutzim poison the soil. The pigeons that came to eat, ate the poison and as a result died.[67]

The tens of thousands of pigeons (*ḥamām* in Arabic) that preferred this area over others are the origin of the name Wādī al-Ḥamām ("valley of the pigeons"). The narrator, who explains the origin of the name, uses the etiological platform to express a romantic yearning for a place where Zionist civilization caused the extinction of the pigeons and the loss of its zoological identity. The hallmarks of the place—that is, the pigeons—disappeared with the change in political reality. The folk etymology tells a sad story that expresses the gap between the "authentic" and "natural" Palestinian past of the place and the painful Israeli present.

In some of the folk etymologies referring to animals, the etiological story involves justifying the name and expressing nostalgia for the primeval natural resources by highlighting the disappearance of the birds. This is the case with

Wādī al-Ḥamām and also with the village of Zarazīr (زَرازير), named after the starlings that were once part of the local landscape. This is also the case in the name of the village of ʿAyn al-Asad with the lion (*al-asad*) who used to drink from the local spring. In another group of animal name folk etymologies, there is no hint of geopolitical changes. For example, the inhabited locality of Umm al-Ghanam (إم الغنم), which means "mother of the sheep," received its name because it was a breeding ground for flocks of sheep from the surrounding villages.

CONTESTING NARRATIVES—ONE NAME, SEVERAL TRADITIONS

Several versions of stories explaining a single name are characteristic of Palestinian toponyms.[68] Below is an analysis of two names of this type and a short demonstration with the help of additional names.

Tarshīḥā (تَرْشِيحا):

First version:

Once a poet passed by a spring near our village of Tarshīḥā. There he met a girl who was drawing water from the spring. He was thirsty and asked her to give him water. After drinking, he raised his eyes and recited a poem. The distich of one of the poem's verses is *wa-rashaḥatnī min māʾihā tarshīḥā* ("and she dripped [upon] me from its waters drop by drop").[69]

Second version:

There was an anonymous poet, who passed through our village Tarshīḥā and was very, very thirsty. He knocked on the door of one of the houses. A very, very handsome girl went out to him. He asked her for water. The girl entered the house and brought a vessel with cold and fresh water and served it to him.

The poet looked at the water and saw that there was straw in it. He began to swallow the water slowly, so that he did not drink the straw as well. After drinking to satiety, he returned the vessel to the girl and said to her: "How wonderful the drink is, except for the dirt [straw] in it!"

The girl replied: "I put the dirt in on purpose. I saw that you were thirsty and tired, and I was afraid that you would drink the water all at once and this would harm you."

The poet marveled at her wisdom and beauty and told her: *wa-rashaḥat-nī al-fatāt min māʾihā tarshīḥā* ("and the girl dripped [upon] me from its waters drop by drop"). And so, the name stuck to the village.

Third version:

> In the time of the Crusaders, a commander named al-Mujāhid [a fighter in
> the holy war] Shīḥā was buried in Tarshīḥā. His name was Shīḥā Jamāl
> al-Dīn, and his tomb is today in Jabal al-Mujāhid (جَبَل المُجاهِد).
>
> Shīḥā fought the Crusaders, was killed in battle, and was buried on the
> spot and about this they said: *ṭār Shīḥā*—Shīḥā flew. In time, the guttural Ṭ
> was refined and became T and thus the name became Tarshīḥā.
>
> This story was told to me by Aḥmad Darba from Tarshīḥā.[70] While I was
> at his house, his wife, Basma Darba, told me another story:
>
> In the army of Ṣalāḥ al-Dīn al-Ayyūbī [Saladin] there was a commander,
> a *mujāhid*, by the name of Shīḥā Jamāl al-Dīn, who was killed on the
> mountain of Jabal al-Shīḥ. After his death his head was cut off, and it rolled
> from the mountain down to the place now called Tarshīḥā, because people
> said: *ṭar shīḥā*, "Shīḥā's head flew off."

Fourth version:

> A long time ago there was a monastery in the village. The explanation is
> that the village is named after the monastery and the broom shrubs (*shīḥ*)
> that grew in the area: Dayr al-Shīkh (دير الشِّيح) ("the monastery of the
> broom plant"). The Bedouin who came to the place called it Ṭūr Shīḥā and
> sometimes called it Dayr Shīḥā (دير شِيحا)[71]—from all the changes in the
> language we came to the name Tarshīḥā.

The etiological element explaining the name's meaning and its origin appears
in all the legends, despite their diverse contents and the many ways they are
constructed. According to the first two versions, which will be discussed together because they are thematically similar, the origin of the name Tarshīḥā
is a love story between a poet and a girl who met as a result of the poet's
thirst: the poet sipped the water the girl served him bit by bit. The etiological
explanation is simply an illustration of a love affair in traditional Arab society, against the background of the rural space. In other words, the content
given to the name is drawn from variations of a classic Arab story about love
between a boy and a girl who meet because the boy, usually a shepherd or
farmer, is thirsty.

In the plot's development, the name has a poetic meaning and was used
by an Arab poet in response to the girl's thoughts. The poet and the girl took
advantage of the meeting to explore and seek a love affair by demonstrating
their skills—hers and his. The girl is blessed with several virtues: she behaved
according to the rules of hospitality and quenched the guest's thirst as well as
being handsome and intelligent. Apparently, she innocently threw the straw

and chaff into the water to do the poet a good turn. But in doing so, she actually resorted to a ploy of putting the poet to the test before forging a bond of love.[72] The girl's cleverness is also evident in her background in folk medicine: She feared that the poet would swallow the water all at once in his state of great thirst and therefore made sure that he would swallow the water slowly.

Even the fact that the poet began to utter poetry—*wa-rashaḥatnī al-fatāt min māʾihā tarshīḥā* ("and the girl dripped [upon] me from its waters drop by drop")—cannot be attributed only to his receiving water and drinking it slowly. He addressed the girl with a general term, *fatāt*, and with words of poetry, which are a form of praise and a signal to the young woman that he was interested in her. At the same time, these are a means of demonstrating the lyrical poet's eloquence and beautiful style.

The main motif in the story revolves around water: thirst motivated the poet to come to the village, the girl drew water and dispensed it, and as a result the poet praised the way the water was served and the girl who served it. Drinking water serves as a connecting link between the poet and the girl, and these two made good use of the natural resource to start a love affair.

The characters are nameless. It is possible that this anonymity is rooted in the values that impose taboos on such encounters, a fortiori when it comes to the public dissemination of lovers' names. The interactions between the poet and the girl are also reflected through the spatial objects and their location. Spaces bear encrypted messages and serve as a metaphor for beliefs and social relations (Lévi-Strauss 1967, 13–21). As mentioned, the meeting place is at "the nearby spring," and according to another version, the two met on the doorstep of the house. In cultural traditions, the spring serves as an ideal space for a meeting between a woman and a man. For example, at the well Moses met the daughters of Jethro (Exodus 2:16–17), Isaac met Rebekah (Genesis 25:16–18), and Jacob met Rachel (Genesis 26:9–10).[73]

Encounters between the sexes at a spring are permissible in the Arab tradition, while in other places, whether on the road or outdoors, such encounters are forbidden. These permits and prohibitions are anchored in the reality of rural life because the men came to the spring to water their flocks and the women came to draw water for drinking, cooking, and cleaning. This realistic necessity turned the spring into a romantic "umbrella" under whose shade acts of love and marriage could occur. The word *nearby* implies the spring's liminal location. Liminal locations—in our case, the spring, or, in other examples, the threshold of the house—are symbolic places of transition from a state of lack of connection between the sexes to the realization of such a connection.

In addition, water in popular belief is a symbol of fertility, a sexual and erotic symbol (Cirlot 1978, 364).

The etiological story about the meeting between a boy and a girl that creates the village's name serves as a reminder of Arab social norms, among both Christians and Muslims, for relationships in earlier times.[74] It is also possible that the story explaining the etiological element seeks by this means to challenge the patriarchal understanding that does not recognize feminine wisdom, let alone a woman's longing for a man. The repressed female voice makes use of the etiological story and resides in its realm.

Unlike its two predecessors, the third version explains Tarshīḥā's name in the context of the activity of the religious-military leadership and establishes its origins in the distant and significant past for Muslims in Israel/Palestine. The name's origin is explained in two minor narrative images: the arrival in the village of the commander Shīḥā, who fought in Saladin's army, on the one hand, and his battle with the Crusaders who threw his head from the top of the mountain, on the other. This dramatic scene left its mark on the locals, who were amazed, and said, *ṭār Shīḥā*—Shīḥā's head flew. That is, the folk etymology merges the two words, *ṭār Shīḥā*, into one—Tarshīḥā—and creates from them a linguistic signifier identifying the locality. The name in its linguistic incarnations loses the long vowel *a*, and the guttural consonant *ṭ* is converted into alveolar *t*.[75]

The folk etymology skimps on presenting the qualities of the heroic warrior, who is characterized by his actions and by the adjectives *fallen* and *mujāhid*, a warrior in a holy war, which indicate his willingness to sacrifice himself. This manner of characterization illuminates the representative dimension of this figure. That is, attributing the name to a Muslim hero who participates in historical events is merely part of a communication system that expresses interreligious rivalry and opposition between Muslims and Crusaders. Against the background of this relationship, the self-awareness of the "ethnic self" is revealed. The Muslim hero acted on behalf of Saladin, and his actions aroused admiration among the members of his group, who kept his memory green by preserving his name as a signifier for the village.[76]

In the fourth version, given by a Christian narrator, there are two explanations for the name. In both, the trick is to break the linguistic form Tarshīḥā into two words. The second word, *shīḥ*, is the same in both explanations, while the first word is different: *dayr* / *ṭūr*. The first explanation explains the name's origin in relation to a Christian religious institution (*dayr*, a monastery) in conjunction with an item from nature (*shīḥ*, the plant Spanish broom). This gives the space a Christian identity in the Arabic language, even though in this story there is no evidence of Arabic locality. Following a linguistic trick, *dayr* and *shīḥ* merge into one word, Tarshīḥā. The consonant *d*, the first in the word *dayr*, becomes *t*, and the long vowel *a* is added to the word *shīḥ*, which becomes *shīḥā*. Thus, the meaning of the name is the monastery surrounded by bushes of Spanish broom. The monastery is a tangible expression of the physical and spiritual existence of the Christian community in the place. The narrated time is the distant past—the Byzantine period in which Christian settlement began in the place. In the Christian conception, this period of time has an emotional significance. Time and space come together to give the place a Christian identity and to appropriate it for the benefit of the narrating society.

Moreover, according to the fourth version, *al-shīḥ*, the Spanish broom, is a natural item present in the name of the locality. More than being derived from the village's natural environment, the word *shīḥ* serves as a formal expression consistent with the word *shīḥā* in the signifier Tarshīḥā. Thus, the folk etymology aims to emphasize the centrality of the monastery rather than that of the natural environment. Evidence of this is the repeated mentions of the monastery compared to the onetime reference to *shīḥ*.

The second explanation in this version, attributed to the Bedouin, is partly reminiscent of the Christian version of Dayr al-Shīḥ and partly focused on the natural environment. The Bedouin used to say *ṭūr shīḥā*, Mount Shīḥā, and over time, the word *ṭūr* became *tar*. In other words, the folk etymology makes use of similar pronunciations in the Arabic language to give a Christian meaning to the geographical name.

From the versions detailed here, it appears that the local consciousness of the community in which the traditions about Tarshīḥā's name appear is complex and heterogeneous. The name Tarshīḥā can express themes of social identity—among which is the gendered manner of acquaintance with one's future spouse in traditional Arab society—as well as historical-Islamic identity, religious Christian identity, and an identity that perpetuates immediate and local natural features. The village is a tapestry of places with different identities. These various spaces conduct a spatial dialogue, built on oppositions: a space with an Islamic status versus one with a Christian identity; local space versus collective-ethnic space.

In the story of the poet and the girl, a benevolent space is described, with a positive image, characterized by grace and gaiety, in which the poet found satisfaction for his physical and mental needs. In the rural space, the poet and the girl got to know each other and the door to emotional satisfaction was opened here. On the other hand, in the story centered on tossing the warrior's head down the mountain, the space's image is terrifying. At the same time, the description of the village as the scene of battles and as a place where a fighter fell in the holy war gives the village a spiritual significance and glory that transcends localities.

Another issue to consider is the ethnic identity of the storytellers. As mentioned, the stories about Tarshīḥā were recorded by a Christian Arab student who documented them at a certain point in her studies. Through the stories, the ethnic identity of the narrators is revealed: a member of the Muslim community, Aḥmad Darba, linked the origin of the name to a commander in Saladin's army; in contrast, the Christian community member, Afwu Bishāra, explained the name in connection with a monastery and the Byzantines. It follows that the explanation for the origin of the name does not have an independent status but is influenced by the narrator's identity and the message that the stories are intended to instill in listeners.[77] The Muslim and the Christian versions of the legend, each in its own way, link the space to a religious identity, thus seeking to appropriate the space to the group to which the narrator belongs. The version that connects the name to the girl and the poet is one of compromise and balance between social forces, the Muslims and the Christians that share the same sociocultural tradition.

Another aspect of villages' multifaceted identities is reflected in the parallel between the ideas anchored in the signifier Kafr Kannā / Qanā. The meanings of the name are as follows: the paradise of the Galilee, the reed (i.e., the plant that grows in the vicinity of the lakes), and jealousy (the locals are characterized by vigilant concern for their good name). This version is derived from the Hebrew root *q-n-'*; *kahanā*—in the sense of Jewish sages, whose legend does not explain in what period they lived and acted—and here they become Kannā, Qanā / Qana. Here we find expressions of various Hebrew traditions and an Arab tradition that includes treating Jews as part of the history of the landscape.

In order to understand the phenomenon of several versions explaining the meaning of a single place-name, it is necessary to distinguish between literary-stylistic discussions related to names and those concerning beliefs and opinions. This is also one of Yair Zakowitz's principles of analysis, when dealing with the personal names and geographical names that are explained in the Bible more than once. The reason for the diversity of content elements explaining the origin of a particular place's name in relation to different factors, is not the name itself. The source of this diversity is the linguistic form foreign to the Arabic ear. At the same time, this diversity signifies faith and identity more than historical truth. Due to the composite identities present in the name, different narratives compete for space. The phenomenon of simultaneous explanations for the name of a particular place signifies its indeterminate nature and the absence of an exclusive and victorious story of the place.

ARABIC PLACE-NAMES—POETIC LINES

The Palestinian names of inhabited localities and villages refer to events and figures that occurred over hundreds of years and are a form of time travel to the distant past in the geographical area where Palestinians and Israelis live today. These names span a very broad chronological canvas of spatial memories. They relate to events, to the commemoration of warriors and leaders from the dawn of Islam, and to Saladin as well as to figures from ancient religions and cultures and local personalities and tribes.

In the explanations of names relating to cultural traditions and historical periods, there are references that date from antiquity and continue to the present: from biblical times to Roman and Byzantine rule and the period of the Mishnah and Talmud, the reigns of the first Muslim caliphs and then of Saladin and his generals, and finally Ottoman rule, British rule, and Israeli rule, respectively. The last period is mainly characterized by the borrowing of semantic elements from modern Hebrew. The names used by Palestinian society testify to the antiquity of human settlement in Israel/Palestine. The folk etymologies interpreting the origins of toponyms reflect a historical image of about fifteen hundred years, thus the names create a multitemporal space that exists in several periods of time and memory. The long period of time represented in the Palestinian toponymic nomenclature demonstrates the formation of names as ancient linguistic layers and serves as a cultural and linguistic expression of the cumulative consciousness of the waves of peoples and cultural identities that have passed through the region.

The Arabic toponymy of the names of inhabited localities that emerges from folk legends and folklore is a panoramic act, a mosaic of traditions and religions. Traditions reflect the place's historical map and the complexity of spatial identity. The Palestinian map reveals openness to other views, religions, and beliefs. Hence, the space of non-Arab ethnic traditions does not cease to exist and is not erased. The people who gave the villages their names and applied their interpretations to them did not intend to achieve political power over the space while denying the Other. That is, the mere connection by the locals of the place where they live to the Islamic tradition, for example, can constitute a political statement regarding Islam's hold over the place. However, the local tradition does not mark the space's ethnic past in dichotomous terms that distinguish each group from each other alone but rather creates continuity between different ethnicities.

The names used by Palestinians are not singular in their origins and do not make the Other foreign; rather, they entail intermediate shades of languages and content. These names were formed in connection with the long-standing traditions of the residents of the area according to the definition of Arab Palestinian localness as well as by the diverse perceptions of the ethnic, religious, and national identities of the peoples who came to the place. The names gradually evolved in response to major historical events of the Muslim Arabs and other peoples who visited and resided in Palestine and in response to local intrasocial events.

The Islamic presence, associated with the actions of Muslim generals and fighters, is the dominant factor in legends that attribute the names of the villages to leaders. The names of fighters who are associated with the wars of the first caliphs, and especially with the campaigns of Saladin and his warriors, are the result of clashes between Muslims and Byzantines and between Muslims and Crusaders. The story of these names is rooted in historical contexts that form part of the Muslim collective memory. These names together create a narrative according to which the place was granted to its inhabitants by the Muslims' religious commanders. The construction of the names in the depths of the ancient past creates a space with mythical and emotional meaning and, at the epistemological level, gives the Arabs priority and historical right over the space described through the names.[78] This construction emphasizes the persistence and continuity between the Muslims' past and present in Palestine. It seems that names of this kind seek to narrate the contribution of the territory of each and every village to the story of the whole umma and to highlight the spatial part and status of each village in the history of the entire collective. The relative prominence of Muslim spatial memory versus the relative marginality of Arab Christianity in the names of villages originates, perhaps, in the demographic composition of Palestinian society in Israel, which today is predominantly Muslim, rather than in the absence of a Christian tradition related to the place's cultural identity. The dwindling of the Christian population has limited the availability of their oral tradition.

The impression that emerges from the etymologies is that only a few of the names of Palestinian villages were created in response to actual deeds of a Muslim figure or of an Arab leader within the village and its vicinity. Most of the names within this conceptual theme are imagined and invented. It is possible that Saladin or his commanders came to the entrance of a certain village or fought near it, but what happened, following the sociologist Maurice Halbwachs (1992, 84–120), is a process of "decentralization of memory" to other and different places. Attributing a name's origin to warriors not only is an expression of appreciation for the leaders and their deeds but also, on a psychological level, strengthens the image of the place and its inhabitants. The map of Palestinian names reveals the emotional and mental images of those who determined the names. In other words, the names of the localities that are not clear to the Arab population are "spaces" that have neither meaning nor content. Some of the names of the localities in which Palestinian society currently resides have ancient linguistic foundations unknown to Arabic speakers. The explanations that the speakers of this language invent to explain these names' origins are a response to an inner contemplation that is revealed through the interpretations.

From the gender aspect, the vast majority of the names of Arab localities attributed to human figures are of a masculine-paternal nature and relate to men's actions. High-ranking heroes (a caliph, a sage, a Muslim or Byzantine commander), local leaders, and tribal leaders are "adopted" to explain the Arab names of the villages and mark their origins—these figures are mostly symbolic and typical, perpetuating an important idea for the Arab nation or the villagers. One can clearly sense a conscious trend of choosing names. The Arabic interpretation of these names' origins locates them among people from general history, exemplary and prominent Muslim figures, local leaders, founding fathers, and tribal leaders.

The impression given by many etiological legends is of an interethnic binary division, as well as of an intraethnic-Arab binary division of "us" versus "them"—the Muslims and the Arabs on one side and the Byzantines and the Crusaders on the other. These legends seem to show that a certain tribe struggled with another one. Quite a few of the names of the villages and their onomastic identity in the Arab folk tale signify religious and local conflicts.

At the basis of the development of the etiological legends and the crystallization of Palestinian names of localities, one senses both population movement and migration from distant places and the intraregional migration of locals. Intrusions from outside the borders of Israel/Palestine, constant mobility between the villages, and nomadic or seminomadic lifestyles—all these are a dominant factor in the formation of the Arabic names of inhabited localities, which were created in an extended and prolonged process, consisting of many layers. The names developed in a manner expressive of a dialectic between sedentary life and nomadism. The status of the place in the context of names is shaped by a play between ephemerality and temporality, on the one hand, and between permanence and locality, on the other. This idea is partly explained by the nomadic or seminomadic past way of life of the culture in which the name legends are told. The impression that emerges from the etiological stories, centered on local Arab Palestinian figures and non-Arab figures alike, is that the names of the villages are read from "outside" as well as "inside," according to Palestinians. On the one hand, the naming emphasizes the role of generals, nomads, and passersby, and on the other hand, there is also an echo of the local geography and of the locals' character.

Palestinian collective memory is not identified only with Muslims but rather is linked to the common heritage of local Arab society. Customs and social values, such as hospitality, loyalty to the tribe, blood covenant, and courage, are some of the materials "adopted" by the Arab narrators to provide meaning to the names of their inhabited localities. These names are ethnographic expressions that reflect the social identity of the narrating group.

An examination of the Palestinian names of inhabited localities that originate in nature reveals that these names are supposedly committed to ideas that present nature and its resources in a positive and sympathetic light. A prominent motif is that in the consciousness of the Arab narrator, only "our village," and not any other village, was blessed with the geographical, topographical, and climatic virtues that gave rise to its name; only "our village" was known for the quality of its water and vegetation, which in some cases even provided locals and passersby with cures for their diseases (Rubinstein 1990, 23–24). The shaping of the spatial reality is fully revealed by the clear fact that the benefits that the space provides are the exclusive domain of Arab Palestinian and Muslim figures in the stories. In contrast, the Other is not described as enjoying the place's virtues and beneficence. The construction of space as a factor that benefits the Arab but not the Other is a statement that the "stranger" and "foreigners" find the place exotic and mysterious. The beneficence of the area was bestowed on both local Palestinians and Muslims and on Arabs who came from foreign countries. Both groups praised the features of the place, and their sayings and thoughts became names.

At the center of the names associated with Muslim generals stands religious identity, but under certain circumstances, religious identity becomes an element in national identity. In a reality where Palestinians suffer discrimination and dispossession of their lands, the names attributed to Muslim fighters and the lush natural environment are ethnolinguistic expressions, indicating Palestinian narrators' right to memory in relation to a particular place at a particular time. For the narrators, the past is not something bygone but a pulsating and living collective memory associated with the place and its names.

Palestinian naming serves, in miniature, as a reminder of the indeterminate nature of the space, ethnic perceptions, and Arab identities, all of which struggle to control it and present its history. The identity of the space is not unequivocally worded, and it has multiple meanings: the space is conflicted and is subject to controversy. Peoples and nations come to it and others leave and abandon it, one tribe struggles with another tribe. The status of the place exists at the crossroads of conflicts between the ethnic groups that have arrived there over the generations. On a smaller scale, the status of the space also exists through the struggles that took place between the local Palestinian Muslim Arab identity and the Christian Arab identity of this region.

Honko (1981) emphasized the adaptation of a narrative tradition and the changes that take place in it when it is absorbed in a particular sociocultural context and in a new area. In this spirit, it can be argued that associating supralocal stories drawn from extraterritorial cultural spaces and borrowing narrative traditions from the past to justify the name of a specific village point to a process of adapting these traditions to the new cultural environment. The Palestinian narrators drew on foreign and ancient explanations in order to decipher some of the names of inhabited localities that were foreign to the Arab ear and to create a sense of belonging and ownership vis-á-vis the place. The growing impression is that some of the names precede the legends and that these textual units were created to give meaning to names that were obscure to Arabic speakers and to domesticate the landscape through their language.

The interpretation applied by Palestinians to the names of the inhabited localities in which they lived is not limited to the representation of the concepts of the outside world or to the "objective" and "factual" representation of the terms denoting the villages. This interpretation is an active factor in creating a folk etymology and its reasoning and in creating a geohistorical narrative that connects the narrators with their natural environment, their past, and the other societies that have lived and still live in Israel. It would therefore be accurate to say that in many cases, according to the Palestinians place legends indicate the existence of additional names and other cultural interpretations, not necessarily Arab ones.

At the center of the interpretation of names lies the relationship between signifiers, the names, and the signified, the meaning of the names. The relationship between the signifiers and the signified is built on limited arbitrariness, in the words of Ferdinand de Saussure (1974, 67–68). The names of localities are symbols whose hidden meanings are in some cases different from the obvious ones.

The interpretation given by Arabic speakers to the names provides meaning to the symbol, mediating between the signifiers and the signified. The fact that there are different interpretations of the name means that the interpretive field is extensive, and hence the connection between the signifiers and the signified is not absolute and limited and can be broken down. In other words, there is no necessary connection between the common signifiers in the speech of Arabic speakers and the linguistic and cultural Arabness of the names.

THE NARRATIVE OF THE LAND AND NATURAL LANDSCAPE IN PALESTINIAN NAMES

SINCE THE 1980S, ANTHROPOLOGISTS' AND cultural historians' interest in the names given by local peoples to their natural environment has increased. Anthropologists consider the terminology of natural landscapes a cultural document that provides information about the experience of the natural surroundings and how it is perceived and conceptualized by locals (Dodge 2007, 4–9; Ryden 1993, 63, 78–79).

Studies indicate four factors that contribute to the processes that tie traditions to a specific physical environment: exploiting nature, controlling the environment (milieu dominance), the local-historical framework of events, and place-names (Honko 1981, 20–21). These factors help explain, albeit partially, the formation of the traditions related to a particular place. The fourth factor, place-names, is the most relevant to our study, and it forms the focus of this chapter. Following the Swedish ethnologist Albert Eskeröd, Lauri Honko proposed the term "dominant factor in the environment" to denote natural features that stand out from their surroundings, commanding the field of vision. The shape and dimensions of dominant factors in the environment may ignite the imagination, generate stories, and engender names. However, the most common phenomenon is that they become the focus of existing traditions (Honko 1981, 20–21). Honko's and Eskeröd's explanations emphasize the environment's role in the creation of traditions about, and names of, natural features, but sometimes the formation of legends, traditions, and explanations of place-names should be attributed not to a dominant factor in the environment but rather to historical events (Honko 1981, 22).

Claude Lévi-Strauss (1969) coined the term "totemic geography," that is, the organization of space according to rituals and myths that link human origins to animals and natural features. The categories of natural species and the myths associated with them may also be used to organize space. An example of this is the totemic geography of the Alurija people, a Native American tribe in the United States, who matched each bump or depression of a rocky site within their area of residence to a certain stage in their cultic rituals and gave each place a name and a meaning. They see this rocky mass as an illustration of the structures of their myths and of their ritual array. The names assigned to locations in the rock describe cultural-tribal beliefs and express ideas and beliefs concerning the tribal members' attachment to the totemic father (Lévi-Strauss 1969).[1] In fact, totemic geography emphasizes that the understanding of nature is constructed under the influence of two factors: the context-laden environment, on the one hand, and the human observation point and cultural context, on the other.

Hunter-gatherer societies, such as the Temiars in the Malay Peninsula, are characterized by their intimate relationship with the land. The names these hunters and gatherers gave to places are drawn from the natural environment, from the vegetation, and from the cracking sounds of breaking branches. These societies believe that spirits and demons are present in the natural environment, inspiring the composition of songs and the bestowal of place-names (Roseman 1998, 110–13).

Other researchers insist on the connection between unique sites in the geographical environment and the culture expressed in the names. According to the geographer Edward Relph, a place's identity is related to its physical environment. A monotonous environment without unique features alienates people. Conversely, a diverse physical environment, with clear physical foundations, will increase awareness of it. Another element of a place's identity is the meaning that people attribute to the environment and the human activity that takes place there (Relph 1976, 44–49).

Indeed, around the world one will often find names of natural features indicating the owners of the place (possessive names), the founders, or the tribes living there. There are also names of natural features that originate from a specific event (incident names) that occurred in a certain place (Room 1997, 4–5). On the Palestinian map, too, there are names and traditions about natural features that are associated with the names of people; I have described many of these cases in the previous chapter. The purpose of the present chapter is to develop this discussion framework and emphasize the uniqueness of the process of formation of Palestinian names of natural features in order to understand their meaning and cultural values.

Local men and women figure prominently in the Palestinian names of natural features. The characteristics of names of both sexes are evident in the gallery of personas and in the difference in cultural values. In the spirit of the words of the American ethnographer and folklore researcher Dell Hymes (1996, 14), it can be said that place-names and their stories were created in relation to a combination of sociocultural factors: the nature of social life, roles and statuses, duties and rights, transmitted values, environmental restrictions, and differences in community members' access to natural resources. In the following sections, we detail these factors with reference to names.

TOPONYMS INFLUENCED BY MEN FROM ARAB LANDS AND BY PALESTINIAN MEN

The names of natural features inspired by men who came from Arab countries and Palestinian men are divided into three types: names of natural features inspired by people from a low socioeconomic status; names of natural features inspired by Druze men;[2] and names of natural features inspired by personalities from the British Mandate period.

Names Inspired by People from a Low Socioeconomic Status

Qabr al-ʿAbid (قَبِر العَبِد)—"the slave's tomb"
Al-ʿAbid is an Egyptian who was married to a woman named Turfanda. He came to our country almost two hundred years ago and lived with the Qāsim Muḥammad Badārna family, whose socioeconomic situation was good. He would serve them in all their day-to-day tasks, but over time their financial and social situation deteriorated somewhat.

His masters asked him to find him another family, or to find another source of livelihood. Their request did not allow him to rest, and he took his wife, Turfanda, and headed to Wādī Sallāma to look for a source of livelihood. But due to his grief and because his future was shrouded in darkness, his health failed, and he died. Qabr al-ʿAbid is named after the Egyptian slave and his wife who lie there.[3]

Qabr al-ʿAbid in Sakhnīn is an earthen mound identified with an Egyptian slave who died while passing through the village and was buried there. This man died of hunger and sorrow while unsuccessfully trying to make a living for himself and his family. The source of the name is therefore an enslaved man, and the legend tells of his unhappiness and his doom. This gloomy atmosphere is conveyed already in the first part of the name, *qabr*, "grave, tomb," while the second part indicates the character's social status. The name legend summarizes the story of the slave's life of constant sorrow and details stations in his life—his Egyptian origin, his enslaved status, the worsening of his health, and his tragic end.

Many other natural features are named after slaves and servants. A fig tree in the south of the village of Nīn, far from the houses of the inhabited locality, is called Tīnat Abū Sālim (تينة ابو سالم) after the person who planted it. Abū Sālim was a slave who served a master from the village. At the end of the working day, he used to go to the tree, take off his clothes, and sleep under it. In this case, naming the tree for Abū Sālim indicates his ownership of it but also serves as a reminder of the slave's lifestyle and the position assigned to him by society to fulfill his desires: after all, this is a fig tree, a small natural feature, and one located at the edge of the inhabited locality. A similar idea is expressed in the name al-Ṣaʿīdiyya (الصُّعيديّة), which was given to a fig grove in the village of Dabbūriyya, the area of which later expanded. This grove is called al-Ṣaʿīdiyya after an enslaved girl from Upper (southern) Egypt (Ar.: al-Ṣaʿīd) who was entrusted with guarding it.[4] The name directly indicates the slave's geographic origin and her position and work—she was entrusted with guarding the grove.

Stories like these teach about the social structure of parts of the Palestinian population even under Ottoman rule. The stories provide evidence of waves of immigration and a polarized social stratification (higher class versus lower class; masters versus slaves). It is possible that the commemoration of enslaved individuals in natural features was meant to arouse compassion toward this group and make its voice and the hardships of its existence heard.

Class differentiation is reflected in the location and size of the place bearing the name: the plot called Qabr al-ʿAbid is located in a liminal area, between Sakhnīn and Wādī Sallāma, and Tīnat Abū Sālim is in the south of Nīn, on the outskirts of the inhabited locality. In other words, the location of the sites named after characters whose social origin is inferior is on the edge of the locality and not in its center or within it, in an empty and uninhabited space. The name of the enslaved man or woman is identified with a natural feature whose area is small—a plot of land, a tree, a grove. In this way, the content and location of the name reflect the relationship between social structure and spatial structure: the social polarization between the local Palestinian residents, who are placed in the center of the village, while slaves and servants are in the geographic periphery.[5]

Traces of the Roma people (Ar.: *al-nawar*, lit. "gypsy") are also evident in the Arabic nomenclature. The use of the term *gypsy*, as a historical reference, may encode the sedentary residents' negative attitude toward nomads, because their image is that of wanderers who create a commotion around them, beggars, and thieves. Names that refer to Roma usually indicate collectives, for example, Manzalat al-Nawar (مِنزَلة النَّوَر), "the gypsy camp," in the village of Buʿayna. One of the areas between Ṭamra and Iʿblīn is also called Khalāyil al-Nawar (خَلايِل النَّوَر),[6] because Roma from Jordan used to settle there temporarily, coming out to beg in the local villages. A large piece of land in the southeast of Jaffa was called Manzal al-Nawar (منزل النَّوَر), "the gypsy camp," since Roma came every year and established a temporary residence there, from where they went out to beg and sell handcrafts. In these cases, the geographical name creates meanings related to the Roma's foreign origin, low socioeconomic status, and nomadic way of life. Similarly, some of the places called after locals of low socioeconomic status refer to acts of piracy and robbery.

> Maqtal Mulāzim (مَقْتَل مُلازِمْ)—"the place of Mulāzim's murder"
> Mulāzim from the tribe of al-Mawāsī said to his uncle: "I wish to marry your daughter."
> The uncle told him: "Her bride-price (*mahr*) is seven heads of cattle."
> Mulāzim said, "Very well," got up and headed in the direction of al-Mafālaḥ in Ṣaffūriyya. A woman lived there who owned seven cows. He stole the first, second, third, fourth cow . . . and gave them to his uncle. He still had to get the seventh cow. He went and stole her, but due to fatigue, he had difficulty controlling the cow that shook him from left to right.
> The plowmen saw him and called the woman, and she said to them: "O my relatives, seven heads of cattle, of which I still have only the young cow, which he has just stolen. I don't know where he came from."
> They went out to look for him, they saw a man plowing his land, "Did you see anyone?"
> He said: "By God, yes, a man and a cow with him, he is before you, before you."
> The thief reached the edge of Marj al-Billan ("valley of the thorny burnet") and there he got tired, tied the cow to a jujube tree, and slept near the jujube.
> The pursuers continued to look for him until they reached him and saw that he was sleeping. They immediately put a gun to him and murdered him.[7]

On the one hand, the name legend reveals a personal story, the troubles of an individual bachelor, in the face of the demands made by marriage customs. On the other hand, it reveals the community's commitment to protecting a weak woman. Thus, the legend ties the place-name to the individual's hardships in the community and to the ways of dealing with them, against the background of the conditions of tribal life in the past. Mulāzim, who wanted to marry his cousin, was required to pay seven head of cattle for her, since he was unable to pay in cash.[8] He went to the Falāḥāt tribe and stole the number of cows necessary to pay the *mahr*. The young cow revealed him. He was shot and killed, and the scene of his murder was named after him. The character of the place, the jujube tree, the site of the murder, and the cow resonate in the background of the name given to the plot of land. A feeling of sadness and restlessness is expressed in the first word of the name, *maqtal*, that is, the place of the robber's murder.

The reality of robberies is hinted at in the linguistic signs of some streams and caves known as Ḥarāmiyya (حَرَامِيَّة), that is, "robbery" or "the robbers": Wādī al- Ḥarāmiyya in the hills of Jerusalem and Maghārat al-Ḥarāmiyya, "the cave of the robbers," in Kafr Kannā and Kābūl. These places, because of their closed, narrow topographical nature and because they were usually far from inhabited localities, were repeatedly the target of robbers who attacked the passersby and the herdsmen's flocks.

Besides reflecting the existential and economic reality of local society in the past, names influenced by folk figures often also refer to the activities of peasants and shepherds. The name Arḍ Abū Yaʿqūb, "the field of Abū Yaʿqūb," originates from the fact that a farmer from the village of Jishsh dug a *jurn* (water hole) so that birds could drink from it. As a result, the water hole was also called Jurn Abū Yaʿqūb. In ʿAyn Māhil, Wādī al-Mashtā, "the stream of shelter from the winter," is a stream (with a cave in its area) where shepherds found shelter from sudden rainstorms. ʿAyn al-Ḥajj Qāsim, to the northeast of ʿAyn Māhil, is named after Qāsim, the owner of the plot of land in which the spring is located.[9] Qāsim was a farmer who worked the land and used to maintain the spring, raise vegetables and flocks, and water them from the spring water. The commemoration of Qāsim's religious title, *al-ḥajj*, stems from the fact that he was the first person in the locality to make the pilgrimage to Mecca, riding a camel, probably in the Ottoman period. Names inspired by peasants sometimes express courage. Jabal al-Ghūl, "the mountain of the ghoul" in the village of Iʿblīn, is named after a peasant nicknamed al-Ghūl. This man had a piece of land in the mountain, and he used to remove the rocks with his own hands and transfer them from place to place. It is also said that he found a neighbor's horse grazing in his plot and wanted to make it disappear. So that the animal's tracks would not be discovered, he picked it up and hid it in another plot of land. Due to these deeds, the man received the nickname al-Ghūl, which became a name for the mountain. Thus, the geographical noun combines the physical attributes of the name's subject with the people's attitude toward him: they gave this person his nickname out of admiration for his strength and to express their fear of him. The name Jabal al-Ghūl uses a cruel mythical figure as a metaphor for the power of a human being (whose real name is not given at all) and the attitude of the local people toward him, which has changed over the generations: Jabal al-Ghūl was changed to Jabal al-Nūr, " the mountain of light," perhaps because the mountain's previous name included "ghoul," now considered by its inhabitants to have a negative image that might label them as superstitious.

Sometimes names were also inspired by the narrowest world of the individual, as the following name legend demonstrates.

> Karm al-Miskīn (كَرم المَسْكين)—"the poor man's grove"
> This man, after his mother gave birth to him, his father died. He and his mother lived alone, and he himself had no children. That's why they called him al-Miskīn. This name followed him all his days.[10]

Karm al-Miskīn is an olive grove in Iksāl village. The grove got its name not because of the economic poverty of the owners, as one might think at first, but because of a biological feature. The nickname of the grove's owner overshadowed his given name, and the locals used the nickname instead of the real one to name the place. The man was considered to be ill-fated because he was deprived of the power of procreation and an orphan, although initially, according to the narrator, the place was called Karim Ḥāmid after al-Miskīn's father. *Al-miskīn* is an emotional metaphorical expression, indicating the surroundings' attitude toward the individual. Through the name, the givers express the man's unhappiness and remember their compassion for him.

The names of natural features can also express respect for local men of religion. Natural features bear the names *al-khaṭīb*, "the preacher"; *al-shaykh*, a Muslim cleric who leads public prayer; *al-khūrī*, "the priest"; and *al-rāhib*, "the monk."[11]

> Qāriṭāt al-Shaykh Aḥmad (قَرْطَات الشَّيخ أحمد)[12]—"Shaykh Aḥmad's plots of land"
> A *shaykh* came from Jabal Nāblus to the village, and his name was Shaykh Aḥmad. He addressed [the people]: "O friends, I want to support my family, I want to serve as a preacher." In the old days there were no schools, and the *shaykh* gathered the children in the mosque, or in one of the far houses in the village and taught them. He would call to prayer and lead the people during prayer. That is, he served as imam and teacher in the village.
> The villagers said to Shaykh Aḥmad: "What do you think, Shaykh, we have a plot of land, we will plow it for you, we will harvest it, we will bring its grain to the thresher and thresh it, and this will be your salary." (The land involved was twenty-five dunams.) The man gave his consent and continued to preach and teach the little children.
> Seven or eight years later, approximately, the people began to say *qāriṭāt al-Shaykh Aḥmad*, and to this day, they call the area by that name.

The origin of the name given to the plot of land in Ṣandala is a personal story concerning the positive role played by the cleric Shaykh Aḥmad in the local community. The name given to the plot of land is a consequence of an intra-social religious identity. Through the name and its story, details concerning the structure of Palestinian agrarian society and its lifestyle are revealed: the education of boys, the teacher, and the role and place of the mosque. The name came into existence in the Ottoman era. At that time, there was not a single literate person in the entire village.[13] The preacher, who came from another locality, was also the teacher and imam who led the prayer in the mosque. Schools began to develop in Arab villages only at the end of the nineteenth century and, within the mosque, taught boys the Qur'an, reading, and the basics of arithmetic. Shaykh Aḥmad, whose name became the signifier of the field, represents the shaykhs who served as teachers, suffered in poverty, and survived on the charity given by the locals and the students' fathers in the form of coins, wheat, or fields sown with legumes. The name legend links the explanation of the name's origin with the preacher's living conditions and the nature of education in the Palestinian village in the past. The name of the field, Qāriṭat al-Shaykh Aḥmad, is a reminder of the preacher's lifestyle, an expression of gratitude and identification with him and his work as a man of religion.

Gratitude also exists in the name ʿUyūn Mūsā (عيون موسى)—Mūsā's springs. The name ʿUyūn Mūsā was given to the springs in Jabal Sīkh on the outskirts of Rayna. The main theme in the story of ʿUyūn Mūsā is the peasants' existential concerns in the face of the ravages of nature. The name was given after the priest Mūsā, known for his piety, led a joint prayer of Christians and Muslims on the mountain in the middle of a drought year. Even before he finished his prayer, water flowed from the ground. The story echoes episodes in the Bible and the Qur'an.[14] It is possible that the story of ʿUyūn Mūsā seeks to glorify Christian superiority over Muslims. Such superiority is symbolized in the figure of the priest, who besides leading the prayer, also brings rain after a year of drought. According to this interpretation, the priest's spiritual act (prayer), which affects the order of nature, perhaps also contains a statement about the appropriation of (local) nature for the benefit of Christians.

We now turn to the names that indicate the lands endowed to mosques and churches. Plots of this type are referred to as *arḍ al-waqf* in a number of variations,[15] with the conjunction *al-jāmiʿ*, "the mosque," or *al-kanīsa*, "the church." In some cases, plots were donated by the locals, motivated by the desire to perform charitable deeds and benefit the village poor, those who study the Qur'an, and religious institutions. Endowment land was leased, or its grain and crops were sold, to finance the purchase of kerosene and mats for the prayer houses as well as religious pamphlets. Part of the endowment, in cash or in kind, was given as a gift to the needy and to those who study the Qurʾan or the Scriptures.

Names of the arḍ al-waqf type emphasize the lands' belonging to the house of prayer, the social aspects of religion (e.g., giving charity), and the commandments of good deeds between humans and their fellows. These expressions give the space a religious-social meaning. As such, the space becomes even more blessed and respected.

Names Inspired by Druze Men

The names of natural features attributed to local figures also include toponyms influenced by the Druze religious identity. This identity is expressed in two ways: (1) place-names based on the motif of seclusion and asceticism and (2) place-names connected to the deeds of the prophet Sabalān.[16]

Seclusion and Asceticism

Shaqīf al-ʿĀbid (شَقِيف العابِد)—"the cliff of the pious man"
Between the village of Jaththh and the village of Yarkā there is a chain of cliffs called Shaqīf al-ʿĀbid. It is said that ʿĀbid, God's servant, used to live there. There is a cave in the place, and it is very difficult to get to it—you can't go up to it from below and you can't go down to it from above.

One day, one of the locals decided to approach and befriend God's servant and learn from him the principles of religion and worshipping the Creator. He walked until he came close to him and called to him, saying: "O servant of the Creator, I wish to follow your path and learn from you."

He [ʿĀbid] said to him: "Welcome! But are you able to bear hardships and suffer the way I do?"

He said: "I will try, with God's help."

It is said that he lowered a woven basket to him and said to him: "Go down to the spring, ʿAyn al-Majnūna"—which is located below Shaqīf al-ʿĀbid—"fill the basket with water and return to me."

The man was puzzled and said to him: "But this is a woven basket and how can it hold the water, how can I use it to transport water?"

He said to him: "Since you do not have faith in the ability of the Creator, may He be praised and exalted, to help you to carry the water, you will not be able to live with me."

The man was convinced, said goodbye to God's servant and returned to his home.[17]

The cliff received its name because it was the abode of God's servant, an ascetic who dedicated himself to worshipping the Creator. The various aspects of the etiological story—the place, the person who wants to know the principles of religion, the dialogue between the characters (the event) and the way the story is designed—symbolize certain aspects of the Druze religious experience. The abode of God's servant is a liminal natural place, between Jathth and Yarkā. On the allegorical level, the place corresponds to a *khalwa*, the Druze prayer house. The literal meaning of *khalwa* is "seclusion" or "isolation," and sometimes the prayer house was removed from any inhabited settlement. The worshipper of God who seeks solitude symbolizes the piety of the Druze believer, who strives to conduct his religious affairs peacefully and confidentially. The episode in which the person who seeks to know the secrets of the religion fails is a parable for the obstacles in the way of those who wish to discover the main principles of the Druze faith and to become one of the faithful. In addition, this person's return home, without having discovered anything about the secret of the believer's asceticism, is a testimony to the closed nature of the Druze religion and an example of the curious "outsiders" whose efforts to learn its secrets founder.

The cliff Shaqīf al-ʿĀbid is located at the edge of the settlement, just like Maghārat Mahanā al-Makannā (مغارة مهَنا المكَنّى), a cave named after Mahanā, a Druze cleric from the village of Jathth. He stopped digging a cave intended for storing rainwater, instead preparing himself for the world to come.

The names and their stories are suited to the places' religious purpose and location. The places are designed as thresholds or liminal territories. It is precisely because of this quality that they are suitable for asceticism, abstinence from social life, and devoting oneself to matters between humans and the deity. In the explanations of these names, in some of which empirical motifs characteristic of saints' legends are evident, the etiological element serves the folk narrator as a poetic tool marking the religious uniqueness of the Druze community.

The Deeds of Nabī Sabalān

There are names that are explained by recounting the miracles of the prophet Sabalān and the wonders he performed thanks to his devout faith in God. For example, the name Wādī al-Ḥabīs (وادي الحَبيس), "the stream of the trap," in Ḥurfeish originates from a story in which Sabalān sought God's intervention against his persecutors; God summoned a cloud that sent torrential rain at the height of summer, and this rain captured (*ḥabasa*) the infidels who tried to harass Sabalān in a wadi that would later be called Wādī al-Ḥabīs.[18]

The blessing and healing properties of ʿAyn al-Dirra (عين الدِّرّه), "the spring of the nipple," in Ḥurfeish derive from the fact that the prophet Sabalān drank from its waters. The women of the area, whose breast milk was not enough to feed their babies, anointed their nipples with the blessed spring water and their milk supply increased.

The place-names inspired by Druze believers symbolically express aspects of Druze religious identity. The natural features named after Druze believers are located in remote places and designed as territories with liminal characteristics. The name legends illustrate the belief that prophets and Druze believers can influence the forces of nature and cause them to act to their or their community's advantage.

Commemorating Palestinians Killed by the British Forces

Most of the names in this group are based on local characters, represented by titles of various kinds. These titles were given to figures or geographical objects following events that occurred during the British Mandate period (1918–48) as a direct result of the exploits of British soldiers or due to the general mood prevailing in Arab villages during that time.

The names commemorating rebels, martyrs, and traitors are related to events that affected the future of the Palestinian population. Signs of these events are also evident in the folk art of those days.[19]

> Maghārat al-Shuhadā (مُغارِة الشُّهَدا)—"the martyrs' cave"
> Seven *shuhadā*, martyrs, sons of Safed families, were murdered in Wādī
> al-Qaḥāb by British soldiers due to an informer. The British arrived prepared,
> in three groups. They reached the spring, found the seven rebels, and killed
> them.
>
> When this became known to the residents of 'Akbara and of Safed, they
> moved their bodies to the cave and buried them there, changing the name of
> the cave from Maghārat al-Bayādir (مغارة البيادر) to Maghārat al-Shuhadā.[20]

The name of Maghārat al-Shuhadā in the village of 'Akbara, is an outcome of political events that affected the Palestinian population and Palestinian villages during the period of the British Mandate in Palestine. The takeover of Palestinian lands by British forces left its mark on their terminology and spatial design. The cave's original name was Maghārat al-Bayādir, "the cave of the threshers." Changing the name due to the death of the rebels[21]—a group of Palestinian militants during the Great Arab Revolt of 1936–39—is a transition from nature to Palestinian national history. From a place associated with normal human and agricultural activities (shepherds' lodging with the herd, shelter from the rains, storing grain, etc.), the cave becomes a burial place for fallen fighters, that is, an element in shaping the Palestinian patriotic identity. The name *shuhadā*, martyrs, also recurs in *arḍ al-shuhadā*, which is a plot of land in Kafr Kannā, where three martyrs of the battles of 1948 were buried.

The names Maghārat Ḥasan, "Ḥasan's cave," and Balāṭat al-Banāt, "the rock of the girls," also came into being against the background of the clash between the locals and the British forces. Ḥasan, a resident of what was then Transjordan, arrived in Kafr Sulam and worked together with people from the village against the British forces, who were besieging the village with tanks. Ḥasan fled with his allies to the mountains until he was captured by his pursuers. The origin of the name Balāṭat al-Banāt, "the rock of the girls," is related to the tragic story of the girls from Dayr Ḥanā, who, returning home from the fields one day during the harvest season, were gunned down and killed by a British plane. They died on a vegetation-covered rock under which they were trying to hide.

The names of the Palestinian martyrs killed by British forces constitute a form of memorial to those who were killed by the British occupiers, shaping the place as an element of the national narrative. The names evoke historical memories of Palestinian society during the mandate and express the feelings of loss and political distress experienced by this society.

Other terms inspired by the conflict between the Palestinians and the British reproduce the feelings of separation and discord that existed within the local community.

> Bi'r al-Qutalā' (بير القُتَلى)—"the well of the killed"
> When the rebels suspected someone of collaborating with the British, they went and took him, shot him, and threw him into Bi'r al-Qutalā'.
>
> A man named Dhi'āb 'Abbūd from Nazareth, an income tax official, was said to be collaborating with the British, and the rebels went and brought him from his home at night, and shot him in the village of Wādī Rummāna. According to the rumors, they brought him while he was tied up and shot him, but he did not die immediately and he would scream and say: "I, if they had untied the rope from my shoulders—my God, that would be enough for me."
>
> Thus, he screamed and finally died, and his clothes were left on the road. I still remember: I, along with other women, went and played with his clothes.[22]

Bi'r al-Qutalā' was named after Palestinians who were thrown into it after being suspected of treason. The explanation of the name's origin reproduces the atmosphere of suspicion that prevailed among the local population during the period of resistance to British rule, and it evokes the division and separation between two Arab groups with contradictory political motives. Each of the groups reacted differently to the presence of the external factor, the British.

On the one hand, there is a group of "collaborators" with the enemy, who were labeled *khawana*, in the sense of traitors, even though in the name legend they are merely called "killed." On the other hand, there are the rebels, *al-thuwwār*, who revolted against the British enemy. Both nicknames reflect two opposite points of view regarding the deeds of those suspected of collaborating with the British. The scream heard by the passersby is a cry against the many injustices directed against the innocent, and it expresses the loss of the trusting relationships that prevailed in the community before the British occupation. The local girls' enjoying playing with the clothes of one of the dead men, Dhiʾāb ʿAbbūd, shows the extent of their contempt for the traitors.

The idea behind the name Biʾr al-Qutalāʾ is also repeated in the name Khalāyel al-Maqbara, "the burial chamber." This place served as an interrogation site for those suspected of collaborating with the British. If the suspect's guilt was proven, he was executed, and his body was dumped here.

These names are a reminder of the bitter fate and subsequent infamy of the accused collaborators. The spaces depicted in these terms are revealed to be terrifying. The naming society preferred not to give places derogatory nicknames fitting the actions of the traitors, instead choosing neutral ones, devoid of negative or positive connotation, perhaps to disguise the identity of the collaborators, who were a source of shame for the village and its residents. This trend also expresses the name-givers' desire to erase the memory of these figures from the space or, in any case, to avoid labeling the land and the place with ugly names. One way or another, the names of these natural features, whether referring to rebels or to collaborators, are a response to the political and existential crisis of the British Mandate period within the Palestinian community.

DEVIANT, PEASANT, AND BRIDE: THE PALESTINIAN WOMAN IN NAMES OF NATURAL FEATURES

Literature and folklore researcher Galit Hasan-Rokem (2000, 82–84) noted that folk literary creations are polyphonic and reveal hidden voices in society, including the voices of female characters and female symbols. The multivocality that characterizes folk creations provides a framework for understanding the presence of female figures in place-names originating from Palestinian folk culture. This multivocality opens the door to new insights, since onomastic studies generally tend to avoid dealing with the meaning of gender relations and the appearance of women in geographical names. It is not impossible that the reason for this is the lack of female representation in formal names that are determined "from above" by name committees, compared to their prominent representation in popular culture.[23]

My research shows that geographical names inspired by local women and their activities are found in many Palestinian villages. Markers of this type include three subgroups for names of natural features: those inspired by women accused of dishonoring the family, peasant women's traditional work, and marriage customs related to the bride.

Women Murdered on the Excuse of Forbidden Sexual Relations

These women became part of the local nomenclature due to their murder by their relatives under the pretext of having forbidden sexual relations.

Maghārat al-Mathūma (مُغارِة المَتّهومه)—"the cave of the wrongfully accused girl"

Maghārat al-Mathūma is one of the caves in the mountains, on the northern side of Iksāl, that is, in the Nazareth Mountains. It is located in a ravine called Wādī al-Mathūma.

The legend tells of a girl whose mother passed away, and her father married a second time. The girl grew up, and as often happens, disagreements between the daughter and her stepmother arose.

The stepmother noticed that the father was very devoted to his daughter and believed that the daughter was sharing her husband and therefore tried to get rid of her. Out of jealousy, she accused her of dishonoring the family.

The father, who wished to preserve his honor, immediately led his daughter to a distant place, to a ravine, butchered her in a cave, and stained the cave's entrance with her blood. To this day there is a dark stain at the entrance to the cave.

After he committed this deed and avenged his honor, it became clear that he was wrong and that this daughter was innocent and was falsely accused of wrongdoing.

To this day, the people tell this story, which is passed down from generation to generation. And when you reach the entrance to Maghārat al-Mathūma, you remember the story of the pure girl who was falsely accused.[24]

The origin of the name Maghārat al-Mathūma, in the village of Iksāl, is related to the desire to understand the meaning of the "dark stain at the entrance to the cave" (a red stain, according to local testimony). This natural phenomenon is explained in a story that revolves around the issue of blood ties in Palestinian society and murder for the crime of "dishonoring the family": a girl was accused of having extramarital sex and was murdered by her father in a cave.

Throughout the story, an atmosphere of conflict is felt between stepmother and stepdaughter, indicating the centrality of the concept of "family honor." The stepmother plots to remove the daughter based on two motives: first, the lack of obligation to protect a girl who is not related to the mother by blood ties and, second, jealousy and desire for exclusivity in the love of the man, the girl's father.[25] Her mother's death and her father's second marriage make the daughter's situation worse: she is separated from her father, suffers false accusations, and is finally murdered. The family's honor, which guided the father's actions, reflects cultural patterns that prohibit women from having sex outside of marriage. The girl's murder was intended to remove the disgrace that might adhere to the family's name and the head of the family due to illicit sex. Staining the entrance of the cave with his daughter's blood, the father made his actions public to restore his honor and that of his tribe in the eyes of society.[26] He is regarded by his society as a purifier who "returns honor," not as a murderer. The publicity involved in this act is also a warning to other women who may be tempted to violate the sexual taboo.

However, the father's admission, in retrospect, of his daughter's innocence, suddenly and entirely changes the relationships among the characters as well as the readers' relationship to the narrative. This discovery reveals a new facet of the girl's character. Her innocence, revealed only after her death, is the reason for her nickname *al-mathūma*, "the wrongfully accused girl," corresponding to her "new" status in the eyes of the community. This nickname also includes a critique of the horrific method by which the girl was killed, but it is a mild one because the murderer is not punished. The cave in which her fate was decided receives the girl's nickname, as does the nearby stream—Wādī al-Mathūma. From this moment on, the space bears witness to the unfortunate life of the murdered woman.

The name given to the cave is a monument that keeps alive the girl's tragic story, integrity, and innocence and ensures their perpetuation for generations. People who pass by the cave "remember the story of the pure girl, who was accused falsely," and they sing the song:

She went to Wadi	al-Mathūma at night
To the famous cave	until she reached a remote place
In the dark, an owl	flew by and screeched
About a woman who died, oppressed,	and men conspired to blame her![27]

The song sung in her memory is a continuation of the conceptual line expressed here, being a lament for the girl's fate. Her tragic tale awakens even the nocturnal birds, the owl—which dwells in caves and ruins—crying out against the injustice done to her and reproving her father as well as the men and the society that libel women.[28] As in other cultures, the owl in Arab culture symbolizes gloom and warns of an evil to come. The owl that utters the victim's cry in the story of Maghārat al-Mathūma foretells bad things for the society that takes human life.[29] The short poem is meant to not only describe the girl's fate but also turn the listeners' hearts to the girl's side and arouse opposition to men's cruelty. The name of the cave is linked to cultural patterns in gender relations and family ties in traditional Palestinian society. The name legend gives vivid expression to this reality but, at the same time, tries to challenge some of its principles.

Another example concerns the name Jalālat Ḥasna (جلاله حَسنَه). A *jalāla* is a narrow strip of land behind a terrace. Its nickname refers to the circumstances of the murder of the woman Ḥasna in this place, which was where she lived until she was murdered. Ḥasna was as her name is—that is to say, she was beautiful and also known for the beauty of her actions and for her generous reception of guests. It turns out that these virtues of hers and her living in a terrace, rather than a village, were sufficient reasons for spreading false rumors against her and throwing her corpse into a well.

Like the previous case, naming geographical objects after women is the result of male violence against female society. Throwing a woman into a well was meant to hide the shameful act she had committed. Here, too, as in the previous legend, a geographical site and the story associated with its name are used to commemorate a woman and the injustice done to her due to the cruelty of her parents and relatives. Ḥasna rebuked her murderers and slanderers with these words: "I am Hasna the innocent, innocent of guilt. By Allah! I will destroy your seed, your seed."[30] These words of Hasna are a kind of prayer to God to avenge her blood and bring her righteousness to light. In addition, hospitality and generosity to guests are an important custom that is deeply rooted in Arab culture since ancient times. The murder of a woman who observed the commandment of hospitality is a violation of the rules of conduct in this society.

In the place-names described in these stories, the women do not rebel against the male code but claim that they have not sinned. In contrast, the story of Khallat Zaynab (خلة زينب) describes the tragic fate of a woman who transgressed the patriarchal code for sexual relations in a traditional society. Zaynab's story is also told in the novel *Arabesques* by Anton Shammas (1988, 116): "At the turn of the century, Zeinab was the most beautiful woman in the Galilee. Folk poets spent many long nights rhyming songs in her praise. Men from all over the Galilee made their way up to Saʿsaʿ, the village of her birth, to behold if only for a moment her rare beauty." The locals believe the story of Zaynab to be true.[31] According to the common story related by the elders interviewed for this book, Zaynab murdered her husband in order to sleep with her lover. These actions infuriated her relatives and the village priest. Therefore, they brought her to the outskirts of the village, placed gunpowder in her genitals, and murdered her. After her death, her name was given to that plot of land.

Identifying a place with a woman's personal story can help understand the patriarchal forces that underlie traditional Palestinian society's approach to women's sexuality. Zaynab's behavior can be seen as an attempt to reject a husband forced on her by her family and to choose a partner herself.[32] Such an attempt undermines the main framework of this society—the family. The men's behavior must therefore be interpreted as a patriarchal struggle against Zaynab's rebellious nature and as a punishment for her husband's murder. Putting gunpowder in the woman's genitalia and murdering her is an act of violence whose purpose is to make amends and restore the family's honor that has been lost due to the woman's sexual behavior. This story is less critical of the idea of family honor than the two previous ones, because in this story the woman is not seen as innocent. Perhaps this is also the reason why the story is more brutal.

Here it is worth noting that the name Zaynab recurs as a geographical identifier in other villages as well: for example, Qanāt Zaynab, "Zaynab's water canal," in Ra's ʿAlī. This place received its name from the story of a different Zaynab, an unmarried girl who was murdered by her brother, who suspected her of having sex with a British officer.

The main motif in the stories reviewed here is the killing of a wife, sister, or daughter, due to promiscuous sexual behavior. The scene of the murder, according to the narrator and according to the generic component of the names, is a cave, a well, a *khalla*, a *jūra*, a *jallāla*, or a *khānūq*—the last four terms all indicate a narrow stretch of land between hills. In these places, women were suspected of violating sexual taboos, or they were dragged to these places and killed there. These natural formations have a resemblance to the female genital organ, so we cannot rule out the possibility that some of the places were associated with stories about women's honor due to their shape.

These places were linked to women's stories also because they are natural sites. The earth and nature are often referred to as female. Even in ancient literature, the mother was identified with the earth, and the woman, with the field. In many cultures, the archetype of Mother Earth prevailed.[33] Enclosed or bounded places (such as a garden, cave, island, valley, and forest) serve as common images for women, and the female body may have been identified with the earth due to their shared functions of reproduction and nourishment

(Lutwack 1984, 83–99). On a larger scale, cities, countries, and continents are also imagined in terms of women and mothers. In the words of the biblical prophets, Jerusalem is described as a mother: "For as soon as Zion travailed, she brought forth her children" (Isaiah 66:8); "That ye may suck, and be satisfied with the breast of her consolations" (Isaiah 66:11); and "As one whom his mother comforteth, so will I comfort you; and ye shall be comforted in Jerusalem" (Isaiah 66:13). Carolyn Marchant (1983, 20–32), who examined literary similes to study cultural relationships to nature, notes that in ancient cultures, especially in Native American culture, the earth is identified as female: a nurse, a nurturing mother, sensitive and protective, a vital and loving figure.

Permitting women's blood to be shed and throwing them into a well, in a cave, and onto agricultural terraces, even as they protest their innocence, reinforces the comparison of women to the earth (Slyomovics 1998, 207–9). Hence, in the Palestinian mind, the land has the image of a woman, one who has been harmed and her world destroyed, under the influence of the patriarchal concept. In this spirit, and as a result of this, these stories express a tendency to subvert the patriarchal structure and challenge the patterns of social behavior concerning gender relations. In this manner, the name legends associated with women represent a double discourse—first undermining the patriarchy and then confirming it.

The names of natural features that commemorate women whose blood was shed are sad and despairing expressions, and so is the status of the space created through these names. They are a form of linguistic monuments to the unfortunate past of Palestinian women and Palestinian society's attitude toward female sexuality, female dignity, and the value of female lives.

Peasant Women's Traditional Work

The geographical locations described in this group of names are sites where, or in whose vicinity, the peasant women (sing.: *fallāḥa*) used to perform tasks related to the household or agriculture. In some of the natural features and sites, the woman's first name is present, and in others, the nature of the tasks that women used to perform there appears.

> ʿAyn al-Nawm (عين النّوم)—"the spring of dozing"
> ʿAyn al-Nawm is a spring with little water, but it is not dry in the summer
> months. The women in Bayt Jann, like all Arab women, would get up at dawn
> to arrive on time and draw water from the spring, prepare provisions for the
> household and wash clothes.
>   The water of this spring was scarce, and by the time the women would
> fill the jugs, a long time would pass, and the women, due to fatigue and lack

of sleep, would close their eyes and doze off a little. Therefore, the spring is called ʿAyn al-Nawm.[34]

The name ʿAyn al-Nawm was given to the source of water because the women of Bayt Jann used to doze in its vicinity when they came to fill their jugs. The women of the village used to go to the spring to get water for the home and family. This chore caused fatigue and lack of sleep, and the forced wait by the spring only increased their fatigue. The combination of the woman's work and lifestyle and the scarcity of water from the spring gave the water source its name. The imprint of rural women was stamped on the geographical name due to their ongoing activity in the place—coming to the spring to draw water for household chores. Along with nature and the human factor, the time factor is also woven into the fabric of the name: that is, the women who had to wake up before daybreak to fetch water for housework fell asleep at the site.

The connection between the formation of the name and the female role of transporting water is also expressed in the name Bi'r Salmā, "Salmā's well." Salmā from the al-ʿAṭṭār family of Jishsh went to draw water from the well, and her shoe fell off and into the well. Since then, the well has been named after her, as has the area around the well.

Another example of the influence of the reality of Palestinian women's lives on the names of natural features is related to the collection of firewood.

Ḥajr al-Ḥaṭṭābāt (حَجر الحَطّابات)—"the rock of the [female] woodcutters" This stone was called Ḥajr al-Ḥaṭṭābāt because the woodcutters, who brought kindling from the forest, would, on their way back, rest their bundles on the stone. They would rest and then return to the village. As is well known, until the beginning of the twentieth century, there was no electricity in the village, and they did not use kerosene but relied on wood and kindling for cooking, baking, and bathing.[35]

Ḥajr al-Ḥaṭṭābāt, in Kafr Kannā, received this name due to the role it played in the lives of the woodcutters when they returned from the forest. This is a rock that was a place for women to rest from the drudgery of work and their heavy burdens. According to the testimony of the villagers, the stone was located in the east of the village, and it was intended for the woodcutters, for women alone. Men did not rest next to it because they used to gather wood in other places, usually away from women—in the north of the village in the Turān mountains. The men also had beasts of burden that carried the bundles of twigs, so they did not need rest. The designation *ḥaṭṭābāt* as an identifying element originating from women's work, repeats in the name Darb al-Ḥaṭṭābāt, "the path of the woodcutters," that the women of Lūbiyya[36] (Heb.: Lavi) walked back and forth on their way to collect kindling on Mount Turān.

Another aspect of the work assigned to women is found in the following example:

Khallat al-Ṭaḥḥānāt (خَلّة الطّحَانات)—"the *khalla* of the [female] millers"
Once upon a time there was a path that connected ʿAylūṭ and Ṣaffūriyya, and its name was Khallat al-Ṭaḥḥānāt. Women who had a *tahana* of wheat [a quantity taken for grinding], or burghul,[37] or *dura faranjiyya*,[38] or of local produce—made their way to Ṣaffūriyya on beasts of burden to grind the *tahana*. Since this road was on the outskirts and safe, these women walked it with their children.[39]

The origin of the name Khallat al-Ṭaḥḥānāt is from the women of ʿAylūṭ, who passed by this place on their way to and from the flour mill in Ṣaffūriyya (Heb.: Tzippori). The Palestinian women are commemorated in the context of the traditional work they performed: grinding grains of wheat to make bread.

The name legend reveals that the women used to walk in certain paths and not in others: there were ways that were considered safe, because they would not be harassed by men, and ways that were considered less safe. The spatial separation between women and men in the Palestinian perception affected the concepts that this society used to identify places and guided the men and women of this society in territorial gender relations.

Besides the woodcutters, millers, and drawers of water, washerwomen also left their mark on Palestinian toponymy. Wādī al-Ghassālāt, "the stream of the washerwomen," got its name from the fact that the women of Ḥurfeish used to wash their clothes and linens there and lay them out to dry on the rocks.

Some geographical features are also known by the first names or the nicknames of local women. Many of the women whose names are embedded in plots of land were widows or orphans who stood out for their skill in working the land and overseeing the agricultural crops. This is the picture that emerges from the following names, such as Naqarat Imm al-Ḥaysh (نقـرة إم الحيش). A *naqara* is a stony field, and the name Imm al-Ḥaysh refers to an elderly woman from Majd al-Kurūm who bore this nickname. Her original name was Khalwa al-Sulaymān. Her nickname was given to her because the members of her community appreciated her positive qualities; she knew how to improve the stony and barren soil and planted fruit trees in it for her livelihood. Her advanced age, the hard life that left her divorced and childless, her personal qualities as a farmer and tiller of her land—all these are summed up in the geographical name, which praises her virtues and also indicates her ownership of the land.

Another example is the name Tūtāt Mīlāda, "Mīlāda's mulberry tree," in Yāfat al-Nāṣira (Heb.: Yafiʿ), which Mīlāda used to watch over after the deaths of her husband and son in the Great Arab Revolt. Ruwaysat Umm ʿAlī[40] is a low hill on the eastern side of the village of Jathth. This plot was named after Umm ʿAlī, a poor widow blessed with many children. This woman was known for her hard work: she prepared fallow land, tilled it, and uprooted thorny burnet plants; she and her sons made a living from agriculture. The locals marveled at the widow's diligence, named the hill after her, and also made up a proverb based on it: "Learn the act of heroism from the low hill of Umm ʿAlī" (*taʿallam al-marjala min ruwaysat umm ʿalī*).

In these latter cases, we are talking about widows or spinsters, that is, women who are not protected by a spouse. In a somewhat paradoxical way, their "problematic" status as unmarried women gave them priority over other women because they owned assets, particularly the most important asset of all—land.

Marriage Customs Related to the Bride

The names *al-ʿarūs* (the bride), *al-ʿarayis* (the brides), and *al-ʿursān* (the grooms) are linguistic evidence of Palestinian wedding customs in the past. These names were given to places in the countryside or to plots of land at the outskirts of villages because they were meeting points for transferring brides in exchange marriages between two villages or because female ceremonies were held for girls on their wedding day in these places. In other cases, flat, spacious, and shady sites were given names from this semantic field because the intended bride and groom were brought there to celebrate with dabka dances and folk singing.

In many names of this type, the word *al-ʿarūs/al-ʿarayis/al-ʿursān* is the second part of a genitive construction, and the first part is commonly a tree (*shajara*) or a spring (*ʿayn*). The tree is usually an olive tree or carob tree,[41] because it was preferable to celebrate a marriage near olive or carob trees, ancient trees that were known for their shade cover.[42]

Hawdaj al-ʿArūs (هودَج العروس)—"the bride's litter"
Hawdaj al-ʿArūs is an area in the territory of our village, the territory of Rayna, at a distance of four kilometers west of the village. It served as a meeting place for Rayna, Ṣaffūriyya, and Kafr Mandā.

Villagers used to wed in exchange marriages; a man from Ṣaffūriyya would marry an ʿarūs, a bride, from Rayna, and in return a man from Rayna would bring a bride from Ṣaffūriyya. Their relatives went out in wedding processions to meet each other, and the first arrivals to this area, which later became known as Hawdaj al-ʿArūs, would have the camel kneel down. The two processions would meet at this point and alternate between themselves:

al-ʿarūs from our village is led to Ṣaffūriyya and *al-ʿarūs* from Saffuriya is led to Rayna. And the generations passed on the matter by word of mouth, until today we still say *hawdaj al-ʿarūs* (although it is known that nowadays we have begun to transport her by plane).[43]

The name Hawdaj al-ʿArūs was inspired by the customs of exchange marriage in Palestinian society on the day of the wedding. We know that in exchange marriages between two villages, the villagers used to celebrate both weddings on the same prearranged day. Both bridal processions arrived at the meeting point at the same time. The practice was that the residents of one village would not hand over a bride until they received the designated girl from the other village.

Befitting a celebration, it was customary for the bride to be led in a procession riding a camel. The camel was led to the meeting point and made to kneel down in a place called Hawdaj al-ʿArūs. There the bride waited, while remaining on the litter, for the procession from the neighboring village to arrive and for the farewell ceremony separating her from her family and the people of her village to take place.

The named place is a border area between the villages, a liminal space in Victor and Edith Turner's (1978, 249–50) terminology. Its liminality symbolizes the transition from lack of connection between the groom and the bride to the consummation of this connection. The meeting point is the dividing line between the two villages, but at the same time, it is also the place where a ceremony is performed that marks the beginning of a connection between the villages, which will bring blessings and fertility.[44] The name alludes to the cheerful sides of village life and of rural lifestyles in the past. The narrator's statement that nowadays, even in Palestinian society, the bride has begun to be transported by plane, signifies the changing times and the dynamism of customs: the contemporary bride, so the narrator implies, can make requests that deviate from the ceremony's traditional customs.

Other explanations for the origins of the names show that nuptial ceremonies for brides were held only at certain springs. For example, ʿAyn al-ʿArūs ("the bride's spring") was a spring far from human settlement, where the residents of Ḥurfeish and the surrounding area used to bathe brides before the wedding day.

In some cases, the bride mentioned in the geographical name is a fictional character, as the following legend demonstrates:

Jabal al-ʿArūs (جَبَل العَروس)—"the mountain of the bride"
According to the narrator, a bride's wedding procession stopped at this place on its way [to the ceremony]. Among the participants in the procession

was a woman whose son did not restrain himself and defecated. Since this happened during the bridal procession, it occurred to the mother to clean her son's body with a loaf of bread, instead of with the handkerchief that the Creator, may He be praised and exalted, brought down to her. The mother wiped her son's excrement with the loaf of bread because she did not want to give up the handkerchief. Therefore, God, may He be praised and exalted, the Creator of the Universe, corrupted the form of all the participants of the procession and turned them into *kuwaym*, heaps of stones.[45]

Jabal al-ʿArūs in Nāʿūra was known to the local Bedouins as Kuwaym, meaning a pile of stones. The etiological explanation of the two names of the place is found in the same story, which is widespread among the villagers. On different occasions, they tell of the mountain in their village that is strewn with many stones and about the rocks in the shape of humans and camels: "the Creator of the Universe, corrupted the form of all the participants of the procession and turned them into *kuwaym*, heaps of stones," as the narrator says. The stones shaped like humans and camels is the reason and explanation for the mountain's name and story. This natural phenomenon, unusual in its environment, is explained not by climatic and environmental factors but through assumptions and imaginations that gave birth to an etiological legend.

The story provides an example of breaking a taboo, which ends with a severe punishment from the hands of a divine power. God is angry that the mother does not use a handkerchief. Setting the bride as the signifier of the place, Jabal al-ʿArūs, instead of naming it after the sinful woman, might be due to two reasons: first, the violation of the taboo and the divine punishment emphasize the arbitrary polarity that separates celebration and joy from calamity. Folktales tend to emphasize the polarities and extremes that characterize the human condition, and it is probably for this reason that the narrator preferred to mention the bride in the place-name rather than the participants in the procession. The second reason derives from a legend that expresses the same motif and ends with the sentence: "Among the stones, to this day, one stone is more beautiful and bigger than the others. This is the bride."[46] The large and beautiful stone, standing out from its surroundings, is missing from our story (it may have been omitted), and it is that which might explain the identification of the mountain with the bride who turned into stone.

The idea behind the story is the denigration of the sanctity of bread. Among the ordinary people, bread is extremely sacred and revered. Bread was the main food of Palestinian peasants, who experienced famine in the past. The explanation given for the curious natural phenomenon is intended to highlight the necessity of this existential commodity through a poignant description of the collective punishment that awaits anyone who harms it.[47]

The motif of the desecration of bread by a woman is present in various Palestinian place-names: the theme of the legend of Jabal al-'Arūs is repeated in its entirety in the name legends of Qalā' al-'Arāyis, "the cliff of the brides," in Buqī'a, and al-Maskhūṭa, "the ugly woman." The name al-Maskhūṭa refers to a stone in the village of Kawkab Abū al-Hijja, whose name was later transferred to the surrounding plot of land. The stone got its name from the words of a mother who wiped her son's buttocks with bread. In this case, the etiological legend is intended to explain the strangeness of a topographic phenomenon found in the place and does not describe an event.[48]

The names explain the unusual sights as a supernatural reaction to the sins of women. As such, the names reflect the rural community's negative attitude toward women. The space created through these expressions is shrouded in mystery, and it has a popular religious meaning for the local community.

—⁓—

The place-names attributed to female characters are a distinct product of gender and social power relations. Despite the difference in their content, these names create a text that describes the role of women and their image in the life of the Palestinian family in the past: a peasant woman works the soil, draws water, cuts wood, and grinds wheat. At the root of the place-names that commemorate women's communal crafts—woodcutters, millers, and washerwomen—are activities belonging to the daily routine. Archetypal cultural concepts identify women with the fertile element of the earth and the earth with the female body (Menicucci 1999, 88–89), and from this perhaps arises the need to give women's names to various objects. The names are a consequence of an actual time and place, and thus women are embedded in the space as realistic figures. Marking them in the space testifies to the division of gender roles and perpetuates their traditional duties. Women's presence in space conveys the village's daily life, customs, and values, including its justification of women's murder for real or imagined violations of sexual social conventions. This naming practice is based on the need to express attitudes and feelings regarding femininity or gender relations.

Names commemorating women's figures reflect on the one hand, women's valued crafts or their desirable qualities as a peasant and a bride. Yet on the other hand, they convey patriarchal stereotypes that condemn women as lacking in restraint and morality.

Marking space with women's names does not give expression to an individual female voice. The names identify the rural space as one stamped with the typical image and representation of the Arab woman during the periods of Ottoman and British rule and earlier. At that time, the peasants depended on the flocks and harvests for their livelihood and blood ties were then very important. Some of the names commemorating women in the geographical environment were inspired by repeated actions in the space. Other names, as we have seen, were born from communal customs. Therefore, it should not be surprising that these names contain a typical element and are repeated, with minor changes, in many villages, both Muslim and Christian, that maintained a similar lifestyle.

Despite the absence of an individual female voice in these names, the marking of female identity in space, especially in sites where daily female activity took place, indicates the appropriation of space for the benefit of women. The earth serves as a resting place for women's bodies, and the female image is intimately connected to nature and merges with it. In this way, nature helps embed women's identity in the natural environment. The topographic formations that have forms comparable to female-specific body parts, such as wadis and caves, reinforce the female identity and feminine character of these spaces.[49] 'Ayn al-Nawm, the secluded and hidden path where the millers passed, the Rock of the Woodcutters—all these are places where women are present without men. A dual practice is visible in the division of the territory into spatial segments in which women exist: On the one hand, in certain spaces, such as those previously discussed, there is cultural permission for the presence of women. On the other hand, it is clear that this cultural privilege also enables women to be controlled and restrained, since their presence is limited and confined to the areas determined by patriarchal authority.

Some of the place-names referring to women's names include expressions of joy, fertility, and peace, while other names instill sorrow and discomfort. This is another manifestation of the fact that the presence of women in Palestinian geography conveys ambivalent messages: on the one hand, the marking of femininity in the natural environment presents women as active subjects who, in their routine actions in space, give the village's land an essential part of its onomastic identification. On the other hand, they are presented as objects, whose presence in the natural environment is passive and marginal. The names reflect a tension between women's activity in the physical and linguistic shaping of space and the theory of the woman as a passive element, submissively integrated into nature.

The image of peasant women toiling on their land and marching in a line to and from the fields with jugs of water and bundles of wood on their heads is evoked by the geographical formations that bear their names and titles. The ideas conveyed by the names refer to the historical period when these notions were established in the geography of the Palestinian countryside. The names were created at a time when it was possible to witness these actions on a common and everyday basis, a time when the Palestinian family made a living from working the land, before Palestinian women went to work outside the village. This was the case before the establishment of the State of Israel, before the new state brought about major changes in the nature of employment in Palestinian society.

METAPHORICAL NAMES

This group of name legends comprises folk explanations and ethnographic memories that describe the origins of geographical place-names and the uniqueness of nature using figurative language. The figurative language of the names helps enrich the place's visual description in various ways or establish its topographical, agricultural, and climatic character. By clarifying the operation of figurative language in place-names, it is possible to understand more clearly the ways in which such names employ various rhetorical strategies to establish a parallel between the named place and a human figure, one animal or another, an idea, a social reality, or any other element relevant to community life.

Metaphorical toponyms exist in various cultures. Adrian Room, relying on the historian George Stewart, notes the existence of metaphorical names but refrains from discussing the subject. Room regards these names as a subset of the category of descriptive names, that indicate a geographical feature or geographic direction (e.g., Dragon Mountain, a mountain whose peak resembles a dragon's head). Alongside the descriptive names, according to Room, there are also subjective terms, such as Disappointment Bay—in which explorers searched in vain for what they were looking for.[50]

The metaphorical names used in Palestinian society can be divided into three main groups: names that praise or denigrate the land, names describing water sources, and names describing the topography of geographical features.

Names That Praise or Denigrate the Land

Karm al-Shaykh (كَرْم الشّيخ)—"the shaykh's olive grove"
The olive trees in the Karm al-Shaykh grove are ancient, Roman,[51] and pillar-like.[52] They called it by the name of Karm al-Shaykh because all the olive trees in it are old, ancient in days, and bear fruit in abundance.[53]

The title *shaykh*, literally "old man, elder," is usually given to a leader or the head of a tribe (as well as being a honorific for a cleric who leads prayer). However, in the name legend before us, neither a person nor their title is the source of the place-name Karm al-Shaykh. The olive grove's name derives from the special properties of the trees there, which are ancient and rich in yield. The metaphor of Karm al-Shaykh is meant to refer to the extreme age of the grove's trees and to indicate that it is unsurpassed in the production of fruits and oil, compared to the other olive groves in the settlement of Abū Sinān. Another example of the use of a human adjective in a similar metaphor is the Arabic name for Mount Hermon, Jabal al-Shaykh (the mountain of the shaykh), in the sense of "the old man's mountain." It is so named because of the snow covering its summit, giving it the appearance of a man with white hair.

Another name that elevates and praises the yield of the olive trees is Ḥitam Ṭayy (حِيتَم طَيّ) in Maghār. Ḥātim al-Ṭayyʾī (Ḥitam Ṭayy in the local dialect) was a pre-Islamic poet famous for his generosity. According to the name legend, the nickname was given to the grove to emphasize the abundance of fruit and oil that the olive trees yield. The theme of a blessed yield is repeated in other names, highlighting the rich harvest of the crops in a particular agricultural area, such as al-ʿArāyis (العَرايِس), the brides.

> Al-ʿArāyis (العَرايِس)—"the brides"
> The plot called al-ʿArāyis is located in the west of the land of Kafr Kannā. The land of Mashhad borders it to the west. In the north is ground called *al-ṣadār* (الصَدار) and in the south is the main Haifa-Tiberias road. This piece of land was called al-ʿArāyis, "the brides," thanks to its location above its surroundings, its fertility and its being free from gravel, stones, bushes, and the like. [The land] knew no floods, neither mud nor slime which cause the seeds to wither. It was known for its grain, yielding grain superior in quality to the grain of the other lands in the village.
>
> It was named al-ʿArāyis after *al-ʿarūs*, the bride, because the bride stands out in her beauty, her purity, and her loveliness.[54]

The name al-ʿArāyis was given to this land in Kafr Kannā due to its aesthetic quality and thanks to its fertility. The parallel between the bride and the land reflects the land's appearance and the quality of its yield. The absence of stones from this section and its freedom from mud, in addition to its high position, give it a fine form. Its virtues as seen by the peasants constitute not only a comely appearance but also an excellent harvest.

Another example is the name Wādī al-ʿAsal (وادي العَسَل), "the stream of honey," in the village of Bayt Jann. The name originates in the quality of the stream's water. The application of the term *al-ʿasal* to the stream highlights the sweetness and purity of its water and signifies the special affection the locals have for it. This attitude is repeated in the name Bīr al-Sukkar (بير السُّكَّر), "the sugar well," in Ḥurfeish, whose waters are as sweet as sugar syrup.

In contrast to terms that praise the land, the locals also use metaphorical terms that denigrate it.

> Umm al-Sharāyiṭ (إِم الشَّرايِط)—"the mother of rags"
> Umm al-Sharāyiṭ is barren land. You sow it and the seed does not germinate properly, the wheat is low, and the ears are so tiny . . . that is, there is no use in it and there is no purpose to it, and does the rag have a purpose? Not always. This land does not bear fruit, does not yield a harvest, and today it is full of construction.
>
> Umm al-Sharāyiṭ has a worthless harvest; if you come across a rag—will you pick it up? In other words, the land is not suitable for cultivation at all, and whoever owns a little land in this place, his land remains fallow. Even when they sowed it—there was nothing to harvest.

The name Umm al-Sharāyiṭ is given to a piece of land in ʿArrāba because of its aridity. The etiological explanation uses the word *rags* to describe the dryness of the earth and thus emphasized the common properties of the rags and the land. The word *umm* is intended to highlight this defect and not to indicate a woman's ownership of the place. The symbolic name Umm al-Sharāyiṭ expresses a kind of sarcasm toward the land because it does not produce wheat and does not provide its owner with bread. The name invented by the peasants expresses their frustration at the barrenness of this plot.

Denigration of plots of land also occurs in other names, such as Umm al-ʿIẓām (إِمّ العْظَامّ), "the mother of bones," in ʿIlabūn. The plot was so called because it has no agricultural use and is similar to the exposed bones of the sacrifice, which do not have even a shred of meat on them. This division of names also includes terms indicating difficulty in tilling the land.

> Al-Khanzīra (الخَنْزيره)—"the sow"
> The name al-Khanzīra refers to mountainous ground with many bumps and cracks that cause scratches.
>
> There is little agricultural land here. And yet the peasants tilled it, even though its yield is low, and its soil is stony, hard, and harmful to those that enter it.
>
> The land was treated like a sow, because not only is it not productive, but it causes harm to those who come near it. In other words, if you pass through it, it causes impurity, there is no benefit from it.[55]

The name al-Khanzīra is given to a plot of poor, bad, and harmful land. The comparison between the characteristics of the (female) pig, an unclean animal for Muslims, and the inanimate object, the plot of land, is intended to emphasize the magnitude of the suffering and damage that this plot caused to the workers of the land, the residents of Majd al-Kurūm, and passersby in its area. Just as in Islam, the pig is a symbol of all impurity and is harmful to those who consume it, so, too, this plot, due to its topographical location, caused suffering to those who worked it. Using the word *pig* to indicate the plot of land is also intended to emphasize its ugliness, since it is a mountainous area with many bumps and ruts.

The existing denigration in the name al-Khanzīra is also repeated in the name Khallat al-Mawt (خلة الموت), "the chamber of death," in Naḥaf. The same motif is also expressed by giving names of demonic creatures to geographical features, such as Ḥajar al-Ghūl (حَجَر الغول), "the stone of the ghoul," between Kafr Kannā and ʿArab al-Shiblī.[56] A mass of rocks and the plot of land around it are called Ḥajar al-Ghūl. According to one explanation, this stone got its name because of all the hardships and difficulties caused to the locals by the bumps, stones, and uneven surfaces.

Names Describing Water Sources

ʿAyn al-Majnūna (عِين المَجنُونِه)—"the spring of the mad woman"
ʿAyn al-Majnūna lies in the south of the village of Naḥaf. Its waters flow in a channel called Wādī al-Zīra (وادي الزّيرِه).

> Sometimes it happened that we passed there and did not find water in the spring. The water did not flow; however, on our return we found the water of the spring boiling and flowing strongly from the south side, and we watched it—the movement of the flow and the water that erupts and descends into the wadi. And again, it happened that after a day or two we discovered that the water was gone. For that reason, and because of these antics, the people called the spring ʿAyn al-Majnūna   because it flows and disappears quickly.[57]

The name ʿAyn al-Majnūna derives from the properties of the spring's waters, which may at one moment flow violently, as if activated by an unseen hand, but immediately afterward stop flowing. This phenomenon caused astonishment among the peasants, who passed by the spring on their way to and from their plots of land, and the name they gave it expresses their wonder at the mysterious natural phenomenon.

A spring by the same name near Jathth is explained differently. This spring flows in strong pulses that sweep the ground, uprooting the olive trees and the stone fences that were built as a dam against the spring's water. The damage caused by the spring drove the landowners mad and left them helpless.

The adjective *majnūn/a* derives from the noun *jinn*, a demon or spirit, and therefore the meaning of the word is demon possessed. The root *j-n-n* in literary Arabic signifies "to hide." The demons are hidden from human eyes (Ibn Manẓūr 1988, 1:515). In general, it can be said that since the causes of these geographical phenomena were invisible to the locals, they called them *majnūna* and thus attributed supernatural and mysterious powers to them.

> Wādī Kasīlān (وادي كسيلان)—"the lazy river"
> I asked an old man why the stream was called Wādī Kasīlān.
>> He said: "From the word *kaslān*, lazy."
>> "And why is that?"
>> He said: "This stream flows once every ten years."
> Wadi Kasīlān—[so-called] for being lazy.[58]

The name *the lazy river* was given to a seasonal river in Maghār because rainwater flows in it very rarely, once every decade. This name is related to the aridity of the stream and also expresses the peasants' disappointment with it.

Sometimes the names and accompanying explanations imply pathos and mockery. For example, Wadi al-Aʿmā, "the blind stream," was so named because, similar to the unsteady gait of a blind person, it does not flow in a fixed course and its water channels intersect randomly. There are also metaphorical names to indicate the depth of the water sources.

> ʿAyn al-Jamal (عين الجَمَل)—"the spring of the camel"
> ʿAyn al-Jamal is located between Bayt Jann and Buqīʿa. The waters of the spring are very chilly, very cool, but it is very difficult for man and beast to reach them. The goats and cows are unable to drink, and only the camel, thanks to its long neck, reaches the water. Since the camel is the only animal capable of reaching water and drinking not much of it, the place was called ʿAyn al-Jamal.[59]

ʿAyn al-Jamal in Bayt Jann is unique in its depth. The locals named the spring because the only animal able to drink from its deep waters was the camel, thanks to its long neck. The relationship between the geographic feature and the camel is intended to enhance and reinforce the image of depth. The picturesque name indicates the camel's characteristic height, even as it indicates the place's dominant feature: depth.

Denoting the place's great dimensions and depth is also repeated in the signifier Ghadīr al-Jamal (غدير الجمَل), "the crater of the camel," in Shaʿb. According to the name legend, the deep and full water hole sufficed for all the animals in the village, even the camel, which would not be able to empty it even if it drank its fill.

Names Describing the Topography of Geographical Features

Maghārat al-Rāhib (مُغارِة الرّاهِب)—"the hermit's cave"
They called it Maghārat al-Rāhib because the paths to it are difficult. Neither
the shepherds nor the goats were able to follow these paths.[60]

The name Maghārat al-Rāhib in the settlement of ʿArab al-ʿAramsha, is based
on the place's difficult topography. The paths leading to the cave are narrow and
rocky, preventing man and beast from reaching it. The word *hermit*, which is
used to refer to the cave, creates an analogy between one aspect of the hermit's
life and the cave's location as seen by humans—both are secluded from the
world. The name and its explanation make the cave seem like a remote place
that cannot be visited, just like the hermit's remote abode in the mountains.

—w—

Figurative names arise as a way to describe the parallel between the concrete
characteristics of plants and inanimate objects and human, animal, and topographical factors in the peasant's immediate environment, such as a slow-flowing
stream being called lazy or a deep water hole being compared to a camel. By
using metaphors of this kind, the name-givers sought to bestow a human significance on physical places and provide them with visibility.

These names often were given based on Palestinians' attempts to explain
prominent characteristics of natural features: a bountiful harvest of agricultural crops, the aridity of the soil, the incomprehensible behavior of a topographic entity, or an unusual feature of the environment. The strangeness of
natural features aroused wonder and required the agricultural community to
provide an interpretation of their significance. The Palestinians, who wanted
to express their impressions of the sights and secrets of these features, began to
recount names and tales about the natural features surrounding them, through
which they gave meaning to events. The poetic descriptions of nature preserved
in the names reflect the vantage point of the local peasants, who through the
conceptualization of nature gave expression to the subjective and communal
experience of space that developed in their natural living environment. The
subjective-communal dimension of naming is reflected in the fact that plots
of land with negative characteristics are never given masculine names, with
the exception of Wādī Kasīlān ("the lazy"). These plots of land are always described as female or with names ending in a morpheme indicating a feminine
grammatical form.

The figurative names metaphorically bridge and mediate between nature
and the people who gave the names. On the more pragmatic level, they activate

social power relations on the land and enable appropriation and orientation in
the natural environment.

TOPONYMS DESCRIBING THE PHYSICAL
FORMATION OF PLACES

Physical Qualities

ʿAyn al-Bārida (عين البَارْدِه)—"the icy spring"
ʿAyn al-Bārida, [so-called] because the waters of al-Bārida, the chilly ones,
surpass in quality the waters of the surrounding springs: they are cooler,
clearer, and tastier.[61]

The origin of the name ʿAyn al-Bārida in al-Jishsh is the coldness of the spring's
water, which distinguishes it from the other springs in the area. This feature is
considered a virtue by the patrons of the spring and indicates its essence. The
folk explanation about ʿAyn Umm al-Fulūs (عين ام الفلوس), "the spring of the
coins,"[62] near al-Sākhina (الساخنة) also highlights the water's quality: "The clar-
ity of the water in ʿAyn Umm al-Fulūs is such that even if you were to throw a
coin of ten Palestinian piasters into them, you would see it with your own eyes."

Unlike the last two examples, ʿAyn al-Malīsa (عين المُلِيصه), "the spring of oili-
ness," in Maghār is known for its thick and viscous waters—qualities that are
seen as disadvantages.

> Al-Baṭūf (البَطّوف)—"the father of floods"
> I learned from the residents of the area and the neighbors of al-Baṭūf, that
> al-Baṭūf's name used to be Abū al-Ṭūf, "the father of the floods." And this is
> because there are many floods there, and the water remains there until after
> the month of May, and this is harmful to the winter crops.
> They used to wait until the water dried up and then sow summer crops.
> And I would hear the local Bedouin women, those who live near al-Baṭūf, sing
> a kind of song, and say:
>> Baṭafa (flooded with water) al-Baṭūf and al-ʿUzayr will look [on al-Baṭūf][63]
>> And al-Shafā (الشَفَا)[64] is known for its marrying off of bachelors.[65]

The name al-Baṭūf received its meaning by echoing two words in Arabic: first,
Abū al-Ṭūf, "the father of floods." The name was given due to the seasonal floods
that afflicted the valley in the winter. Second, the word ṭūf is reminiscent of
the word ṭūfān, the biblical flood that destroyed all living things in the days of
Noah. The two meanings intertwine, as the floods and the destruction of the
agricultural crops in the place allude to the great flood, al-ṭufān.

As is the way of the popular creator, the narrator harnesses the etiological explanation to mention other matters concerning the conditions of life. Thus, another idea expressed in the name al-Baṭūf is explained by two verses of poetry that the Bedouin women used to recite. The song shows that when al-Baṭūf was flooded and the agricultural crops did not flourish, the bachelors who were about to get married turned to the area of al-Shafā (present-day Ramat Poriyya, which means "fertile plateau" in Hebrew), which was characterized by a bountiful harvest. Here they sowed and reaped to finance the marriage ceremony. The form of the verses in Arabic implies that the bachelors married the land of al-Shafā.

Natural Features in the Landscape

Umm Bābayn (إم بابين)—"mother of two gates"
The area was called Umm Bābayn because there is a large cave with two entrances. The farmers, with their flocks, horses, and animals, would spend the rainy days there. The name of the cave became the name of the entire area around it.[66]

The area's name originates from the name of a cave within its boundaries. The Umm Bābayn cave in the locality of Yāfā, received its name due to two natural openings in its walls.[67] The cave's striking and unusual shape is the basis for the name it was given.

The mark of topographical forms is evident in other names: al-Sillam (السَّلَّم), "the ladder," is an agricultural area on the borders of Shaʿab where the terraces are arranged one above the other, like steps in a ladder, and al-Ṣalīb, "the cross," is a junction of dirt roads in Kafr Kannā, each of which leads to a different settlement.

The locals mark even tiny topographical phenomena with geographical names. An example of this is Umm al-Kharārīm (إمّ الخَرَارِيم), "the mother of the tiny holes," in the village of Ṭurʿān. The name was coined due to the multiple holes in the rocks, where ropes were threaded to tie animals. Other examples are names that include the identifying element *daraj*, that is, carved steps. These names may indicate man-made stairs or ones that were formed naturally. Maghārat Umm al-Daraj (مُغارة إمّ الدَّرَج), "the cave of the mother of stairs," in the locality of Nīn, is an example of stairs of the latter type. The root *daraj* is also present, with a slight formal change, in the names of Arab villages, such as the village of Durayjāt—an unrecognized village on the border of the Arad Valley. The village lies at the bottom of Naqab al-Durayjāt (نَقَّب الدريجات), now called Maʾaleh Deragot, hence its name.[68]

Measuring Distance

Geographical sites are sometimes indicated by the names of animals, which imply different distances within the geographical space. Thus, the banks of a stream in the settled locality of Maʿalīyā were called Kamzat al-Muhur (قَمزة المُهُر), "the colt's leap," at a narrow point where they are close to each other. Because of the short distance between the banks of the stream, a small colt is able to jump from one side to the other, even when rainwater flows through it.

Some names indicate a distance between two villages. Ḥajar al-Nuṣṣ, "the middle stone," got its name because it was halfway between Makr and Acre. The stone served as a resting place for the village women who sold milk.

These names and the contexts of their reception provide cultural information about the method of measuring distances between geographic sites. The values practiced in Palestinian society, as expressed in the names, are based on the animal world and details from the natural environment. Bernard Lewis described two main methods of measuring distance that were used among the Arabs of the Middle East: one based on time and one based on the movement of the human body (Lewis 2002).[69] My study of name legends reveals that the Palestinian villagers measured distances also—and perhaps mainly—with the help of fauna, flora, and various natural details.

In some cases, the peasants determined the boundaries of their plots using stones and trees, to which they gave names. This method of measurement is clarified through the name legend of Kharrūbat al-Ṣalīb (خرّوبة الصّليب), "the carob-tree of the cross," which was so named following the names of areas of land belonging to the localities of Ḥasaniyya and Dayr al-Asad. The border between the areas of the villages was determined by engraving a cross in the rock that separates them, and the carob tree in this area is named after that cross.

Names Influenced by Agricultural Resources and Produce

Al-Mūna (المُونه)—"food stored for the winter"
Al-Mūna was a fertile land, where grains—wheat or sorghum or barley—were sown. All types of grain and olive trees were also planted there. People would store and make a living from the oil of the olive trees, store and make a living from the grains, for a whole year. The land was named al-Mūna after this yield.[70]

Food stored for the year or for the winter period, mainly olive oil and flour, is known as *al-mūna*. This term is associated with a plot of land in Abū Sinān because its abundant yield was enough for a whole year. From the name legend, it appears that olive oil and flour (the main crops in this land) are essential to the Palestinian family's food basket.

Another name related to agricultural activity is al-Rubʿ (الرُبع), "the quarter." This name was given to lands in the village of Makr, because of the conditions of its cultivation. Only in one case was this land cultivated in exchange for a quarter of the crop, while in other plots in the village, the owner of the land paid the worker by supplying his subsistence needs. From the name legend, we learn that the landless and the serfs, called in Arabic *qaṭarīz*, worked for the peasants in exchange for a loaf of bread and their basic needs. As mentioned, only in one case and on a certain plot did one of the poor peasants manage to cultivate the land in return for a quarter of its grain.

Another marker associated with the household is al-Manāshir (المَنَاشِر), "the drying surfaces": this is a rock surface, which got its name because the women of Ṭurʿān village used to spread *kishk* (dried yogurt mixed with wheat grits) to dry for a few days in this place, which was open to the wind and the sun. The signifier al-Manāshir is common in the geographical landscape of Arab villages, for example, in Kafr Kannā and Maʿlūl (مَعْلول). Ṭārūq al-Burghul (طاروق البُرْغُل), a plot of land where they chopped burgul, and Ṭārūq al-Mashīḥara (طاروق المشيحره), a plot of land where they used to make charcoal, in the village of Ḥasaniyya, derive their names from rural crafts related to the household.

In fact, all the names described in this subsection refer to unique natural features and signify the particular singularity of the natural environment. The impressions of the senses, of sight, taste, and touch, can be felt at the foundations of these names, which are based on a direct and homologous affinity between the signifier and the signified.

Toponyms Based on Narrative Elements

The names in this division can be roughly divided into those that refer to repeated human activities and those that refer to onetime actions and events.

> Ra's al-Muṣallā (راس المُصَلَّى)—"the top of the prayer-hill"
> Those who would descend from Kawkab to Kafr Mandā would pray (*yuṣallī*)
> in this place. After all, the land is flat and spacious, the weather is cold, and so
> on. They would pray and continue down to Kafr Mandā.
> The same goes for those coming up from Kfar Mandā. If the time for prayer
> came while they were on their way, they would pray in this place.[71]

The origin of the name Ra's al-Muṣallā refers to a religious duty that people from Kawkab Abū al-Ḥijā and their neighbors from Kafr Mandā used to perform when they had the opportunity to go to the top of the hill. The place received its name because the inhabitants of the villages used to pray at this point if the time for prayer fell while they were on the road between the two villages. The worshippers preferred to pray in this place because of its positive qualities: "flat and spacious land, the weather is cold."

The continuous activities of the Palestinians in nature can be seen in other names. Al-Jalasa (الجَلَسِه), "the place of sitting," is the resting place of women woodcutters from Dayr al-Asad. They used to sit and rest on the rocks on their way to gather twigs at dawn. This idea is repeated with a slight change in Shaqīf al-Mustarāḥ (شقيف المُستراح), "the cliff of rest," between the villages of Yānūḥ and Jaththth. This cliff got its name because travelers used to rest in its area. It is interesting that the actions underlying the last three names, signifying rest and sojourn, all refer to a location of flat and spacious rocks, whose properties influenced its choice as a place of rest. Partnership and collective actions form the basis of these names, which result from continuous collective human actions on the spot. The topographical nature of the place resonates alongside the human activities embedded in these expressions. In the following, I demonstrate names that are the result of a onetime occurrence in a place.

> Abū al-Sabʿa (أبو السَّبْعَه)—"the father of seven"
> There once was a bee in a rock on the way down to the wadi. She was inside a cliff, a huge, high cliff—two hundred meters, three hundred meters—only God knows the truth. Caves are carved into the cliff, and the bee has its hive in the middle of the cliff. A man thought to steal the honey, to bring down honey, but he had trouble getting to the place. There are holes in the lumps of rock—from the ground to the bee's hive.
>
> So, the man brought pegs from the trees to stick them one next to the other, in order to hang from them and reach the bee. The man began to stick [the pegs] in and climb in the direction of the bee, but when he stuck the seventh (al-sabʿa) peg, it broke. The man slipped and fell to his death. After the event, they called the place Abū al-Sabʿa,[72] or Abu Sabʿ Wtād—the Father of Seven Pegs.[73]

The name Abū al-Sabʿa in the locality of ʿArab al-ʿAramsha, is based on the tragic fate of a hardworking local. The reasoning behind the name is almost surreal. The man stuck pegs in the rocks, intending to use them to reach the beehive and obtain honey. When he drove in the seventh peg, it dropped, and he fell and died. The name is therefore the result of a meeting between the conditions of nature, the bees' hives, and the plight and failed efforts of a Palestinian villager.

Toponyms Influenced by Spirits and Demons

Names given in reference to spirits and demons express belief in the supernatural. These name stories can be attributed to the literary genre of "folk belief," which centers on meetings between human beings and spirits or demonic creatures.[74]

In Arab culture, belief in demons and their great power is common. This belief is fueled by the fear of forces beyond human control.[75] The peasants and Bedouins view nature and its contents as beings imbued with supernatural souls and spirits. For them, the elements of nature and everything in the universe are all manifestations of a hidden power, over which humankind has no control. The Bedouins believe that mysterious forces control the environment and reveal their existence in various natural and climatic phenomena. Being isolated in the desert, the Bedouins created symbols and interpreted the natural phenomena for themselves (Canaan 1928, 151–52).

The name legends of natural features related to spirits and demons can be divided into two types: in the first, the story and the name are aimed at explaining a natural phenomenon characteristic of the place; in the second, spirits and demons are linked to a natural feature to explain the origin of its name. Below is an example of the first type.

> Khurr ʿUzrayyīn (خُرّ عُزْرَيِّن)—"ʿUzrayyīn's channel"
> This name is attributed to the cold that prevails in the place during the
> summer days. And if you were to sleep in Khurr ʿUzrayyīn on one of the
> days of the summer month of Ab, you would feel as if it was one of the days of
> Shubāṭ,[76] that is, a scorching cold prevails.
>
> Anyone who came to Khurr ʿUzrayyīn in the summer and was exposed to
> the strong cold of the morning there would freeze, feel stomach aches, and
> suffer from illness. Therefore, because of the cold that prevails there in the
> summer, they gave it the name of Khurr ʿUzrayyīn.
>
> It is known that Bedouins stayed there for a while and were unable to
> survive, because some of their people died. Many people woke up at dawn
> to harvest their plots, and being distracted by the coldness of the place,
> they were attacked by a high fever and needed doctors, or found themselves
> dead.[77]

Khurr ʿUzrayyīn in the inhabited locality of Fasūṭa was so named due to its peculiar climate. An extraordinary cold prevailed in the gorge during the summer days, and those who chanced upon the place suffered from aches and pains, sometimes even died on the spot. ʿUzrayyīn (Azrael) is the name of the angel of death. Giving his name to the place indicates the serious harm done to people there and the hidden force that causes low temperatures in the middle of summer. The strange and harmful climatic feature bewildered the locals, who chose to explain it on the basis of their belief in the presence of powerful occult forces, led by the angel of death, Azrael.

A variety of incomprehensible natural phenomena serve as a basis for the formation of name legends. Shaqīf al-Mughanniyya (شقيف المَغَنِّيِّه), "the cliff of the songstress," in the inhabited locality al-ʿUzayr, is a cliff from which sounds of singing emanated at night, causing panic, especially among the shepherds. They did not dare to approach the cliff and find out the source of the sound and attributed it to a demon residing there. In the following, we will deal with name legends of the second type, which focus on explaining the name's origin.

> Wādī al-Malak (وادِي المَلَك، عِين المَلَك)—"the stream of the demon"
> Regarding Wādī al-Malak, the story goes that a huge and strong bull used to come down from Zāwiyat al-Ashrāf (زاوية الأشراف) in the east and continue its way along the wadi making a frightening sound: a very loud bellow that caused panic among the people of the area. The bull continued to bellow until it reached the spring. When it cast himself into the spring, a pillar of fire came out of the spring and reached heaven.
>
> Due to the recurrence of this phenomenon, which was witnessed by more than one person, they realized that it was not an ordinary bull but rather a *malak*, a demon. They named the wadi Wādī al-Malak after it, and the spring was called ʿAyn al-Malak.[78]

The names Wādī al-Malak and ʿAyn al-Malak (the demon's spring) are rooted in the Bedouin folk belief that a demon resides in every water source and controls what happens within it. In the popular imagination of the local Bedouins, the demon (*malak*) was depicted as a huge bull that made a terrifying sound and created a pillar of fire.

In this case, it is the imagined properties of the stream that give meaning to the name. The place's name and identity derive from some ancient tradition concerning the perception of the geographical surroundings and their character. The malak is described in the name legend as a terrifying beast. But contrary to the negative image that emerges from the name legend we quoted, there are parts of Bedouin society who believe that the malak's attitude toward humans is positive. The malak resides in the places where main roads cross, most of which pass along wadis. Thus, every crossroads is a sacred place with healing properties.[79] The sacred character of the place in the popular perception is also hinted at in the name legend of Wādī al-Malak, a wadi whose northern part is located in Zāwiyat al-Ashrāf, a complex of graves of Muslim saints near Tzippori.

Demons and spirits appear in the names of natural features in different variations. ʿAyn Umm al-Ṭabūl (عين ام الطبول), "the spring of the mother of drums" in the vicinity of ʿAkbara, is so called because its waters make the sound of a drum. Because of this noise, the locals believed that the spring was bewitched and inhabited by demons. Another supernatural creature that appears in Arabic geographical names is the *ghūla* or ghoul, an example of which is Khānūq al-Ghūla (خانوق الغوله)[80] in the village of Zarazīr and Maghārat al-Ghūla (مغارة الغوله), "the monster's cave," in Jaththh.

Why are demons, spirits, and supernatural beings absent from the names of inhabited localities and present in the names of natural features? The cultural perception of uninhabited places, such as wells, caves, deserts, and ruins, tends to "locate" supernatural beings in a geographical space that is not "civilized" in human terms (Alexander-Frizer 2008, 51, 313). Peripheral places, such as mountains, caves, and jungles, are characterized by formlessness. As objects that are not subject to distinct human knowledge, these places become terrifying. On the other hand, as populated areas of land, inhabited localities have a relatively fixed form in human consciousness, which makes them familiar, classified, and controllable (Lutwack 1984, 40).

Toponyms Influenced by Animals

The names in this group are divided into two types: those in which animals play a simple and typical role, and those in which animals play a symbolic role. The names of the second type give a place a symbolic and allegorical aspect. These stories belong to the genre of "animal stories" or "animal fables," in which the characters are animals. A central example of this type is Aesop's fables. Even if these stories take place in ancient times, their moral for the human world is appropriate both for the present and for the future (Noy 1976, 138–39).

Animal stories are common in many cultures and are one of the oldest known literary genres. Animals were greatly admired and even sanctified in ancient Arab culture. In Arabic literature, they were often mentioned and admired for their power and qualities. At one point, the Arabs may have consecrated animals out of totemic beliefs (Smith 1966, 231). A connection to different types of animals is very common in Palestinian toponymy.[81] Here is a story of an animal's name that plays a simple and typical role in the naming of a place.

Maghārat al-Nimr (مُغارِة النِّمِر)—"the leopard's cave"
A man named ʿAbdallāh al-Qāsim used to spend the winter in a cave called Maghārat al-Fakht (مُغارِة الفخْت), "the cave with holes," and suddenly we

noticed the depletion of the goats: every day both he and I would lose a goat. We were at a loss. "Did someone steal them? Did a wild animal eat them? The leopard?"

My neighbor started to lie in wait and said: "Surely it is the leopard, I have to get my hands on the leopard!"

I started mocking him and said: "How will you catch a leopard?"

He said: "Wait and see."

One day he came down before me, and it turned out that the leopard had snatched one of his goats and stuck her in the cave.

The man had two dogs. These started in pursuit of the leopard but did not dare to approach the cave. They would bark and recoil. [Al-Qāsim] followed them, went down there, and saw with his own eyes that the leopard was devouring the goat. He said to it: "I have been looking for you for a long time. I have decided to get rid of you."

And he added and said (he told me this after he left the hospital): "I took a stone and hit it, then I felt the leopard hang on my neck, cross its front legs, and hold me from behind. But I was defending myself. We started to struggle, until we rolled to flat ground as it was under me, biting me. At the last moment I remembered the knife in my pocket, grabbed it and stuck it in his mouth while he was biting my fingers. I started butchering him until he fell down and met his death. I lost consciousness and from that moment I did not remember where the leopard was and where I was."[82]

The cave's original name—Maghārat al-Fakht, which means "the cave with the holes"—was changed to Maghārat al-Nimr after a shepherd's successful fight against a leopard. The nearby stream was also called Wādī al-Nimr. The name legend is a type of memorate, and it is told with pride by the residents of 'Arab al-'Aramsha from infancy to old age; the story also became a symbol of the tribesman's fortitude and subsequently a symbol for the entire tribe.

The main idea of the name legend is a metaphor for the forces of nature that threaten the Bedouin's livelihood and their struggle against them. Here the leopard represents wild nature in all its might. When it preys on the goats, it harms a major resource for the Bedouin's livelihood. The Bedouin's intelligence and resourcefulness help him in his war against the forces of nature, and praise for the Bedouin's bravery and courage is at the center of the legend.[83]

Shaqīf al-Nimra (شقيف النّمرﻩ), "the leopard's cliff," in the village of Yānūḥ also bears this name due to an incident in which a local shepherd killed a female leopard. Other animals that appear in the names of natural features in the story corpus are the fly, the horse, and the cow. 'Ayn al-Dhubbān (عين النّبّان), "the spring of the flies," in the locality of Bayt Jann, was named thus because the flies that gathered around the spring revealed the place of the corpse of a dead man from the area. Kaḥayla (كُحَيِلِه) is the name of a mare given to a piece of land in the village of al-Daḥī, following a dispute over the land between the residents of the village and serfs from the nearby village of Nāʿūra. The serfs from Nāʿūra took over a piece of land owned by the people of al-Daḥī, and the latter eventually redeemed it thanks to the intervention of a local woman, who gave her mare to the leader of the serfs. The name's origin, rooted in a local event, testifies to the high value of both land and mare in the eyes of the local community. A name that was common in the Arab villages is Marāḥ al-ʿAjjāl (مَراح العِجَّال)—the field where the cattle herds camped. Every village had a field, usually near a spring, where the cattle were brought to rest during the heat of the day.

In the case of other natural features, animals play a symbolic role in determining their names.

> Arḍ al-Kalb (أَرْض الكَلْب)—"the land of the dog"
> One year, peasants sowed wheat. These were wealthy people and people respected them. The residents said: "We want to offer help to these people, to help them with the harvest," and indeed they went to them and began to help them with the harvest.
>
> They cooked a meal of porridge for the harvesters and brought it to them. Away from the listeners, a dog was lying down. While the dog was lying down and guarding, a snake emerged and sprinkled [venom] into the milk, into the porridge.
>
> When the harvesters came and wanted to dine, the dog threw himself on the porridge and ate it. Since he ate from the porridge, the harvesters avoided eating from it.[84] The dog died while they were watching it.[85]

The plot of land called Arḍ al-Kalb in Abū Sinān received its name thanks to the dog sacrificing itself for the benefit of humans. In the etiological name legend, there are echoes of some ancient legend in which a dog saved humans from a negative figure—the snake.[86] The plot of land commemorates the dog in gratitude for his loyalty to humans and for saving their lives. The name's origin is no more than a parable for the way dogs are perceived in the narrating culture. And perhaps, the name legend also intends to teach about the wonders of the Creator revealed in his creations. It must be remembered that this positive image of a dog is contrary to its status as an unclean animal in Islamic (al-Zuḥaylī 1985, 153–54) and Jewish (b. B. Qam 83a [Lieberman edition]) law.

Animal-inspired names also express gender relationships. The story of Wādī al-Jamal (وادي الجَمَل), "the stream of the camel," in the village of Fasūṭa embodies, implicitly and figuratively, the patriarchal attitude toward Palestinian women. According to the story, the members of the tribe used to tie the large, leading female camel by her front legs so that she and her kind would not wander and stray beyond the tribe's boundaries. Once it happened that a female camel came to the stream, and it overflowed. The tethered female camel was swept away along with the other camels. A symbolic interpretation of this story allows us to see the leading female camel as a woman who is presented as guilty of drifting away from the tribe.[87] Just as the female camel's carelessness caused the rest of the camels to be swept away, so, too, the woman's carelessness and disobedience to her "superiors" lead to a rebelliousness that spreads among other family members.[88] There can also be an opposite interpretation: tying a woman's (the female camel's) feet and narrowing her steps ultimately leads to her death. In this interpretation, responsibility for the death falls first of all on the men who tied the legs of the female camel. In Bedouin and Arab folklore, it is customary to refer to the female camel allegorically, as representing women: "When the Bedouin poet describes the beauty of the she-camel and attributes to her all good qualities—everyone knows that he is referring to a woman. This is done to avoid suspicion that the words are directed at a certain woman" (Levi 1987, 352).

Animals serve as an object of symbolic interpretation due to their distinguishing characteristics—their ways of movement, their forms, their colors, and their relationships with humans (Cirlot 1978, 10). The ties between humans and animals provide a symbolic infrastructure for understanding the connections between humans and their ancestors (Lévi-Strauss 1966, 72–91). The storytelling society views natural features' names that are based on animals as linguistic expressions with symbolic power. These names, more than they commemorate or describe the life or the place, are used by the storytelling culture to evoke an ancient Arab tradition, rich in ancient legends; they allow the community to adopt different traditions and apply them to the local geography, which expresses gender and social concepts and reflects a closeness between the locals and their environment. The folk narrators use names to show a picture of social and family behavior typical of Palestinian society. In doing so, they try to make the space meaningful to and appropriate it for the local society.

CHRISTIAN TRADITIONS

The presence of Christian traditions in the Palestinian names of natural features is minimal, and this fact makes it difficult to offer general and comprehensive insights on this matter. The Christian scriptures refer to two areas of Palestine, Jerusalem and the Galilee, and deal with events from the lives of Jesus and his apostles in these regions. As we know, the Galilee is mentioned many times in the New Testament: the Sermon on the Mount, miracles in Tiberias and Cana, supernatural events near the Sea of Galilee, and more.

ʿĀmūd al-Shaʿānīn (عامود الشَّعانين)—"the pillar of the palm branches"
ʿĀmūd al-Shaʿānīn originates in an ancient agreement between two villages: Judida and Makr. On Palm Sunday or on the holiday of al-Shaʿānīn,[89] the residents of Judida used to pray in Makr, and also vice versa: the residents of Makr sometimes used to pray in the Roman Catholic church in Judida.

Along the ancient dirt road connecting Judida and Makr, there were olive groves. The worshippers who made their way between the villages used to pluck the olive branches from the trees next to the road and bring them to the church. The priest would bless the branches and the worshippers would take them [at the end of the prayer] and be blessed through them throughout the year.

This caused damage to the owner of the plots (who was called al-ʿAkkī [i.e., a Muslim]) who lived in Acre and had plots of land between Makr and Judida. He turned to the priest and said to him: "O my friend, o my lord, you are causing damage to the olive trees by the road. I will give you an olive tree as a gift." The tree in question was large. Since then, the residents of Judida going to Makr would take branches from al-ʿāmūd, from this olive tree, and continue praying in the Makr church. The same thing happened to the residents of Makr: those who came to pray in Judida, also picked branches from that olive tree and brought them to the church in Judida. That's why they called the tree by the name of ʿĀmūd al-Shaʿānīn.

[Why did the residents of Judida go to Makr and the residents of Makr—to Judida?]

Judida and Makr were two neighboring villages, and during the British rule until 1948, the residents of Judida numbered from 300 to 350 people, half of them Muslims and half of them Christians, and the residents of Makr numbered from 300 to 350 and about half of them were Christians and half Muslims. The two villages, the two denominations, the Roman Catholic and the Orthodox, had one priest and two churches. Therefore, they agreed to hold the holiday ceremonies, alternately, in the two villages; sometimes the holiday of Palm Sunday was celebrated in Judida and sometimes—in Makr, that is, they would make mutual prayer visits.[90]

ʿĀmūd al-Shaʿānīn in the town of Judida is the olive tree from which branches were harvested for the Palm Sunday ceremony, the Christian holiday commemorating Jesus's arrival at the Temple in Jerusalem. The circumstances of the tree's name formation bring together the holiday and the branches of the olive tree that, in the absence of date palms, probably replaced date fronds.

The olive tree's role on this special day gave it its nickname and distinguished it from the other trees in the grove. The name, therefore, does not reflect the plant's nature and uniqueness but rather its image in the eyes of the celebrants who needed its branches.

The narrator, a Christian, also explains the relationship between the different communities and within the Christian community itself through the name legend. Al-ʿAkkī, a Muslim, gave the olive tree as a gift to the churchgoers on their feast day, among other reasons—to reduce the damage to the olive grove. In this story, there are references to a period of brotherhood and respect between Muslims and Christians living in the same village. The story also expresses longing for the past, where emotional closeness and religious brotherhood between Muslims and Christians prevailed.[91]

Other names are associated with the Virgin Mary and the events of her life and Jesus's life in Nazareth. These are ʿAyn al-ʿAdhrā (عين العَذراا), "the spring of the Virgin," and Tallat al-Rajafa (تَلَّة الرَّجِفه), "the hill of shaking" near Mount Precipice (the Mount of the Leap of the Lord).

NAMES OF NATURAL OBJECTS—POETIC LINES

A mosaic of motifs and ideas undergird the names of topographic entities. The explanations of these names reveal a rich composition of themes, detailed and extending across a huge number of types and categories: the imprint of everyday life, ancient Arab heritage, collective memories of Palestinian society and its spatial experience, individuals' work, and gender relations, among others. Inspiration for the names of natural features came from the varied forms and features of the geographical surroundings, their agricultural uses, matters related to happy events in the life of the community, the family, and the individual. Places that have been conceptualized include mountains and hilltops; fields, agricultural plots, trees, and footpaths; and the depths of streams and caves.

The versatility of the Palestinian toponymy of natural features indicates a practice in which almost everyone took part. The map of natural features is pluralistic and does not express an exclusive and uniform line of thought—and hence the act of naming natural features is the result of a wide spectrum of human activity that lasted for many generations.

Intracommunal characters, which are absent from the names of settled localities and villages, are present in the names of topographical entities within the boundaries of the villages and their surroundings. The toponymic creation of natural features reveals a long line of lower-class Palestinian men and women. Some of the natural features commemorate the names of local families or saints as well as the names of Muslim and Christian clerics: shaykhs, priests, and monks. Very common are the names of male and female peasants, imprinted on plots and territories that they themselves cultivated and depended on for their livelihood. Marginal social groups, such as robbers, enslaved people, Roma, and immigrants, are also present in the names of natural features. A political consciousness among the villagers during the British Mandate period is reflected in the names commemorating "rebels" and "traitors" from the days of the Great Arab Revolt (1936–39). The traces of these personalities, marked in space through their various nicknames, connect the history of the Palestinian people to the local geography.

The representation of natural features, their perception, and their application depend on categories of consciousness specific to Palestinian culture. The combination of these expressions and signs against the context of time, place, and lifestyle characterizes the naming society, the Palestinians, as a group with a defined ethnic heritage and a local color. Shaping a locality using the terminology of natural features creates, within the Palestinian space, a polyphonic and fascinating variety of places, figures, and social identities that ignore social codes, such as those that adhere to class-social separation.

From a political point of view, the toponymy of natural features that we described in this chapter tells the story of the individual and allocates space to the story of Palestinian society, but it does not refer to the Arabs as a nation with a common overall ideology. Natural features are named using the proper names of ordinary people and not of symbolic heroes. Local identities, gender and tribal identities, and traditions with tribal characteristics, which were absent from the stories about the names of settled localities, are present in the Palestinian nomenclature of natural features and give it its character and uniqueness.[92] Unlike the names of localities that serve as memorials for heroes from the Muslim religious heritage going back to the times of the caliphs and of Saladin, the naming of natural features commemorates local people, the Palestinian rebels who opposed the British occupiers, and Palestinian women who were murdered for dishonoring their family.

The common people's suffering and means of livelihood, their conditions of life, and the system of manners and customs within which they existed are well felt in the names of natural features. The general impression that emerges from this study is that the motifs of these names are based not on a binary national division between "us" versus "them" but on a variety of intrasocietal loyalties. The bearers of the names mark the space with "local color," in relation to individual and community identities. These names may provide much information about aspects of Palestinian social and cultural life for which there are not many sources, especially regarding figures belonging to the sector known as "the common people."[93]

In addition, the names of the natural environment in the Palestinian village are reliable evidence of women's roles and of stations in their lives. Palestinian women's traditional work as peasants and agriculturalists, as well as their role in the household, are revealed in the places that bear their personal names and nicknames or that indicate their agricultural work. The names reflect women's agricultural duties and the division between male and female spaces. Wedding celebrations and the great activity that this event incurred in the life of the local community, caused many places, in almost every village, to earn the name of *al-ʿarāʾis*, "the brides." In this way, natural features immortalized women's status in a transitional stage of their lives.

Gender perceptions of women's sexuality in patriarchal society are expressed in personal names given to features in space, after women who were accused of dishonoring their family were murdered in or near them. As we have seen, that the literary form of some of the names and their origin are attributed to the boundary between realistic and imaginary elements—even as they reflect the hierarchy of men versus women in traditional society—reveals tones of rebellion and struggle against the patriarchal structure and express a challenge to gender conventions.

The diverse religious nature of the Palestinian population has also permeated the geographical marking system. The Druze community, which had no expression in the names of settlements, and the Christian community, which had only relatively little expression, are present in the names of geographical objects within the villages, alongside names influenced by the Muslim community. The meager presence of the Muslim and Christian religious traditions— except for cases that indicate endowed land—can be explained, among other things, by the fact that the Muslims and Christians did not need an exclusive religious marking of the spaces in which they lived. Muslims and Christians shared the space and its resources in their daily lives, so there was no need for names encouraging exclusionary spatial division.

Traces of Jewish figures are also very marginal in the names of natural objects. Kharrūbat al-Dalaka (خَرّوبِة الدَّلَكِه), the carob tree in Dayr Ḥanā, is named after al-Dalaka, a Bedouin whom an Israeli military governor sentenced to stand day and night under the carob tree on the side of the road leading to Dayr Ḥanā. Apart from the suffering expressed in the tree's name, it also implies the Zionist subjugation of the Palestinians. This is also the idea behind the name Khaṭṭ al-Hazīma (خط الهزيمه), "Retreater's Way," where the soldiers of Kaukji's Salvation Army fled at the end of 1948 (Shammas 1988, 114).

There are three reasons for the relatively numerous references to the Jewish tradition, the Hebrew language, and the Israeli version of the names of *settled localities*, compared to the rather scant representation of these motifs in the names of *natural features*. First, the Israeli government did not put its stamp on the setting of natural features in the Palestinian villages. It mainly focused on the presence of the Hebrew form in the names of settlements, intersections, and national roads. The second reason is communication. The Israeli media rarely mentions the names of natural features, and these names are absent, in most cases, from the country's official signage. Third, the names of natural features are endonymic expressions, preserved in the memories of their givers, and therefore, no borrowing of explanations from other traditions occurred.

The philosopher and sociologist Michel De Certeau suggests reading the daily movement of pedestrians in the city as a form of appropriation of the topographical system. Walking on the urban road network creates "spatial stories." It is a living linguistic activity that gives the space its meaning through the experiences, intimate encounters, and stories of those who walk in it (De Certeau 1984, 61–62, 88). The Palestinians who bestowed names are depicted as people who walked among the places of nature on a daily basis, working in the fields, resting in the natural environment, sleeping and praying in the shade of the trees and rocks, plucking twigs, and walking the paths to the fields. The Palestinians' accumulated knowledge of the land and the place became place-names, and their spatial experiences became living linguistic forms of social and cultural communication. The immediate connection between the Palestinians and the natural environment is the essence of many of the names and is evidence of the mutual relationship between society and space: the locals' frequent stays in the space outside the built-up area, their daily crossings through the fields as well as special occasions like wedding celebrations, the uses of the land and the nature of its organization, the economic and ritual dependence of the Palestinians on trees and crops, and also their astonishment at natural sights and strange sounds.

The high frequency of spatial encounters that the Palestinians experienced in the natural environment is analogous to the density of the onomastic terms used by the name-givers to distinguish places.[94] Palestinian society's way of life—which, until the beginning of the twentieth century, was mainly agrarian, rural, and partly nomadic—influenced its toponymic behavior and created a practice according to which each piece of land was assigned a name, distinguishing it from others and reflecting local actions and memories in the space. The names of fields, caves, and water holes not only were used for orientation in space but were also "texts" with cultural meanings and beliefs, which gave the space a deep human and communal meaning. The expressions and concepts associated with the physical elements in the Palestinians' geographical environment are the result of an internal experience of the place. The villagers who gave the names felt the natural features and experienced them as insiders.[95]

The qualities of the natural features—inspired by the natural environment—received their nicknames from the local people according to intense sensory impressions and were also preserved in their consciousness thus. Unusual and prominent land surfaces and odd topographical shapes stimulated the senses and became fixed in the mind through their nicknames. The stamp of the sense of sight, focused on a specific point rather than a wide panoramic view, is very noticeable in Palestinian nomenclature. The conclusion that emerges from this book is that the sense of sight influenced the creation of Palestinian names for natural features more than other senses, strengthening the author's assumption that the use of sight dominates the way humans define and identify their geographical environment and not only with reference to the relationships among them.

In official topographical maps, the appearance of the names of natural features is conditioned by their physical size, usually mountain ranges, lakes, rivers, and valleys. The Palestinian names of natural features, even the smallest and humblest among them, live on in the memories of their givers. They are endonyms specific to the group that gave them. In this way, they create an unofficial but invaluable map for the residents of the area. The local toponymy was used by the locals in their agricultural lives, in hunting, while herding the cattle, and while spending time in nature—a time that derived from their livelihood as farmers and not from hiking.

Familiarity with the land and its stories, with every piece of land and fold of soil, characterizes the Palestinians' attitude to their places and their perspective on the geography near which they live. *Wādī* (وادي), *khurr* (خر), and *shiʿib* (شِعِب)—all of which can be translated as "a stream"—are each a term that represents a different view of the material reality described through them. For example, the term *khurr* indicates the narrow channel of a stream, which only those in its immediate vicinity are able to distinguish by sight. The term *shiʿib* also denotes a narrow streambed (but more open than that of a *khurr*), which can be detected by a person looking at it from a greater distance, while the term *wādī* denotes a much wider streambed that can be seen even from a great distance.

The Palestinian toponymy of natural features is sensitive to their diverse forms and to the multitude of features that characterize the surface of the land. The topographical forms of plots of land differ from each other in their colors, sizes, elevations, and uses. Each one has a nomenclature that distinguishes it from its surroundings: For example, *arḍ*, *jalāla*, *khilla*—all of these can be translated, in the contexts discussed, as "plot." But alongside the geographical features, we also commonly find names attentive to the inner and hidden features of tiny topographical sites, such as a ridge, a den, a small plot of land, and a gorge. For example, the name al-Mindasa (المِنَسه), "the stuck," describes a narrow sunken area surrounded by mountain slopes.

Another prominent aspect of the geographical terms by which Palestinians refer to their lands is the prevalence of the names of family members: *abū*, *umm*, *banāt*, and *ʿaziba* (father, mother, daughters, and single woman, respectively). There are also images and borrowings from the names of body parts to denote the surface, such as *dharāʿ*, *ẓāhir*, and *katf* (arm, back, and shoulder). Applying terms denoting family relationships and body parts is a type of metaphorical use that signifies an emotional closeness between the name-givers and their natural environment. Names relating to the features of the landscape and the land are characterized by the frequent use of various rhetorical figures: metaphors, images, parabolas, personification, or onomatopoeia. In this way, the names give nature the form of a human being or an animal and rescue it from its silence.

Natural features are often called by different names not only because of their usefulness but also simply in order to recognize them. In his discussion of place identification among Indigenous tribes, Lévi-Strauss (1969) claimed that "animals and plants are known not because they are useful; they are considered useful or interesting, because first of all they are known." Among Indigenous societies, the identification of places by name stems first of all from the need to know them. As we have seen, even in Palestinian society, some of the names are used to identify harmful or frightening objects, which have no use. Thus, plant species, springs, caves, plots of land, and other natural features were given names due to being familiar to Palestinian society and not to indicate their benefit or harm.[96]

The dialectic in content motifs and semantics is one of the characteristics of the Palestinian nomenclature of the natural environment. The names drawn from the natural environment and perpetuating its character express an ambivalence toward the space. There are names that praise places and those that denigrate or mock natural features. Thus, the concept of space does not match the romantic image of "good land." There are names that reflect a binary that arises from the landscape's external appearance, from the soil's fertility or barrenness, from the sufficiency or otherwise of the water in the streams and springs. There are names whose ambivalence stems from an emotional impression that the place evokes—calm or threatening, sad or happy.

Together, natural features are a folk creation about a place, whose main protagonist is not easy to determine. The natural features and the geographical landscape have their own presence, and they aroused curiosity and admiration among the locals. These, in turn, gave the natural landscapes their linguistic identity, which thus reflected the mindset of the local people. The names show that human beings not only act in the natural environment and imprint their concepts in it but are also in a sense acted on, in that their concepts depend on the natural environment. Names of this type can be regarded as dialogic events that reflect the place's identity as a result of meeting and mutual inspiration between humankind and nature.

Palestinian peasants created new places in their natural environment on various occasions: to commemorate events, in honor of an ancestor, or simply following the cultivation of the land. Elements in nature were identified and distinguished by proper names that were passed down from generation to generation as a "local topographic package" that teaches about the world of these peasants (Falah 1996, 275). The names that developed after the readying of a plot of land or following an event that occurred in a certain place—these names and the circumstances of their formation created an "additional place" in the minds of the inhabitants. Thanks to the names given to it, the place's identity changed and was restructured, and the place itself split into subplaces. The continuous human activity in the environment produced more and more names alongside the "first" or previous name.

The place plays the role of a hero whose presence is extremely important in the narrative explaining the formation of Palestinian toponymy. The place's centrality and identity are reinforced because it is essential for the emergence of rural, gender, and personal identities. The spatial identity of the name-givers and their territorial feelings are tied tightly to the place and are revealed in the encounter with its people.[97] The rural way of life is closely related to the land and its crops. The natural environment, including its names, biographical memories, and cultural associations, is linked to Palestine and the Palestinians as a cultural heritage. The peasants working in the field and the natural geographical environment that serves as their background (the orange tree, the prickly pear, the olive tree, and the *za'tar* plant) are presented in Palestinian poetry and prose as national symbols and an allegory for the land and the fate of its inhabitants. This representation has overshadowed, in quite a few cases, the folkloristic-cultural aspects that were presented in this study as standing at the foundation of the relationship between the Palestinians and their environment. These last aspects played an important role in Palestinian culture even before the symbols of the land were mobilized in the national struggle against Zionism.[98]

The space created through the naming of natural features is a space with a specific meaning, related to private details and local features of the land and place. The names are focused on a concrete feature of a tiny geographical-topographic entity and the forms of the landscape, thus expressing an intimate familiarity with the natural surroundings and a dependence on the places and concepts that organize the space. The importance of this space for the workers of the land is great because their existence and culture are closely related to nature. Identifying the place through names that focus on concrete properties of natural features reflects intersubjective relationships between the community and nature or refers to nature as if it were a subject. The native Palestinian landscape and the folkloric values of Palestinian society are represented in the space of the names of natural features. The space is significant for the local identity, it is a stage for the locals' work and livelihood, for their joys and troubles, for the memories of brotherhood, and for the reality of conflicts. The shaping of toponymy is a projection of symbolic images and ideas about nature, but sometimes, as we have seen, it also reflects gender issues and Palestinian national attitudes. Reading the namespace of natural features reveals that it consists of conflictual and contradictory spatial sections. Nature is a fertile, beautiful, and pleasant place, but sometimes it is arid, scary, and a place where locals have died or been murdered.

One of the themes interwoven in the names of geographical formations is the time factor. The echoes of time are heard through the explanations of the names and through the space described in the names. Time appears in Palestinian names in different forms. Sometimes the names reflect physical time; in other cases, the names are stamped with a chronotopic perception of time, which develops directly from the space. Sometimes the names are anchored in a concept of time arising from daily activity.

Physical time is present in the causal and circumstantial contexts that gave rise to the names of the natural surroundings and geographical formations.[99] These contexts are anchored in the historical period in which the names were formed. This is mainly a period that chronologically preceded the urbanization and modernization of Israel/Palestine (long before the Ottoman period and the beginning of the days of British rule). In any case, as we have already mentioned on various occasions in this book, the names of natural features express a communal way of life that is not related to the great events written on the pages of canonical history.

The second concept of time that we mentioned, time formed from space, can be clarified with the help of the term "chronotope" (time-place), coined by Mikhail Bakhtin. By means of this term, Bakhtin discusses the way in which literature assimilates historical time and space and the reality within which it is created and exists. In the literary-artistic chronotope, there is a fusion of time in space. Time condenses, becomes concentrated, and receives visual expression in works of art. At the same time, the space becomes more intense by being an active participant in the movement of time, plot, and history. Aspects of time are revealed in space, and space is interpreted and measured through time. Alongside its literary-linguistic character, the artistic chronotope also expresses the values of a certain community or society (Bakhtin 1981, 84–85, 250–52).

In the spirit of Bakhtin's notion of the chronotope, we can say that the stories accompanying the names of natural features drown time within the natural feature. A distinct expression of the meeting of time and space in place-names against the background of the Palestinians' activity in the space can be seen in the names Marj al-Shams (مَرْج الشَّمس), "the valley of the sun," in the settled locality of Dayr Ḥanā, and ʿArīḍ al-Shams (عريض الشَّمس), "the slope of the sun," in the vicinity of Jūlis and Yarkā. These plots of land received these names because already at the beginning of dawn, the sun directs its rays to them and not to other plots in the vicinity of the villages. These names hint at the detailed knowledge of the place on the part of whoever invented them and their attachment to the dimension of time.

As a rule, the Palestinian names of natural features stem from the essence of an agrarian culture and social history that have declined. These names re-create the cultural landscape of the Palestinian village in the past. They express the rural culture that created them, its worldview, and its ways of life. The creation of the names within the villages constructs the space as an ethnographic text and voices the ethnography of the local community.

—ɷ—

DISTINCTION BETWEEN NAMES OF INHABITED LOCATIONS AND NAMES OF NATURAL FEATURES

The Re-creation of Social Class, Gender, and Village Prestige

DAVID HARVEY (1973, 14) HAS pointed out that space carries a variety of meanings, including those provided by its material existence and those that are the product of social power relations, all of which imbue the space with significance. Power relations are operated subtly with the help of manipulation, persuasion, and authority that provide the hegemonic group with consent and legitimacy (Gramsci 1971). As stated in the introduction, according to the French Marxist Henri Lefebvre (1991), space is not only a result of a given social structure but also a factor that shapes that structure. Designing a space is an ideological action aimed at creating an image for that space—that is, creating its symbolic essence as an inseparable part of its material essence (Lefebvre 1991, 73–80).

Humanistic geography has emphasized the subjectivity and diversity of personal space and the relationship between humankind and its geographical surroundings. Places are structured through the meanings bestowed on them, through the actions carried out within them, and through human experiences in them that give them names and contexts (Portugali 2000, 217). According to the literary scholar Leonard Lutwack (1984), who relies on classical definitions, place in literature is an experiential space (*erlebter Raum*) linked axiomatically to human aspects.

Cultural studies also emphasize the connection between language and social and cultural processes. For example, Pierre Bourdieu (1985, 723–25) points out that representations of nature and landscape through language play a central role in the construction of reality since they reflect social power relations. In various ways, language gives a place a tangible dimension and provides it with cultural meaning. Naming a place, telling stories and myths about it, are some of these means (Azaryahu 2005, 14–22; Tuan 1991, 685–92). Indigenous cultures, such as the Apache people, have ongoing and intimate relationships with their environment. In this process, place-names are used as monuments for the acquisition of wisdom by members of the tribe (Basso 1996, 76).

Cultural-political approaches to the landscape recognize its invisible layers and emphasize its being a cultural site. As such, it is shaped by "bottom-up" Indigenous traditions and by hegemonic groups, whether within or outside Indigenous society. These groups use the landscape as an arena for inculcating their ideology. Following W. J. T. Mitchell (2002) and Chris Philo (2002, 121–28), I describe the shaping of this landscape as an arena where power struggles between groups, values, and images within Palestinian society play out.

In chapter 2, we discuss the meaning of the landscape that emerges from the names of inhabited localities, while in chapter 3, we deal with the meaning that emerges from the names of natural features. So far, these two types of names have been discussed separately, but the comparison conducted in this chapter between the two types from social, class, and gendered viewpoints reveals that these two categories embody two geocultural ideas that contrast with each other. The starting point of the current chapter's discussion is that the typology of names in space is the product of two parallel processes: the names express reality and social identity but also derive profoundly from the symbolic relation that the name-giving culture bestows on the space. In other words, social reality and geographical space jointly determine the cultural and communicative activity reflected in names (Pinchevski and Torgovnik 2002, 365–88). Furthermore, I assume that the relationship between humans and their natural environment is reciprocal: that is, society shapes the landscape, physically and symbolically, to suit its values and goals while the landscape shapes society (Boal 1989, 99).

This chapter deals only with the Palestinian place-names of locations determined by the figures or events associated with them. The purpose of analyzing the names is twofold: first, to discuss issues of class and gender power relations in space and the attempt to elevate the village's social image through names and, second, to examine how the Palestinians' differential attitude to space is reflected in place-names and in the topographical location of these names.

The topics that the names deal with both reflect and create class relations, perceptions of gender, and impressions of society in various areas of the village. The meaning that emerges from inhabited localities' and natural features' place-names reveals the internal Palestinian social and ideological forces at play. These forces are expressed differently in inhabited localities and natural features respectively. This linguistic-spatial reality forms cultural-ethnographical evidence of a spatial division that determines a hierarchical-social order. This intricate system of spatial differentiations and classifications gives ideological visibility to hegemonic gender and class values, which highlight masculine or high-class images at the expense of feminine or low-class ones. To illustrate this state of affairs, I discuss the phrase *Arab geographical names* critically. By breaking the expression down into its components, I try to highlight the analytical and critical potential inherent in understanding the difference between the ideology behind the names of localities and that underlying the names of natural features. By the names of natural features, I mean the names of modest and peripheral natural sites, which usually denote small places far from human settlement. On the other hand, the names of inhabited localities indicate an anterior space, whose location is prominent and whose area is large.

This chapter also demonstrates the ways in which the differences among place-names and their spatial location express the organization of the human living space in the studied culture and how the concept of the geographic name is related to the identities that develop from the reality of Palestinian and Arab communal life. As mentioned, the discussion further reveals the difference between the spatial construction characteristic of the names of inhabited localities and that of the names of natural features. In light of this difference, the chapter revolves around two main axes: (1) the practice of spatial construction and the extralinguistic reality that names create in space and (2) the reasons for this construction as explained by the worldview of the culture being studied.

Despite the increase in the number of publications on the subject of geographic naming in Israel and around the world, the study of class and gender relations in the linguistic landscape of names has remained largely outside researchers' fields of interest.[1] Particularly noticeable in its absence is research dealing with the issue of femininity in the linguistic landscape of street and settlement signs, even though the exclusion of women from administrative names is known.

As mentioned, toponymic practices and the names that people and authorities give to their surroundings reveal the perception of the place, the ideologies, and the identity of the society determining the names. Researchers taking this approach include those who have dealt with place-names as part of a discussion of society-space relations. The linguist Kevin McCarthy (1975, 81–84), for example, noted the sectarian struggle reflected in the names of Beirut's streets. Studies of a different type focused on society-space relations in the material-physical contexts of buildings and of visible man-made boundaries. These include Claude Lévi-Strauss's (1963a, 291–92) study of the relationship between the spatial structure and the social structure of the Buroro people in South America, Lefebvre's (1991) study of physical buildings and facilities in the city, and Bourdieu's (1979) study of the gender construction of the tents of the Kabyle in Algeria.

This study also regards place-names as an expression of society-space relations and social power relations, but it differs from previous studies dealing with this topic in two ways. First, this study distinguishes and compares two categories of geographical entities that exist in the Palestinian space: localities inhabited by humans, on the one hand, and natural features or natural entities, on the other. This is different from studies that focused on names of the same type, such as the names of plots of land in the Lesser Antilles (Berleant-Shiller 1991, 92–93) or the inspiration and influence of Zionist symbols in the choice of names given by the governmental naming committee to settlements established in the Occupied Territories from 1967 onward (Cohen and Kliot 1992).

Second, the current study examines place-names as an ethnolinguistic product of social perceptions existing in space over a long time and that are not the result of short-term political and historical developments. This is also different from studies that analyze place-names that result from changes in the national identity of the power controlling the space or of short-lived political forces. An example of the latter type of research is a study on the Judaization of the Arab names of streets in Jerusalem's Old City (Suleiman 2004, 183–202).

In analytical terms, my discussion is based on the ideas of Lévi-Strauss (1963b, 1969), who perceived cultural contrasts as foundational elements of human language and as analytical tools for producing hidden meanings in culture. Using this notion as a framework for analysis, my discussion centers spatial contrasts such as interior-exterior, central-peripheral, public-private, visible-hidden, and anterior-posterior. The comparison between the names of inhabited localities and the names of natural features in terms of binary contrast will help us uncover the ideological concepts they embody and reveal the power relations they embed in the space. However, contrary to Lévi-Strauss's approach (1969), the two categories of place-names do not have equal status but are influenced by practices of control and politics. Moreover, the distinction between them is not perfect, and they may overlap in some cases (Fraser 1989; Blumen 2005, 30–32).[2]

The social division of space into areas, including the attribution of values and images to places, is performed in a different and unique way in every culture.[3] For example, the Palestinian toponymic creation is divided into two linguistic systems whose themes and motifs are varied and even opposing—the names of villages or inhabited localities compared to the names of natural features such as fields, wells, and caves. These two toponymic groups constitute two distinct linguistic landscapes, and this thematic division is reflected from the level of the map of the individual village up to the entire area of study. The distinction between two geocultural areas creates two cultural worlds and two social images that are constructed by the positioning of the border separating them. This distinction is not merely the result of objective spatial characteristics; rather, it is mainly the result of subjective cultural meanings related to the landscape (Bachealard [1958] 1964, 5–14) and of daily conduct in the relevant spaces (De Certeau 1984). The subjective meaning attributed to spaces and daily conduct there creates personal or collective mental maps that form the cultural perception of the space (Gould and White 2012) and the feeling of the place (Yacobi 2004, 3–15).

TWO CATEGORIES OF NAMES—CONTRARY JUSTIFICATIONS FOR NAMES OF INHABITED LOCALITIES AND NAMES OF NATURAL FEATURES

In this section, I briefly present names of inhabited localities and names of natural features. These names and the reasons for them have already been discussed at length in this book but not in connection with the issues discussed in this chapter. The place-names are intended to illustrate the space's linguistic design categories and reveal the meanings arising from them in the context of this chapter's foci.

As we saw in the stories that justified the names of the settlements Shafā ʿAmr, Dayr al-Asad, Dayr Ḥanā, Wādī Sallāma, al-Ṭayyiba, and ʿArrāba, the names of inhabited localities commemorate soldiers or other historical figures.[4] They are named after founding fathers, local leaders and tribal chiefs, religious apostles, or leaders of various ethnic groups. Unlike the names of inhabited localities, the names of natural features are derived from persons of the common people, known to the local community. The names of natural features are often inspired by male and female peasants as well as by girls, shepherds, robbers, and murdered people. The names of natural features also represent concepts from the life of the nuclear family, as depicted in the stories about Maqtal Shākir, the place of Shākir's murder near Dabbūriyya, and about Maghārat al-Mathūma, the cave of the accused girl.

In the names of natural features, the place of local women is also prominent. For example, Ḥajar al-Ḥaṭṭābāt—the (female) woodcutters' stone—is named after the women of Kafr Kannā, who used to chop wood for firewood, and ʿAyn al-Nawm—the dozing spring—is named after the women of Bayt Jann, who used to come there early in the morning to draw water. Traces of Roma and enslaved people are also embedded in the Palestinian nomenclature of natural features. Thus, Manzal al-Nawwar, the "gypsy camp," is an area that was used as a camp by the Roma who came to the village. Other natural features bear the names of slaves and servants: a fig tree in the south of the village of Nīn, far from the village houses, is called Tīnat Abū Sālim, the fig of Abū Sālim, after its planter, the slave Abū Sālim.

What is the spatial text that the names create? The meaning of the landscape emerging from the linguistic markers of the place-names presented here is linguistic-spatial evidence of the ideological use that Palestinian social forces made of these markers. The extralinguistic reality hidden in names reflects the limits and hierarchy of human identities. The conceptualization of space, by means of the Arabic language and through the notions of Palestinian culture, reflects and establishes class and gender differentiation; a conceptualization achieved through the social image arising from the name of a locality or village. This concept is expressed in two layers: (1) the name's content and (2) its location in the space of the signified place, its size, and its essence. These two layers apparently have a mutual relationship, and they correspond to the distinction made between the names of inhabited localities and the names of natural features. The names of inhabited localities are associated with noble personalities, heroic figures, and patriarchs as well as public affairs, historical events, the ethos of the expansion of *dār al-islām* (such as in the name of Shafā-ʿamr), deeds and wars of Christian military commanders (such as in the name of Dayr Ḥanā), popular values (such as hospitality, in the name of al-Ṭayyiba), and tribal conflicts and gaining an advantage over the Other (such as in the story about Wādī Sallāma and Dayr al-Asad). Because of their centrality and because they are inspiring, the names of inhabited localities denoted large, central, public, and visible geographic spaces. On the other hand, the names of natural features were identified with figures on the margins of society (e.g., Tīnat Abū Sālim), with topics having a private and local aspect (e.g., Maqtal Shākir), concepts from the family sphere (e.g., Maghārat al-Mathūma), and matters that were considered less important. The names of natural features marked places that are not only modest in size but also considered peripheral, private and hidden from view.

As these examples illustrate, in Palestinian society the names of inhabited localities and the names of natural features are two categories whose relationship is binary and conflictual. Borrowing from the distinctions made by Maurice Halbwachs (1992), the names of inhabited localities establish a collective identity shared by the Arab nation, the Palestinian village, and a historical narrative of armed struggles.[5] On the other hand, the names of natural features commemorate particular identities related to the local identities of the place's inhabitants, to local events, and to "herstory" topics and subjects (Ohana and Wistrich 1995). This division runs like a scarlet thread throughout the name legends and indicates the existence of an agreed-on sociocultural hierarchy of values that the names express. The form, location, essence, and size of the identified locality/landscape match its social and cultural significance. This categorization circumscribes the boundaries of what is permitted and what is forbidden in the Arab Palestinian discourse.

LOCATION IN SPACE AS REFLECTING STATUS

The Arab Palestinian interpretation of geographical names determined these names' locations and classified them in relation to space and topography. The allocation of names in space indicates a place's social status. For example, the map of names in the Palestinian local consciousness reflects a categorical division, which gives a person their status according to their location in space. The space is conceptualized as a hierarchical one, sorted and classified according to internal social power relations. One place was designated for the powerful and the privileged, and another was designated for popular and lower-class figures. There are public spaces and private ones, places identified with patriarchal values of male supremacy, and ones identified with women's marginal advantage.

Studies tend to indicate a direct relationship between a person's social status and the extent of the territory in their possession. A person's economic and social status has a decisive influence on their location within a territory. Persons of high social status who play important roles are located in central and prominent places;[6] in contrast, people of low social status are pushed to the edges of the territory and are given limited space (Altman 1975, 137–42; Ley 1983, 55–67). The compatibility between an individual's social status and the space under their control is also reflected in the fact that members of the upper classes usually settle in high places, while members of the lower classes settle at the foot of the mountain or on a slope. The same is true when it comes to signage: street signs bearing names get their importance from their locations for physical reasons, not only from the names' themes (Zvinashe, Muwati, and Mutasa 2018, 436).

This idea is true for gender identity, as well. In the western metropolis, areas identified as feminine spaces are located on the outskirts of the city and are separated from masculine areas that constitute the urban center, where political, economic, and administrative activity takes place (Saegret 1980, 96–98, 107).

Constraints of authority, laws, customs, and cultural values affect human mobility in space and determine the individual's position in space (Hägerstrand 1976, 332–33). These spatial constraints create "spaces of discipline" (Gregory 1989, 360–63). The geographer Tovi Fenster (1998, 234–35), who studied the mobility patterns of Bedouin women in the Negev, found that patriarchal power relations excluded women from space and limited their mobility.

As seen in Palestinian folktales, this conceptual framework is relevant for the analysis of the relative spatial positioning of both genders and classes in traditional Arab society. The linguistic-spatial practices of this society have ensured ideological and cultural visibility for male and other hegemonic images. This hierarchic shaping of space through traditional nomenclature is a key dimension of the formalization and enshrining of values in this society—a semiotic expression of cultural constraints that dictate the use of space, mobility in space, and the names of spaces. In what follows, three aspects of this hierarchy are discussed in turn: social class, gender, and village prestige.

Social Stratification

In Bedouin society and traditional Palestinian Arab society, individuals' roles and statuses are related to their age and gender. From childhood, women and men are set on different social paths, and the division of roles between them is clear at all organizational levels. Traditional rural Arab society is patriarchal. The nuclear family and the extended family were subordinate to the *shaykh*, who was the head of the tribe, and he represented its values and norms. Due to the shaykh's representative status, his tent served as a central place of accommodation, which is still called *shaqq*. The location of the shaqq was prominent, set at a certain distance from the rest of the tribe's tents, at the northern end of the encampment near a stream or ravine. This central and accessible location was intended to facilitate guests' access to the tent, on the one hand, and to prevent them from observing what was happening in the residential tents, on the other—that is, to prevent the exposure of women and dishonoring the family (Krenawi 2000, 40–42; Ben-David 1981, 35–41, 87–97).

The identification of Arab-inhabited localities with the names and deeds of the nation's leaders and its prominent figures stands in contrast to the names of women and common people, which were used to indicate marginal places located at the rear of natural and public spaces. This binary contrast gives a semiotic expression to the class ranking prevalent in traditional Arab culture. It even illustrates how the constraints of culture determined the individual's place in this cultural space. Out of respect for the leader, and as befits a person of high status, an inhabited locality with a large area and a prominent location was named after him, as in the case of Wādī Sallāma. On the other hand, the lower classes, including the women, were removed from the settlement's anterior to its outskirts and were territorially separated from the members of the upper classes through names such as Maghārat al-Mashtā. The names of the lower classes were used to indicate natural geographical entities. These entities are hidden and internal, their area is small compared to the area of the locality as a whole, and their identification is not relevant for visitors from outside.

The phenomenon of identifying Arab settlements with the names and deeds of leaders, compared with the identification of natural features in the "backyard" with the names of figures from a low socioeconomic status, such as in the case of Manzal al-Nawwar, is a type of linguistic-onomastic encryption. The linguistic markers inspired by figures from the fringes of society—such as Roma, enslaved people, robbers, and murderers—remain hidden from foreign eyes and from visitors and guests because their nicknames may provoke ridicule and disgrace the local residents in the eyes of others.

Gender Relations

Traditional gender relations in Palestinian society are articulated in the numerous names related to women given to natural features and their nearly complete absence from names of inhabited places. This also mirrors a more general tendency in human society of associating towers and vertical buildings, common in urban landscapes, with phallic masculinity (Lefebvre 1991), while inner, round spaces in buildings and non-man-made features, such as hills and valleys, are considered feminine or linked to women's spaces (Rendell 2002).

As discussed, in patriarchal societies, gender dictates not only different social statuses but also different spatial mobilities. Specifically, the code of female modesty defines men's honor, on the one hand, and marginalizes women, on the other (Abu-Lughod 1986). In the rural Middle East and North Africa, these norms have dictated the creation of distinct and physically separated geographic spaces for women, which are charged with deep symbolic meaning. This gendered architecture has restricted women's range of activity and limited them to the private domestic space dedicated to reproduction and nurturing (Steinmann 2005, 91–93, 119–20). In opposition to these approaches, feminist research explores the conduct of women in space and their participation in producing a geography while being subjected to masculine supervision (Lubin 2013, 30–37).

In traditional Arab society, the living space is divided in two. Whether in a tent, a shaqq, or a stone house, there are usually two separate sections or rooms—one for men and one for women, who often also use separate entrances as well. Erving Goffman (1959) termed those two sections "front" and "rear": the rear section is dedicated to routine and instrumental activities, while the front section is dedicated to public activities, including the presentation and serving of the rear section's products. Access to the rear section is restricted, in order to prevent strangers from seeing the activities of the womenfolk and the family. Accordingly, it is usually less tidy and presentable than the front section, which is used for hospitality.

In his study of the Muslim Kabyle people of Algeria, Bourdieu found this domestic architecture to be symbolic of the gendered stratification of society. Moreover, it is manifested in space, even beyond the immediate residential area: the women's path to the spring is different from the men's, enabling them to go there without fear of having another man see them. Where no such spatial separation is possible, the women go to the spring at designated hours, at dusk, for example (Bourdieu 1979, 121). This is echoed in the folklore collected for this study by the story about ʿAyn al-ʿArūs.

In keeping with this spatial hierarchy, Palestinian toponymy privileges the village as a geographic entity: it is accessible, large and prominent, and visitors and other foreigners need to know its name, which is therefore male or male-related. Conversely, natural features are smaller and known mainly to locals, as they are located "in the back" and are relevant only to insiders, with others having no reason to visit them or learn their names. Many of these names emphasize the woman-nature nexus by including the word *umm* (mother) in names of natural features, such as reeds in the riverbed in Wādī Umm al-Qaṣab or poplars around the spring in ʿAyn Umm Ṣufṣāfa. Note that in these two cases, as in many others, the names refer to places that are not only inward facing, small, and concealed but also physically lower than where a village would be located.

From a feminist perspective, a militaristic society generates socialization processes that cultivate a view of masculinity in terms of superiority and power (Allen 2013). Writing gender relations into the spatial text is not only a passive mirroring of an unfortunate social reality but also a coercive act by the patriarchy to reinforce its hegemony over both the local villagers and neighboring communities, as in the story of Wādī Sallāma. The narratives woven in this way are grounded in male social authority and the memories of wars and conflicts and designed to give the village a semiotic edge, so to speak. In other words, the male-oriented toponymy of place-names articulates a local Palestinian discourse in which each village stakes its claim to power and leadership.

The converse identification of the female gender with natural features may be explained, as seen, by their relative distance from populated areas and their ability to provide protection, privacy, physicality, and intimate social inter-actions (Grosz 1992, 244–52). Trees, shrubs, and narrow footpaths provided Palestinian women with a space for activities and encounters, enabling them to free themselves temporarily from the physical and normative restrictions of the rear section of the house. This notion is supported by studies that show how a distinctly feminine space allows women to express themselves more freely and to talk about their lives as women (Baker 1998, 16–17). In the postco-lonial literature, the subaltern struggles against the hegemony through daily practices of using, walking in, and discussing their space (De Certeau 1984, 88). De Certeau calls this concept "everyday space," and we can see it in use in the feminine spaces created by Palestinian women. They take advantage of fleeting opportunities to exploit the space used by the hegemonic class to attain limited freedom—to escape the male gaze, form a space of their own, and claim space for their bodies (De Certeau 1984). Thus, while the linguistic mechanism names villages after fearsome warlords, it names natural features after women to protect their privacy, supervise their modesty, and make sure their movements remain hidden.

Another, more general cultural explanation for the frequent use of female names in the Palestinian toponymy of natural features is the tendency to iden-tify nature or the land with women, as both are associated with reproduction and nurturing. As demonstrated in the previously detailed stories, places as-sociated with women are rhetorical performances. That is, the rhetoric of the place is created by a specificity requiring a certain type of discourse rather than by any discourse imposed on it by its female visitors (Endres and Senda-Cook 2011). These stories tell us of caves, springs, and gorges named after women or feminine activities and habits. Relatedly, their concealed nature and shapes, which are reminiscent of female organs—physically associated with reproduc-tion and nurturing—may have also played a part in this toponymic connection.

The converse of this intuitive association, although less frequent in these sto-ries, is also true. One example is Jabal al-Shaykh—or the old man's mountain (in Hebrew, Mt. Hermon)—so named because of its snowy peaks that look like a white beard. This mountain, which towers over the entire northern region of Israel, is visible on a clear day from many parts of the Galilee.[7]

The mother-nature nexus relates not only to the spatial marginalization of women and to the physical similarity of natural objects to female organs but also to the traditional division of labor. Palestinian women played a major role in agricultural activities, and many names reflect this by referring to an event that occurred in a specific space and time that reproduced their domestic and agricultural roles in the village geography. Although limited, this role may have gained paradoxical prominence after the Nakba and the ensuing destruction of the Palestinian village as a physical and cultural entity (Tamari 1999). Once relegated to the margins, Palestinian identity has sought to reestablish itself through that which is more difficult to destroy—the land and its natural features. Women might play a more central role here; Hagar Salamon (2016), for example, showed how women preserve and revive the motherland by weaving geographical maps hung in the front section of Palestinian homes.

Theoretically, the discourse about natural features can be better understood through Homi Bhabha's notion of the third space. A third space is a symbolic and tangible space that challenges various types of hierarchic binaries, affording an intermingling of figures, motifs, interactions, and identities (Bhabha [1988] 1995, 206–9). Following Bhabha, spaces located beyond the control of the monolithic imagery of place-names can be seen as third spaces, despite traditional society's constant attempts to extend its segregationist control to these spaces as well. Thus, the linguistic construction of natural space challenges the division into front (male) and rear (female) and subverts the boundaries of the hegemonic practice that organizes the toponymy according to male interests. The result is a nonbinary division of roles in Palestinian space: men without women in place-names, and women beside men in the names of natural features.

Increasing the Village's Prestige

As suggested, village names are often used to glorify their identity as seen by Palestinian society. In general, names provide answers to the questions: How do we want others to see us? How do we define ourselves? Toponymic stories not only glorify the village in relation to others but do so at the expense of the natural features in its surroundings, thereby articulating the fundamental assumption shared by both modern and traditional societies, that (masculine) human culture is superior to (feminine) nature.

The location of a human settlement is representative of its relationships with its environment. These determine its status among all other settlements in the area, the entire country, or even the world (Ben-Artzi 1997). In literary texts and cultural practices, we find that a location's name acts as the display window of its self-image. In turn, it becomes associated with situations, meanings, or symbols that express its history and collective identity. Some examples include Chicago, the Gangster City, or Paris, the City of Lights.

In Palestinian society, the image of the village is even more central than in other cultures, since many Palestinians still identify themselves first by naming their place of origin. For example, many Palestinians from al-Khalīl (Hebron) first define themselves as "Khalīlī" (Khalidi 1997). Relatedly, despite its small size, Palestine can still be mapped according to its many Arabic dialects, with the regional dialect being a marker of identity and status. Due to its importance for its inhabitants and those of neighboring villages, the village's name is iconic and central to social discourse, more so than the names of natural features, neighborhoods, or streets; indeed, many Palestinian localities still lack formal street names (Dahamshe 2017, 104).

As in the construction of individual, national, and other identities, however, the image that villagers seek to project is also designed to conceal certain layers of reality. The Indigenous authors of name legends associate their etymology with values or events that speak of power and glory and are a source of pride for tribesmen and villagers. A typical example is the village Majd al-Kurūm, whose name—meaning "Glory of the Vines"—was given to it, according to a local tradition, because of its wealth of fine vines, olive groves, and fig trees. Other place-names glorify the entire Arab nation, as in the case of ʿAyn Māhil.

By using such a strategy to give names, in conjunction with highlighting the feminine narrative, harsh daily realities and internal conflicts that can tarnish the village's reputation are sidelined. Routine themes, such as farming or family life, and negative ones, such as crime, are thus displaced to the backyard of nature. Similar to the innocent girl from the cave story, negative themes are pushed away to maintain the village's good name.

This linguistic-cultural mechanism provides a selective view of reality as positive and heroic, contrasting with the negativity and banality of the villagers' lived experience. This is related to the fact that village names are official and used mainly in the "front section" of intervillage communication, as the villagers themselves have little need for them. Conversely, names of natural features are used mainly in intravillage communication and are therefore of little use for increasing the village's prestige.

This inverse relationship is supported by studies on the sociology of space. The description of a certain space as a "real chronotope," to use Mikhail Bakhtin's (1981) terminology, indicates that a place associated with a certain sociohistorical reality may dictate the activities of its inhabitants and the nature of their social contacts. Places dictate different manners of speech and behavior, and together with the nature of social contacts, these are actualized, according to real chronotopes. A person's behavior in a natural environment is different from that on the city streets. As shown by Maoz Azaryahu, the beach is an example of a "liminal territory" because it allows the reversal of social norms, as in clothing or gender relations (Azaryahu 2005, 272).

These theoretical approaches provide another explanation for the fact that local and personal matters have inspired the naming of natural features as entities hidden from public view. These include recurring meetings of village women under the tree or on the path to the spring as well as negative events and daily hardships. Thus, the names on the Palestinian map of peripheral or liminal territories straddling the boundary between culture and nature echo the freedom and intimacy provided by distance from the disciplinary male gaze.

Thus, Palestinian Arab toponymy is much more than the sum total of the places and natural features it names. The distinction made by Palestinian society between names of inhabited localities and those of natural features symbolizes and shapes that culture's differential approach to nature. This distinction is translated into social boundaries and patterns of exclusion and selection of people, practices, values, space, and time. The terms Palestinian society uses to identify its environment reveal how space is used as a platform for the (re)production of social values and their spatial locations. Palestinian space is a mnemonic—an instrument of cultural power that imposes and reproduces hierarchic distinctions and discriminations based on class, gender, and geographic differences and, in the process, mediates them for the users of the space. Finally, this distinction may also be designed to create an internal Palestinian discourse about the perceptions and memories evoked by the two types of space and the need to express the complexities of Palestinian identity through the mechanisms used for the differential naming of places.

According to this distinction, settlements are marked as special spaces that give publicity to collective memory, important and "official" events, class and masculine hegemonies, and the values that the patriarchy is interested in promulgating. Conversely, natural features are seen as private spaces for personal memories, women and ordinary people, everyday conduct in space, female concerns, and other issues, which are seen as secondary in importance. Despite this difference, both types of naming are more than part of the constitution of identity or society and articulate the spatial inspiration for highly site-specific social practices and interactions. Thus, the cultural production of space and its relations with human society, as conveyed by this rich fabric of name stories, draws a kind of "map of the soul" (Cajete 2000).

Furthermore, this toponymy is a spatial projection: the meanings that Palestinian society attributes to names are irreducible to etymological aspects alone. They belong to a broader discourse related to the marking of the boundaries of public space; ideological, class, and gender mediation; desirable images; semiotic perspectives; and spatial memories and beliefs.

This chapter examines Palestinian oral toponymic constructions as a discourse dependent on a geocultural context that has mostly disappeared due to and since the Nakba and subsequent modernization. Given its exploratory nature, it should be considered a point of departure for future studies. For example, it would be interesting to examine if and how formal and informal naming in traditional and nontraditional cultures create class/gender/image differentiation in the intrasocial context. It would also be interesting to examine whether these constructions differ between formal and informal naming.

ARAB PALESTINIAN TOPONYMY—
FROM ARABISM TO HEBRAIZATION

IN PALESTINE, PLACE-NAMES ORIGINATED IN oral expressions that people used to mark events, indicate the properties of natural features, and express their understandings of and associations with life and nature. These experiences and characteristics, as well as the knowledge gained about these places, are reflected in present-day place-names. Palestinian names were not formed within the framework of written culture, and few of them were recorded on road signs and directional markers, although among the relevant cultural interfaces for their formation are written sources: local chronicles; travelogues of Muslim, Christian, and Jewish pilgrims, geographers, and merchants; sources in Arabic and other languages; and various scriptures. Those who determined the names did not regard them as merely part of the national narrative and did not try to use them to promote political ideas aimed at dispossessing others from the land. This is probably why names from other languages have been preserved by Arabic speakers.

The origins and meanings of Palestinian place-names are rooted in historical legends, biographical legends, and local memories. This map is a cultural deposit of local memories and a meeting place for the cultural relics of the various peoples who lived and worked in the land. The motifs of the names' origins belong to the ethnic and religious traditions that entered Israel/Palestine, but the content of Palestinian names derives from the lifestyle of ancient Arab society and the distant past. They originated in the human reality of the Ayyubid period in Palestine, family-tribal and gender loyalties, and social ideals. Some place-names preserve aspirations and views from Arab tribal society's tales about life and nature, and some are drawn from previous traditions about Muslims versus Crusaders and Christians and traditions about intertribal battles.

This means that the answers to the question "How did a specific place receive a certain name?" can be found, at least in part, in ancient Arab stories or in etiological tales from the culture of local Palestinian communities.

These stories are a kind of prototype and were "planted" among local Palestinian name legends. Name legends were sometimes created in response to concrete human circumstances identified with the site or out of a need to mark or document a visible geographic feature. Some name legends tried to explain a name's strange sound and, for this purpose, made sophisticated use of textual trickery or folk etymology. Sometimes the motivations for the name legend are rooted in an attempt to understand the meaning of odd natural and climatic phenomena.

The representation of the place in the Palestinian name map "does not tell its past, but contains it" (Calvino 1974, 11), that is, contains its story and implicitly leaves room for other narratives. From the historical aspect, Palestinian explanations for the names of inhabited localities express the places' genealogical and symbolic dimensions. These dimensions play an important role in what Pamela Stewart and Andrew Strathern (Stewart and Strathern 2003, 6) defined—following Michel Foucault—as "the archeology of the meanings of space." In other words, the names used by Palestinian society reflect the historical map of the region and the marks left by time on the space, partly in the form of memories or cultural practices. The Palestinians consciously preserve a linguistic and cultural past that is not merely Muslim or Arab. The Jews and the Christians, including the Crusaders, are also part of the land's past. The Palestinian name map thus indicates that this community's sense of place consists of different and distinct layers that represent various historical periods. The Palestinian consciousness of place flourishes at the meeting point between the space's distant past and its present; the interpretations and realistic details that comprise the place-names reflect thousands of years of history that did not find their way into any written documents and that endure from ancient times to the twentieth century.

The character of some of the name legends indicates that these texts maintain a dialogue with earlier ones. Sometimes the name legends give a concrete dimension to a story "adopted" from some other source, one that is neither Arab nor Palestinian. The explanations for the names provide a general story, Arab or non-Arab, with a unique local character, and the tale undergoes a process of localization and historicization. At the same time, the place-names reveal expressions of a covert Palestinian culture, a hidden social history and a latent local geography.

The Palestinian place-names were formed as a "text" gradually, from ancient historical periods to the recent past. They reveal a process of dynamic spatial crystallization. The different layers of the map of Palestinian place-names disclose the stages of their formation as well as the intercultural communication that characterized the connections between the religious denominations and national groups that inhabited the land in the past. The map of Palestinian inhabited localities creates a spatial dialogue between the marking systems of several ethnic and linguistic groups and serves as a site of multiple identities, traditions, and languages. Despite demographic and geopolitical changes, Palestinian names preserve the ethnic and sectarian Otherness that previously marked the area. However, the traces of non-Arab and non-Palestinian ethnic groups in the names of natural features are greatly limited. In a semiotic reading, this phenomenon means that nature, the land, the fields, the topography, and all knowledge about them are experienced only by the Palestinian natives and belong to them and not to the Other. Furthermore, the Palestinian Arab identity derives from the land and from belonging to it, in a contrasting analogy to the inhabited localities, whose foreign, non-Arab inhabitants may change and pass away, as is evident from the name legends themselves.

It is sometimes possible to learn about a site's history from the pronunciation of its name by Arabic speakers. These continue to use names from Roman and Greek sources as pronounced in the original language or with a slight phonetic change. A Greek or Latin name established by the Hellenistic or Roman authorities was generally used only in official and literary circles. These names are common among Arabic speakers. For example, Bīsān, or Beth Shean in Hebrew, was called Scythopolis in the Hellenistic-Roman nomenclature, while Baniyās is the Arabic form of the Greek name Paneas.

The vital character of the stories describing the origins of names according to Palestinian society does not derive only from the reliability of the facts they present or the correctness of the etiological explanations they provide. Although in many cases the stories provide us with significant factual truths, their vitality stems from the fact that they give us access to the interpretive framework used by the community and the culture in the process of creating names and in the process of asserting their meaning. The narrators who explain the reasons for the names' formation do not rely only on the existing local tradition. They provide extensive and very important information about the ways in which the community occupies the place, about the ways by which the place was given its linguistic identity.

Many parts of Palestinian names reflect local identities or social and family ones. Personal stories and autobiographical elements of poverty-stricken locals; ordinary men and women; trivial matters; and the broad spectrum of the village community, farmers, and shepherds—all of these find expression in the names of natural features within the inhabited localities and in the natural environment. Many of the linguistic signs in fact form the essence of the cultural tradition or the historical heritage that gave the places their names. Some of them can be read as a text that unfolds Palestinian daily life in natural spaces.

The Palestinian interpretation of toponyms referring to human figures, or to actions related to them, determined these toponyms' location and classified them in relation to the space. Determining which names and images are suitable for inhabited localities and which are appropriate for identifying natural features is influenced by a culture's hierarchical perception of the environment. In this cultural concept, geographical space is divided into two separate areas: the first is at the macro level, which comprises the names of villages or inhabited localities; the second is at the micro level and is composed of the names of natural features, such as fields, wells, or caves. In this view, the interpretive process of naming places creates two regions in the same geocultural context, each of which is a metaphor for a cultural essence with contrasting relations. The binary spatial concept is also evident in the gender division, as men's names were determined as the names of inhabited localities, while women's names and images were used to indicate natural features.

In this manner of conceptual separation, place-names construct a space that is not created only as the result of a material-concrete organization or of a human action that occurred there, but is mainly a symbolic and semantic one. This construction is derived from cultural concepts concerning differences in social class, gender, and social ideals while illustrating them. Another conclusion is that in Palestinian terminology, the naming of a certain space hints at the naming of another space and exists by virtue of contrast with it. The linguistic system of the inhabited localities references the system of names of natural features, and vice versa.

The Palestinian human reality that gives names their meaning ranges from marking a local identity to marking the collective and shared identity of the Palestinian people or society. The names provide the geography that they distinguish with an ambivalent image: they amplify the village's modest dimensions to historical-epic ones while reducing it to its immediate and local features and the local human reality. This ambivalence is also evident in the tendency to exaggerate and attribute imaginary virtues—especially in the names and name legends of villages. This phenomenon is less common in the names and name legends of natural features within the villages. This spatial design also stems from the narrators' interpretations and can be explained by the desire to present the village, which is an ordinary place in the discourse of the nonresidential media, as a unique location through its name and to enhance its image in the eyes of the local residents as well as among their neighboring inhabited localities. An example of this is the name Majd al-Kurūm, which means "the glory of the vineyards."

The Palestinian map not only narrates the actions of men and women but also the movement in space-time of men and leaders, as compared to the movements of women and ordinary people.[1] A constant movement of people and population in space can be felt at the base of the development of names of inhabited localities and of natural features. The motif of men's long journeys from distant places is prominent in the names of inhabited localities that commemorate the actions and movements of male figures in space, as are motifs of migration from foreign countries and of long-term movements of figures who arrived from beyond the borders of Israel/Palestine. On the other hand, beneath the names of natural features lies a motif of local women and men's routine movement in their living area, and short and frequent daily transitions in the vicinity of the villages. The names explained by the name legends indicate a difference between feminine and masculine movement. Feminine movement is usually short-term, and the route is cyclical and lasts one day: the woman goes to the field or to the spring, works or draws water, and returns to the family residence. On the other hand, masculine movement is often long-term and lasts for many days, because men and soldiers took part in wars, foraging, and robbery. The names reveal a tension between the local population and waves of migration from external and nomadic groups, which can also be formulated as an archetypal tension between sedentary permanent residence and localness, on the one hand, and nomadism, on the other.

In the spatial consciousness of Palestinian society, the manner in which geographical names are determined (or in its scientific name, toponymics) leads to the conclusion that these expressions were born naturally. According to Naftali Kadmon, the term *natural birth* refers to a name that derives from a topographical or geographical essence. For example, the Dead Sea is so named because of the high proportion of salts it contains. On the other hand, when a name is given by administrative order, this is a kind of "in vitro birth" (Kadmon 2004, 12). Such is, for example, the name of the town Kiryat Motzkin, called after the Zionist leader Aryeh Leib Motzkin. Unlike Kadmon, I demonstrate that even names given to the environment by natural birth do not necessarily represent a geographical and topographical essence characteristic of the place. Such are the names in Palestinian culture: they were created by the ordinary people, out of a natural inclination, spontaneously, in response to an action or an event—without the deliberate authorization of an official body.

In Palestinian folk naming practices, the same name can be given to different natural features and even to different villages, for example, the name al-Ṭayyiba, which refers to a number of Arab-inhabited localities in Israel and neighboring countries. Other examples of places that bear the same element in the Arabic language are names in which the second element is *al-tīn* (التين), "the figs," or *al-tīna* (التينه), "the fig," due to the fig trees that exist or existed there, such as Wādī al-Tīn (وادي التين) in Kafr Kannā; Wādī ʿAyn al-Tīna (وادي عين التينه) in the center of the Western Galilee and in the Menashe plateau; ʿAyn al-Tīna (عين التينه) in the Miron ravine and the Ginnosar valley in the northwest of the Sea of Galilee.[2] Using the same name for different places can be seen as a social code that emphasizes a collective popular perception of the essence of natural phenomena or of the place's properties. Since the names of natural features in Palestinian society were mainly used for intracommunity communication, repeating them over and over at different sites was not an obstacle to communication for their users.

Another toponymic practice customary in Palestinian naming is to call each part or tributary of a stream and each section of a mountain by a separate name. Thus, several names are found simultaneously along the course of a stream or up a mountain. For example, in the Arabic language, six names were used to indicate the route of Naḥal Jephthahel in the center of the Lower Galilee. The names are Wādī al-Maʿāṣir (وادي المعاصر), "the river of the [wine] presses"; Wādī al-Mughur (وادي المُغر), "the river of the caves"; Wādī Jarabān (وادي جَربان), because of the ugly and winding shape of the wadi, resembling the appearance of a person suffering from the skin disease called *jarab*; Wādī al-Aʿwaj (وادي الاعوج), "the crooked stream," so named because its course is crooked; Wādī Rummāna (وادي رمانه), after the village of Rummāna; and Wādī al-Khalādiyya (وادي الخلاديه), after the ruin of Khalādiyya, which was a temporary residence for Bedouins. The differentiated Palestinian naming was due to the fact that each village, in whose vicinity the course of the stream passes, gave a different nomenclature to each section according to its perception or point of interpretation, and the status of this section of the stream in the daily agricultural life of the village. Linguistic differentiation emerges from the naming in Arabic, and thus the nickname Jarabān used by the residents of Kafr Kannā is blunt compared to the nickname al-Aʿwaj used by the residents of Mashhad. The Palestinian terms also indicate an economic function because they were used to mark the borders between village lands, and as such, they were useful in everyday life. For example, al-Aʿwaj and the lands adjacent to it are owned by the village of Mashhad, while al-Mughur and the plots around it belong to Ṭurʿān.

The names of this type reveal the sociolect—the language used in Palestinian peasant society to define their natural environment. This language reveals the cultural inspiration, the influence of the agricultural culture on the generality of terms for the space, and reflects the linguistic dialects that characterized the local people.

Another practice is a content-related connection between the name and the place signified by it. The signifier—that is, the name—is linked to the signified, or the place that exists in reality. This feature is particularly noticeable in names inspired by the natural environment. According to this approach, plots of land and natural formations were given special names deriving from their geographical character or climatic-agricultural properties, according to the crops or the actions taken there, or due to the effect of a deed or action inherent to the site.

In the Palestinian practice, names were given not only to prominent external natural features and unusual formations but also to details of natural features that were hidden and distant from inhabited localities. Why did the need for such individual identification arise? And what are the reasons for this toponymic richness? The abundance of Palestinian names for features of the natural landscape and plots of land indicates Palestinian society's constant contact with its environment, its familiarity (more than those who try to impose names "from above," institutionally, using methods of erasing and drawing new maps) with it, and the need to identify sites and natural features in the daily life of a society whose livelihood and entire lifestyle were tied to the land. This familiarity with the place and the way of life gives the Palestinians priority in naming. The names point to the immediate-local identifying features, to the tiny details of the place that are hidden to the untrained eye, such as the small hidden plot of land that the residents of ʿIlabūn called Warā Umm Khalīl (ورا إم خليل), that is, the plot behind the fields of Umm Khalīl. Moreover, the land is a key element in this society's cooperative heritage.

The names used to identify the natural environment reflect a cultural landscape of close interrelationship between that environment and the culture operating within it. The dependence of the Palestinian peasants on the land and its crops, the existence of ritual actions, community or group events, and the close observation of natural phenomena of nature and their properties—all these experiences not only are individual but also become the voices of sociocultural communication and then names.

Trees, plants, flowers, and agricultural crops of all kinds are abundantly present in Palestinian place-names. The Palestinian exile Muṣṭafā al-Dabbāgh (1988, 121–226) devoted an entire book to the influence of flora and fauna on the formation of Palestinian names, and the following is a small selection from what he recorded: ʿAyn al-Zaytūna (عين الزيتونه), "the spring of the olive tree"; al-Rīḥāniyya (الريهانيه), after the myrtle growing in the vicinity; Wādī al-Kharrūb (وادي الخروب), "the stream of the carobs"; ʿAyn al-Tūt (عين التوت), "the mulberry spring"; Wādī al-Tīn (وادي التين), "the stream of the figs"; Wādī al-Lamūn (وادي اللمون), "the stream of the lemons"; al-Sindiyāna (السنديانه), after the oak trees that grew in the vicinity; ʿAyn al-Ṣufṣāf (عين الصُفصاف), "the poplar spring"; Khirbat Zaʿtara (خربة زعتره), named after the *zaʿtar* (hyssop) plants; Wādī al-Shūmariyya (وادي الشومريه), "the stream of the fennel plants"; Tall al-Shumām (تل الشمام), "the hill of the melons"; Khirbat al-ʿUrayma (خربة العريمه), "the ruins of the wheat sheaf"; Wādī al-Shaʿīr (وادي الشعير), "the barley stream"; Tall al-ʿAdas (تل العدس), "the hill of lentils"; Kafr Qaraʿ (كفر قرع), "the village of gourds," and many more.

Nature in all its richness is expressed also in names derived from animals: large and predatory animals, as well as small animals, reptiles, insects, and birds, are abundantly present in the Arabic nomenclature: ʿAyn al-Asad (عين الاسد), "the spring of the lion"; ʿAyn al-Numayra (عين النُميره), "the spring of the little she-leopard"; Wādī al-Khanāzīr (وادي الخنازير), "the stream of the pigs"; Wādī al-Ẓibāʿ (وادي الظباع), "the stream of the hyenas"; Khirbat al-Dhīb (خربة الذيب), "the ruin of the wolf"; Marāḥ al-Ghuzalān (مراح الغزلان), a plain where the deer camped; ʿAyn al-Baqr (عين البقر), "the spring of the cattle"; Umm al-Ḥīrān (إم الحيران), "the mother of the camel calves"; Tall al-Ḥamīr (تل الحمير), "the hill of the donkeys"; Qamzat al-Muhr (قمزة المُهر), "the colt's jumping place"; Tall al-Wāwiyāt (تل الواويات), "the hill of the jackals"; Umm al-Ghanam (ام الغنم), "the mother of the sheep"; ʿAyn al-Ḥayya (عين الحيه), "the spring of the snake"; ʿAyn al-Dhubbān (عين الذبان), "the spring of the flies"; Ḥajar al-Namla (حجر النمله), "the rock of the ant"; Dayr Ḥajala (دير حجله), "the monastery of the partridge"; Wādī al-Ḥamām (وادي الحمام), "the stream of the pigeons"; Wādī al-Nasūr (وادي النسور), "the river of the vultures"; Wādī Ghurāb (وادي غراب), "the stream of the crow"; ʿIrāq Abū Maṣaṣ (عراق ابو مصص), "the cliffs of the short-toed eagle"; al-ʿIshūsh (العشوش), "the birds' nests."

The names of settled localities and the names of natural features that originate from the properties of the natural environment—crops, springs, and climate—usually praise the immediate environment and extol the land's fertility and abundance. Mainly, they praise its contribution to Arab visitors and Muslim soldiers who came from foreign countries as well as its physical and emotional contribution to the locals and the peasant economy.[3] The land and its natural resources are presented in the name legends as elements supportive of the Arabs and Palestinians and deterring to their enemies. For example, the legend telling of the circumstances and reasons for the name of ʿUyūn Janān ("the mad men's springs") in the mountains around the village of Rayna explains as a kind of microcosm the concept of the land as a factor that benefits the Arabs.

> Saladin placed a garrison on the springs so that the Crusaders could not reach them and drink from them. But the Crusader armies overcame the small garrison there, arrived and camped there. Around the springs grew *tufāḥ majann*, mandrakes. Anyone who eats more than a hundred grams of mandrake falls into exhaustion and frivolity.
>
> When Saladin's soldiers returned to attack the Crusader armies, they found them lying down, drunk and talking nonsense. Despite their large numbers and the few soldiers in Saladin's army, the Crusaders surrendered. It turned out that after eating the mandrakes, *injannū*—the Crusaders went out of their minds.

The purpose of this legend is not to describe the historical processes but mainly to indicate the place's benevolent features. Rural nature made an alliance with the Muslims to put an end to the threat of the Crusaders, who, being invaders, endanger the Muslims and likewise the homeland because they covet it. The Muslim warriors, who came from a distant territory, are familiar with the place's secrets, its plants and their innate properties, while their enemies are described as invaders who are foreign to the place and its owners. The Muslim commanders' knowledge of the place's secrets signifies their ownership of it, because the "truth" of the place is known only to the Muslims, and they possess the place. In the narrative context, the place is given an animistic-mysterious status; this is a place that lurks in wait for foreigners and, at the same time, guarantees the supremacy of the Muslims. Hence, the place is a symbol of the homeland. It is worth noting that the names emphasize more the beneficial power of the village lands and of nature itself and less the virtues of the locals—the Arabs.

Many of these names are picturesque, especially those relating to the features of the landscape and the qualities of the soil. They are highly sensitive to landscape formations and topography and in tracing the life cycles of plants and the functioning of nature. The terminology used by the Palestinians to describe their natural environment has a poetic quality: Palestinian names are full of words that have a lyrical quality, and use metaphors, allusions, images, exaggerations, personification, and onomatopoeia. These linguistic means allow the name-givers to express succinctly the depth of emotion and the depth of thought behind the names. These names are embedded in the genre of the story, and thus the natural world and the actions associated with it are described in a fresh and vivid way that excites listeners and readers.[4] The figurative language of Palestinian place-names testifies not only to the importance of the information about the environment—the referential side, which indicates the environmental reality—but also to aesthetic choices, or the poetic quality of the language of the names. Along with the semantic aspect, the phonetic and the poetic aspects of the name are also valuable to the name-givers. Such, for example, are the phonetic names: al-ʿAlāʾil (العلايل), al-Khalāʾil (لخلايل), al-Dawāʾir (الدواير), al-ʿAlīliyyāt (العليليات), al-Hawāyāt (الهَوايات), al-Ṭāsāt (الطاسات), al-Zahrāt (الظَهرات), and al-Ṣadrāt (الصَدرات).

Many terms express the earth's richness and charms phonemically and have a romantic tune. These names are like expressions of thanks to the places and they present the land as an object of love and beauty. The tendency to idealize and romanticize the environment, as well as the intense feeling of admiration for the place's beauty and its qualities, are very noticeable in the names that the Palestinian peasants used to identify their lands. Sometimes sensuality, grandiosity, and coquetry are evident in the names. This attitude is expressed, for example, in the fields named after young women and boys, after women's cosmetics and adornments, and in relation to their activity in the space: Kaḥil al-ʿAyn (كحيل العين), "the blue-eyed," and Umm al-Asāwir (إم الاساور), "the mother who wears bracelets." So are Marj al-ʿUshshāq (مرج العشاق), "the meadow of the lovers," because young men and women used to meet there. The name Umm al-Zīnāt (إم الزينات), "the mother of the pretty girls," was given to a village known for the beauty of its women, while the path leading up to the village was known as Darb al-ʿUrsān (درب العرسان), "the path of the bridegrooms," because it was where the young men of the area went to look for brides. When they returned to the village of their birth, the girls of the village greeted them with dances and drums, and therefore the place was called Umm al-Dufūf (م الدفوف), "the mother of the drummers." There are names in which a note of beauty emerges from their sounds, such as Ghurūb al-Qamar (غروب القمر), "the setting of the moon"; al-Sahra (السهره), "the evening"; Wādī al-Zarqā (وادي الزرقا), "the blue stream"; Wādī al-Nadā (وادي الندى), "the dewy stream."[5]

Reference to a place's history can testify to humans' love for the land and their loyalty to it (Tuan 1974, 99). Nurit Govrin (1988, 36) states, among other things, "Turning to the past can serve as a source of national consolation. For example: in the past we were free, strong." In cases of asymmetry in power relations, and in regimes where an ethnic minority is controlled by a majority that forbids free criticism, writing about the past is a disguised tool for expressing protest and circumventing censorship (Govrin 1988, 36). The minority creates alternative narratives of collective memory, which oppose the memory practices of the hegemonic majority (Zerubavel 1995, 10–11). Among ethnic minorities who suffer from the expropriation of land and geographic resources, historical stories and narratives work to strengthen the bond between the natives and their land and to secure the rights to it. It is not by chance that Edward Chamberlin (2004) called his book dealing with the relationship between governments (such as those of Canada and the US) and Indigenous Native American tribes *If This Is Your Land, Where Are Your Stories?* In the reality described in the etiological legends, both Saladin and the positive descriptions of the local natural environment in the past have a significant influence on Palestinian name-giving and the construction of the environment. The choice of a historical period characterized by Islamic military superiority and control over territory, and the exaggeration of the contribution of the land and natural resources to the locals and the Arabs, are not disconnected from the political reality that came into being after 1948. The loss of the Palestinian homeland to the Zionist movement influenced the name legends, which refer in hints and allusions to the place's glorious Arab and Palestinian past. Placing Muslim leaders in the space expresses a longing for the umma's "golden age" and its victories as well as expressing a gap between the locale's abundant and fertile past and its present that is experienced as scarce, that is, the painful political reality of Palestinian society in Israel. This reference aims to construct a different consciousness that stands in opposition to the Zionist consciousness. The message that runs as a scarlet thread through all these names is sharp and clear: this place has been ours for a long time, and its value is priceless.

The names centered on Saladin and the plenitude of the lost place are monumental ones. They are intended to provide a verbal narrative for what is no more, to provide a monument that outlines the boundaries of the lacunae that the geopolitical transformations of modern life have created in the reality of Palestinian society. Telling about the place means mourning for what has passed and gone as well as an attempt to reach the soil that has been taken violently and add meaning to the place's past through creating names and inventing their stories in the present. Borrowing from Anton Shammas (2005), we can say that the stories redraw the map of the lost homeland. "The memory that was exiled off the map in 1948 returned and exercised its right to speak through the language of a place." The stories and names of the places used by the Palestinians become part of a narrative that symbolizes their struggle against the expropriation of land by the Israeli government (Davis 2007, 64).

Place-names and their explanations in Indigenous cultures are expressive phrases, articulating the human subjective interpretation of phenomena in reality. Therefore, apart from their etiological-onomastic value, Palestinian place-names serve as a source of social history. They evoke images and abstract matters from the life of Palestinian society, mainly the customs, ways of thinking, beliefs, moral values, and standard of living of this society in the past. Furthermore, they give tangible expression to the social organization of the local communities and the values of folk literature. The purpose of Palestinian names is to make heard the voice of Islamic history and thereby perpetuate the memory of the nation's forefathers and heroes, and at the same time to be a mouthpiece for the voices of local Palestinian society—the voices of Muslims, Christians, Bedouin, and Druze. The names of the heroes who inspired the names of villages are connected to a historical narrative of a people; while the names of local figures given to natural features create a local ethnographic narrative, which ties the geographic space to Palestinianness and local Arabness.

Palestinian toponymy is not the result of state decisions at certain points in time, so it is difficult to date the moment of its formation and the milestones in its development. The linguistic forms of the names were formed in an evolutionary process over generations and shaped the identity of the space according to the events that took place there. The names were created under the influence of the temporary settlement of ancient peoples who passed through the place, through groups of immigrants and nomads, and up to the social activities of locals and their experiences with natural elements. The historical events constructed the Palestinian toponymic creation as a serial tale, layer on layer.

To explain names whose sounds are foreign to the Arab ear, especially the names of inhabited localities, as well as to explain a strange and unique natural feature, the name-givers used place legends and images that were familiar and close to them. Solutions of this type fit what is known as "poetic geography" (Vico 1968, 60–61, 69–76, 285–92; Portugali 1999, 50). That is, cultures make use of images and events distant in time and space as materials for constructing their present and future. In the context of toponymy, poetic geography is an expression of the imagined and interpretive context that humans use in naming the space. An example of this is the way the Greeks named the new lands they conquered after the various regions of Greece. The distinct poetic geography in the naming of places by the Palestinians is a mental extension of folk traditions and beliefs and of the ancient Arab culture, and this means that many layers on the Palestinian map are a subjective representation.

In the Palestinian name map, there is a depth structure of contrasting and different elements and themes. As mentioned, one element in the depth structure is the contrast between the outward-facing names of inhabited localities and the inward-facing names of natural features. Another element is the contrast between long-term movements in space of collective characters, and short-term movements of local characters. The space takes on a private meaning because it is related to a local and individual geography, but it also has a collective meaning, when it comes to names derived from symbolic figures and leaders. In general, the study of Palestinian toponymy indicates that the Palestinian map of place-names is divided into two maps with opposing ideas and themes—the "upper map," which is filled by inhabited localities, and the "lower map," which identifies natural features.[6] Following George Stewart (1975, 6–7), the names of inhabited localities can be considered "great names," in which the stamp of the collective and the inspiration of various ethnic groups resonate glory and courage. On the other hand, the names of natural features are considered "little names," documenting the daily lives of local figures in Palestinian society. These maps reflect and are designed as two different worldviews. Palestinian toponymy fluctuates between these two maps, but it also merges them, according to the principle of mediation in cultural creation according to Claude Lévi-Strauss (1967, 40–47).

Due to their inseparable connection with the places that they signify, geographical names make it possible to know a huge variety of mental, psychological, and emotional contexts (Basso 1996, 76). Name legends provide much information about the identities of the people who created them and give expression to their spatial consciousness and the image of the place in human perception. In his study of place-names originating from folklore and local history, the geographer Ivan Lind found that the content of names is a source of information about the identity and character of the culture that coined them (Lind 1962, 123–27).

These approaches suggest that the givers of geographical names in Palestinian society saw themselves as successors to the toponymic traditions of other cultures and to the peoples that preceded them in time. The Palestinians are tolerant and open to the linguistic-spatial heritage of the Other; they follow it and do not replace it, as occurred, for example, with the founding of the State of Israel.

A recurring motif in Palestinian names is the person who moves in space and connects between places. When this person is Palestinian, there is a mutual relationship: the land usually gives them their identity and, at the same time, they make their mark on it through physical contact and by naming it. This Palestinian geography has a double importance, historical and literary, both in the preservation of the place's past and in the preservation of Palestinian society's consciousness of place through the name legends. In the final analysis, the relationship between Palestinian society and Palestinian space is one of mutual shaping.

Palestinian toponymy creates a temporal division of space, usually according to the seasons and the parts of the day. The expressions of time in place-names indicate stretches of time that cannot be measured in terms of hours and minutes: al-Raḥārīḥ (الرحاريح) are shallow ridges in which rainwater remains after the rain has stopped; al-Shiqāq (الشقاق), "the cracked earth," is a name for the soil that cracks in summer or autumn; ʿArīḍ al-Shams (عريض الشمس), "the slope of the sun," got its name because the morning sun illuminates it. The time markers "evening," "morning," "summer," and "winter" thus do not only mark a point on the moving timeline but also indicate a human climatic essence and an agricultural way of life.

Six main roles can be identified in the local legends connected to the Palestinian spatial map. The first role is that of a "primary legend," which explains the name and its content. The second role is to emphasize the Palestinians and Muslims' age-old ownership of the land. Apart from their ideological-political purpose, Arabic place-names refer to educational-social norms. Therefore, the essence of the third role is to create socialization within the institutions of society. The fourth role is the preservation and shaping of memories of the geographical environment and the preservation of the perception of the place. The names of places are like a portrait of the location, of its consciousness and its past. The folkloric names that people give to their environment are a form of code names, which provide the name-givers with a feeling of security and a sense of belonging to the environment (Ryden 1993, 79). Names and their explanations have a fifth role of interpreting natural phenomena that seem incomprehensible. The sixth and last role that the name legends fulfill is the presentation of human reality in the space—that is, transmitting a message about the ethnic traditions that existed there, especially a message concerning the locals' spatial way of life, their values, and their perceptions.

The relationship between the legendary text, on the one hand, and reality and historical events, on the other, is complex and multifaceted (Yassif 1999a, 217–21). Although the creation of Palestinian toponymy reflected the poetics of its times and creators, that toponomy cannot be used as a reference for the historical moment of the names' formation, especially in relation to the names of inhabited localities, and cannot help in determining their dating.[7] However, it can certainly serve as a cultural document, for both the way the space is constructed and its presence in the Palestinian cultural consciousness.

Thus, the design of the space and landscapes in name legends, to paraphrase the geographer John Kirtland Wright, reveals the most fascinating terra incognita: that which resides in the human psyche.[8] The cultural production of the environment and human-space relations, as demonstrated in Palestinian name legends, touches on the discussions of Gregory Cajete and Scott Momaday, a researcher of Native American culture and a researcher of Native American literature and tradition, respectively. Cajete uses the term "ensoulment" to characterize the deep psychological affinity that develops between people in Indigenous societies and the earth (geopsyche), an affinity that reveals a sort of map of the soul (Cajete 2000, 186–87). Momaday refers to the mutual bond created between Indigenous societies that have been living in a place for hundreds of years and their geographical environment. His term is "appropriation," which means that the person "invests" himself in the landscape and at the same time integrates the landscape into his deepest experiences (Momaday 1974, 179–85).

But this toponymy has had the bad fortune to be depleted, mainly due to political, demographic, and geopolitical reasons. Since the renewal of Jewish settlement in Palestine at the end of the nineteenth century, and increasingly since the beginning of the British Mandate period, there has been a retreat in the status of the "Palestinian map." The Zionist movement's preoccupation with Palestinian toponyms is related to the beginning of this movement's activity in promoting its national goals in Palestine (the Land of Israel). This issue has never left the Israeli agenda and is still relevant today. The status of the "Palestinian map" deteriorated throughout the twentieth century as the "Hebrew map" took shape and took root. The emergence of the Hebrew map involved a political conflict with the Indigenous Palestinian toponymy, and it was intended to dispossess this toponymy and cause it to be forgotten.

This process began during the British Mandate, with the National Committee, most of whose claims about inhabited localities' names the British Mandate government in Palestine accepted (Katz 1998, 110–14), and thus the Hebrew map was created at the same time as the Palestinian map. In 1949 another process began: the deletion of the Palestinian map, on the one hand and the creation of the Hebrew map, on the other. In this year, the Geographic Committee for the Determination of Names in the Negev was appointed, and thus Hebrew nomenclature received the official stamp from the State of Israel. In 1951, the Israeli government established the Governmental Names Committee. At this stage, the dimensions of the "Hebrew map" were enlarged and expanded, and it was seen as part of the Hebrew language revival project. The Hebraization process that began in the Negev gained momentum and spread to other districts and places. Judaization and Hebraization were applied to the entire territory of Israel, including the displaced Palestinian villages and all geographic features, and at the same time the Palestinian map shrank until most of it disappeared.

Up to the middle of the twentieth century, the period during which Zionism—mainly for political and diplomatic reasons—worked to deepen the Hebraization process, the Palestinians did not attribute an ideological-political significance to the issue of toponymy and did not care about the preservation of naming traditions or the creation of cartographic documentation, even though they had a database of tens of thousands of place-names. However, from the Zionist ideological perspective of a people returning to their country and trying to bridge the gap of two thousand years of exile, while attaching ancient names to concrete sites, the native Palestinian names were considered foreign (Bitan 1992, 336).

Zionism's attitude toward Palestinian toponymy is characterized by arrogance and hostility. The representatives of the Israeli government reconfigured the linguistic landscape and severed it from its previous Palestinian identity. The Hebrew naming installed on the ruins of Palestinian names is based on two separate linguistic operations, one on top of the other. First, the Palestinian names were deleted, translated into Hebrew, or transliterated based on phonemic similarity. Second, the suppression and exclusion of the Palestinian names erased linguistic markers that reflected the Palestinian cultural perceptions that stood behind the naming processes. In other words, beyond the denial of Arab Palestinian politics and ownership of the space, the Hebrew naming also had metapolitical and cultural consequences. The process of erasing Arabic included a long series of cultural practices related to forgetting the customs of Palestinian society.[9]

The linguistic policy at the basis of Israeli name-giving is that of uniformity. In the Zionist practice, it is desirable to give a stream or a mountain a single Hebrew name, replacing several names in the Arabic language. An example of this is the name Naḥal ʿAmud, which is a Hebrew translation of the Arabic term Wādī al-ʿAmūd. In Arabic, there are three names for the parts of the river: Wādī al-Lamūn (وادي اللمون), after the citrus groves and fruit trees; Wādī al-Ṭawāḥīn (وادي الطواحين), after the many flour mills used by the Arabs of Safed; and Wādī al-ʿAmūd (وادي العمود), named after the rock column located in the lower part of the stream. As mentioned, these three names were reduced to a single one in the Hebrew naming system.

A logical mechanism that requires a state of monovalence is also salient in Hebrew naming. According to this mechanism, one name should signify one object, and only one object, in order to differentiate places and avoid confusion. This procedure of unique marking, which was forcibly imposed on the Palestinian nomenclature, erased and deleted the Palestinian practice of giving the same name to different natural objects and even to different villages. For example, the signifier al-Bayḍa, "the white," indicated various places due to the white color of the soil or rock, and those places were each called by separate Hebrew signifiers. The place ʿAyn al-Bayḍa (عين البيضه), between ʿAylūṭ and Tzippori, became ʿEin Rabbi (named after R. Judah the Prince, a Jewish sage who lived in the second century CE), while ʿAyn al-Bayḍa in the vicinity of Ḥanita became ʿEin Kovshim. In this way, not only were the two identical Palestinian markers, ʿAyn al-Bayḍa, erased, but the Hebrew naming removed the Palestinian practice of giving the same name to different geographical formations.

The naming also transferred the hegemonic political relationship to the gender and patriarchal contexts. Palestinian feminine images and motifs were displaced from the Hebrew Israeli landscape. This procedure was carried out on several levels: Palestinian feminine names were replaced by male proper names or names whose grammatical gender is masculine. For example, ʿAyn Umm Ḥamīd (عين إم حميد) became ʿEin Ḥomeṭ.[10] The gender significance of places named in honor of brides on their wedding day was also displaced and disappeared from the Hebrew naming. As we have seen, names like al-ʿArūs (the bride) or al-ʿArāʾis (the brides) were given to places where female ceremonies were held for young women on their wedding day. ʿAyn al-ʿArūs was far from inhabited localities, and there the female residents of Ḥurfeish and the nearby settlements used to bathe the brides and prepare them before the wedding ceremony, away from the eyes of the men. This spring was called in Hebrew ʿEinot Ghabāṭa, together with the springs ʿAyn al-Birka (the pool) and Jurn al-Qāq ("the cistern of the hooded crow").

The exclusion of feminine identity is also evident from names that included elements from the semantic field of the female. The term *umm* (mother) in Arabic is the feminine of father. It also indicates a place with a well-known characteristic. For example, ʿAyn Umm Ṣufṣāfa (عين إم صفصافه), "the spring of Umm Ṣufṣāfa [= the poplar]," became ʿEin ʿEfroni ("the spring of the lark"), and Wādī Umm al-Qaṣab (وادي إم القصب), "the stream of the bulrushes," received the name Naḥal Alon ("Oak Stream"). The signifier *umm*, which creates a connection to motherhood and personifies nature as Mother Earth, thus signifying an age-old bond between the Palestinians and the soil, does not exist in the Hebrew names of natural features. The suppression of the term *umm* is a suppression of the gendered lexical pool of place-names and of gendered perceptions of nature.

Following the gender rhetoric created by Zionism, the female subject, which for the Palestinians marked the inner space of the village and inhabited location, was repressed. Its place was taken by vague masculine names, whose gender character tends to be limited and bounded within the grammatical gender. Following the change of Palestinian names, the territory underwent a sexual mutation. The de-Palestinianization of the landscape displaced the locale's feminine image. This displacement is explained against the background of the ideology implicit in Zionist practice, according to which the Palestinian space was empty and desolate until the Zionist settlers arrived (Zerubavel 2008, 205–6).

Another mechanism used by Zionism against the Palestinian names is the giving of beautiful names to replace Arabic names that the Zionist view considered repulsive in their meaning and content. About two years after the establishment of the State of Israel, David Ben-Gurion declared: "The names we found . . . are foreign to us in their sounds . . . bear a derogatory character . . . repulsive in their sad meaning."[11] The labels attached to the Palestinian terminology, as a metonym for Orientalism, characterize it as a wild nuisance that needs to be healed by converting it into an appropriate language—Hebrew. As an example of this change, I will note that ʿAyn Umm Ḥajar ("the spring of the mother of the stone"), so called because its waters come out of stones, became ʿEin Peraḥ ("the spring of the flower").

In a comparative view, the Israeli erasure of Palestinian naming practices is reminiscent of the European map of Southeast Asia in the second half of the nineteenth century. This mapping ignored the local population and served the purposes of European rule (Anderson 1983). Furthermore, the Hebraization of the space not only destroyed the Palestinian spatial heritage but also damaged remnants of ancient times, which are neither Arab nor Palestinian. For example, the name of the displaced village of Qālūniyā (قالونيا), originally a Roman colony, was deleted and Mevaseret Tziyyon was established on the village's territory.

Against the background of the ongoing national conflict whose end is not in sight, the issue of geographical names in Israel has so far remained unresolved for the Palestinians. It has lately shown signs of awakening beyond the academic discourse in Israel, such as in the media, and in spatial practices initiated by Palestinians and Jews for the preservation and restoration of the presence of the Palestinian linguistic heritage in the general Israeli space. The reason for this is, among other things, the gradual transition of the Palestinians living in Israel from a state of survival to a state of challenge—class, intellectual, and conscious—that allows them to confront the discriminatory spatial policy on the part of Israeli rule (Bigon and Dahamshe 2014).

Recently, awareness of the existence and preservation of Palestinian geographical names from before 1948 has increased, but the expression of this awareness is very limited. These are usually the initiatives of individuals or voluntary associations, such as the establishment of alternative signage in Arabic in the general area in mixed cities such as Acre (Shoval 2013, 621–24) and petitions to the High Court regarding urban signage by Adalah, the legal center for Arab rights in Israel (Pinto 2011, 3). In the last few years, the pilgrimage of Palestinians, with the participation of members of the Zochrot association, to displaced villages on Nakba Day, has also increased.[12] As part of the revival of Palestinian collective memory on this day, banners with the names of the displaced villages are waved, and in some cases, the names are placed on temporary signs.

On the other hand, the official Israeli opposition to Palestinian names has recently become more intense and anchored within the framework of the law. Israel established regulations and laws designed to denigrate the status of Palestinian names and the Arabic language. This process culminated in 2018, when the Knesset, Israel's parliament, enacted the Nationality Law, which stripped Arabic of its status as an official language in the country.

An earlier example occurred in 2009, when Minister of Transportation Israel Katz established a regulation, unifying road signs in Israel. The goal was to remove the accepted Arabic and English place-names and to present in their place the transliteration of the Hebrew names only (Olsen 2011, 403). Thus, for example, following this regulation, the inscription أُورشَليم القُدْس (Urūshalim al-Quds, the Arabic name of Jerusalem as it appears in Arabic on Israeli signage)[13] that appeared on signs in the past would be replaced with the inscription يروشلايم, transliterating the Hebrew *Yerushalayim* into Arabic letters. The approach of the Israeli establishment in the last few years reflects a deep politicization of the naming processes taking place on the ground, reflecting a linguistic policy that expresses right-wing orientations and the enforcement of power relations, the result of which is "symbolic extinction" (Gross 1988), that is, preventing Arabic names from appearing in the public sphere. A practical expression of this approach is that recently the Arabic names of cities that previously had an Arab majority were removed from Israeli signage; at the same time, in Jewish settlements the Hebrew names were left as they were and transliterated into Arabic script, replacing the original Arabic name. For example, on the contemporary signage, بيت شان (Beit Shean) appears and not بيسان (Bīsān) as before. As a general rule, Israeli signage in the vast majority of cases does not indicate the Palestinian names of natural features.

The Palestinian terminology of natural features is known to the Israeli authorities, and when the need arises, the representatives of the authorities use it to provide legal justification for the annexation of Palestinian lands. The writer Rajā Shihāda says that a plant called *naṭash* (prickly burnet, *Sarcopoterium spinosum*) was very popular in the Israeli military courts. This is because on various occasions the representative of the Civil Administration (responsible for the expropriation of Palestinian land for the purposes of Israeli settlements) declared to the chair of the appeals committee, which discussed land matters, as follows: "But your honor, the land is full of *naṭash*," meaning that it is not cultivated and hence it is public land that Israeli settlers may take control of (Shiḥāda 2009, 73).

Israeli naming policy has also brought about a change in the spatial consciousness of Palestinians. It erased the place's Arab past, and at the same time cast Palestinians into a process of socialization and acculturation conducted in the Hebrew language and in accordance with the interests of the Zionist hegemony. This policy discriminated against Palestinian names, the Arabic language and its speakers, and established the sovereignty of the Hebrew language.[14]

However, the linguistic reality that took shape in the geographical space of Palestinian society in Israel is characterized by two seemingly contradictory processes: on the one hand, Arab municipalities bestow street names, a small part of which relate to the layers of Palestinian national identity that developed after 1948. In the last two decades in particular, streets have been named after localities displaced in 1948, national heroes (like Yasser Arafat), and Palestinian writers (such as Mahmoud Darwish or Fadwa Tuqan).[15] On the other hand, the Palestinians use Hebrew-language addresses and place-names.

The culture developed by the Palestinian minority in Israel cannot ignore the complexity of the political situation, and it also reflects attempts to resemble the dominant culture and be part of it, among other things through the tactical use of Israeli names. A complex toponymic discourse has formed among the Palestinians: Palestinians use names in Arabic and at the same time, they use Hebrew signifiers to indicate the names of their places of residence. For example, they use the Hebrew name Peqiʻin instead of the Arabic name al-Buqīʻa, and Gush Ḥalav instead of Jīshsh.[16] The use of Israeli names by the Palestinians is not limited to the sphere of names of inhabited localities and national roads. Palestinians in Israel use Hebrew names of state institutions to indicate places inside Palestinian villages, such as "the square near Bank Leumi," "the street by the post office" (*ha-do'ar*). The main reason for this is that the names of landmarks within Palestinian localities are not known to young people and because they do not appear on signs, although in recent years some of these names have appeared on municipal signage in Arab local authorities. The Palestinian toponymic discourse that developed in Israel is a hybrid creation, born from the encounter between the ruler and the ruled. It might be said that this discourse gave rise to a "third map," neither solely Arabic nor entirely Hebrew, an ambivalent map that disrupts the binary oppositions prevalent in the linguistic marking systems of Jews and Arabs.

Beyond the power relations at the national level, the Palestinians' use of Israeli names can also be explained through the many internal changes in Palestinian economy and culture. Agriculture has ceased to be dominant in the life of Palestinian society, and therefore, the direct experiential relationship between Palestinian society and its natural environment is reduced. This reality has caused names of agrarian origin to be emptied of their content and validity. One of the conclusions from this process is that naming practices within Palestinian society are influenced by the name-givers' lifestyles.

The significance of the use of a bilingual toponymy by young Palestinians is that the concept of place that has developed among them is complex, fuzzy, and without clear boundaries. The fundamental structures of attachment to space, which were dominant for a long time in the lives of Palestinians (e.g., the Arab heritage and its values, the ways of life of the Palestinian peasants, rural traditions, and the agricultural heritage) are seen as meaningless or unsuited to the reality of their lives as they have developed in Israel.

In the postcolonial approach, the relationship between the ruler and the ruled is not a one-way, top-down one. Homi Bhabha pointed out the mutuality in the relationship between the conqueror and the conquered, which exists within wide margins (Bhabha 1990). In other words, the Israeli hegemony also takes part in the rebellion against the "Hebrew map." Jewish Israelis working from the bottom as well as official and governmental bodies belonging to the establishment and working from the top use the Arabic forms of names, even though these places have Hebrew names and even though the pronunciation of the forms in Arabic and their content are clear to everyone. I call this toponymic discourse "nevertheless names," because Palestinian names were absorbed by Israelis despite the determination of Israeli state institutions to design a monolingual and monocultural space, free from Palestinianness.[17] A preliminary mapping that I performed reveals that Israelis use Arabic names in five cases.

1. Checkpoints. For example, al-Za'īm checkpoint, named after a Palestinian village located in East Jerusalem.
2. Prisons. For example, Shāṭa prison, whose name derives from its proximity to the displaced Palestinian village of Shāṭa that existed in that area.
3. Landscape features and natural sites, for example, the Saḥneh, which is Sākhina in Arabic.
4. Generic terms for natural landscapes, such as *wādī* and *jabal*.

5. Names of displaced Palestinian neighborhoods and villages. For example, the use of the name Ṭalbiyya, which was a Palestinian neighborhood in Jerusalem until 1948. After the establishment of the state, the neighborhood received the Hebrew name Qommemiyut.

De facto, a local subculture is created here, from below, that disrupts the idyll of a landscape without Arabs and a land without Palestinians and creates an ambivalent reality in which Hebrew and Arabic exist together, side by side.

The toponymic discourse that has developed in Israel is definite proof that a landscape without Arabic and without Palestinians is not possible, even when there is a hegemony working to erase the culture of the Other. The obvious conclusion is that no matter how forceful a policy of erasure may be, it is unable to sever the ties that connect a people to a place, and human memory works to preserve them against all institutional activity. Despite the efforts of Israeli governmental mechanisms, Arabic names managed to survive even though there is no institution to perpetuate them. This is due to the materialistic power of history, which once again defeats ideology through the preservation of names against all odds.

To conclude, the significance attributed to Arab Palestinian names is not stable, but changing and dynamic. These names, which originally were ethnographic names, both symbolic and useful, and which also reflected the traces of the peoples who had passed through Israel/Palestine, became a target for political erasure and the Hebraization of the space by official Israeli name committees, while nowadays they serve the Palestinian citizens of Israel as an ideological means to restore the place's Palestinianness.

NOTES

INTRODUCTION

1. The ancient name of Kafr Kannā, as mentioned in the New Testament, is Cana of the Galilee, which means "the paradise of the Galilee." According to one local tradition, the place's name was due to several virtues that distinguish it: Christian pilgrims from all over the world come to the village, considering it the place where Jesus performed his first miracle; the pomegranate orchards are known for the fine taste of their fruit; the spring water is palatable; the climate is pleasant; and it is surrounded by mountains and hills that protect it from the desert's east wind while being open on its west side to the sea breeze.

2. The terms *Palestinian society, Arab Palestinian society, Palestinians in Israel, Palestinians, Israeli Arabs, Arab society,* and their derivatives are synonymous in this book. The term *natural features* includes related terms, such as *natural formations, geographical entities,* and *geographical landscapes.*

3. A mental map (also called a cognitive map) is the hermeneutics of physical space. This map is not intended to describe the objective characteristics of a place, as a cartographic map does; rather, its purpose is to express a subjective representation of a particular space as perceived by an individual or a group (Portugali 1999, 70–73).

4. The term *linguistic landscape* refers to linguistic objects that mark public areas, including landmarks, sites, streets, buildings, places, street signs, and the like (Landry and Bourhis 1997).

5. Toponymy is the study of place-names, or the study of geographic names, and is a subdiscipline in the field of geography and the field of linguistics. The term originates from the Greek words *topos* (place) and *onyma* (name). This subdiscipline deals with all the scientific and theoretical aspects associated with

geographical names. The term *toponym* means "place-name" and is derived from the word *toponymy* (Kadmon 2000, 10). This book also includes related terms, such as *geographical name* and *toponymic creation*.

6. Details at the website http://ifa.haifa.ac.il/index.php/he/home.

7. Personal communication via e-mail, Dr. Haya Milo, coordinator of IFSA, October 8, 2018.

8. The Green Line: The armistice border established in 1949 after the war between Israel and Jordan, Egypt, Syria, and Lebanon. It was called *green* because it was drawn in green pencil on the map used in the discussions leading to the Rhodes Agreements (Shenhav 2010, 10–11).

9. Obtaining female informants was not an easy task. This is shown by the small number of female interviewees: 15 women (8.6%) compared with 160 men (91.4%). The cultural code of Arab society emphasizes the importance of segregating the sexes, in particular when it comes to an encounter with a stranger who is not a resident of the locality. In my meetings with the interviewees, I would address them by the nicknames *khālatī* (my aunt) and *ukhtī* (my sister), to relieve tension and to make it clear that my relationship with them was like that of a family member. Researchers who wish to conduct field research on the identity of members of the opposite gender in a traditional society encounter quite a few obstacles. In her research on the relationship between men and women among the Bedouin tribes in Egypt, Lila Abu-Lughod (1986, 9–24) was helped by her father to gain the trust of the tribal men under study.

10. Cultural anthropologist Clifford Geertz (1976, 224–25) urges ethnographers who are looking for the symbolic forms of culture to use internal cultural terms.

11. Except for a few short articles on the interpretations of place-names in the British Isles and the US. See Baker 1972 and Nicolaisen 1976.

12. The multilayered model I propose in this chapter is a poetic model and an outline for those dealing with toponymy in its narrative context. The five levels are intended to guide those dealing with place-name legends and not necessarily a proposal for a binding order or a rigid model.

13. Tel Aviv originated with the establishment of the Ahuzat Bayit association in 1906. The association purchased the land of the Jibali vineyard from the Arabs of Jaffa, and in 1910, the construction of the neighborhood houses was completed.

1. THE STUDY OF PALESTINIAN PLACE-NAMES

1. The maps and surveys prepared by European expeditions, including the Palestine Exploration Fund, were often tools with multiple functions: first, to map and publish the sites of Israel/Palestine and their names in order to revive the ancient land—the "Holy Land," the land of the Bible and the New

Testament, and second, to prepare the ground for the future conquest of Palestine. See Ben-Arieh 1970, 194, and Abu-Sitta 2004, 32.

2. The term *lands of al-Shām* refers to historical Palestine and Syria (present-day Syria, Lebanon, Jordan, and Israel/Palestine). The two countries were often seen as belonging to one geographical-political unit. This is how the Greeks, Romans, and Arabs saw them. (According to Arabs, this term refers generally to the land north of the Arabian Peninsula.) The precise meaning of the term *al-Shām* changed frequently (Prawer 1971, 17).

3. The most well known and quoted are Ibn ʿAbd al-Ḥaqq 1954–55 and al-Bakrī 1976.

4. Victor Guérin (1868) also reviews a multitude of Arabic place-names, but the subject of his book is not toponymy.

5. According to the perception of David Ben-Gurion and Yitzhak Ben-Zvi, the Arab and Bedouin peasants are the descendants of the ancient Jews, who during times of persecution abandoned their religion and remained in historical Palestine. They also claim that a quarter of the villages that existed in Western Palestine (i.e., west of the Jordan River) are called by Hebrew names from the Bible and the Talmud (Ben-Gurion and Ben-Zvi 1979, 195–205, esp. 202–5).

6. It should be noted that there are also publications on the administrative aspect of the "Hebrew map," such as that by Hana Bitan (2013).

7. The term *oppositional toponymy* is borrowed from the lecture "Oppositional Toponymy: Who Lost and Who Gained?," delivered by Miron Benvenisti at the conference The Naming of Places—The Glorification/Exclusion of Person, Place and Time, at Tel Aviv University in May 2014.

8. On the lack of studies that discuss place-names from the linguistic aspect, see Rainey 1982, 11–29. For a critique of the writings of medieval Arab geographers, see al-Ḥilw 1999, 41–44.

9. The names of the inhabited localities and their stories are presented in Dahamshe 2009, 2, appendix to the doctoral dissertation.

10. The term *Muslims* in the context of the religious-sectarian breakdown includes Bedouin, because the Bedouin are in fact Muslims.

11. *Khalla*: A narrow and flat piece of land going up a stream between two mountains or two hills.

12. Pronounced *umm* by Hebrew speakers.

13. For a list of components, see Kadmon 2004, 9.

14. This number does not reflect the distribution of the terms *abū* and *imm/umm* in the Arab communities. These terms exist in many of the names of the Arab settlements in different regions of Israel, such as Umm al-Faḥm, Umm al-Aghnām, and more.

15. In other areas of Israel, I also found place-names with the element *banī*, "son(s)," such as Banī Naʿīm, but I did not encounter this usage in the examined corpus.

16. Ernst Cassirer, as cited in Lutwack 1984, 77–79.

17. *Caliph* is the name or title of the Muslim leader of the Islamic *umma*.

18. In the writings of Muslim chroniclers, the term *al-Shām* was used to indicate the region composed today of Syria, Lebanon, Israel/Palestine, and Jordan. In other cases, the word *Filasṭīn* is used to denote the area today called Israel/Palestine (and part of Jordan): for example, Ibn al-Athīr 1956, 2:402–99 (chap. 13).

2. ARAB HISTORICAL MEMORIES AND LINGUISTIC SHADES OF OTHER LANGUAGES

1. The reasoning for the name of an inhabited locality is discussed in this book as a unique version, sufficient to explain the phenomenon under investigation. This is despite the fact that there are other versions that explain some of the names in this category. The versions are listed in Dahamshe 2009, 2:4–106. The order in which the names appear in this book expresses the frequency of the motifs justifying the names' origins.

2. In order to facilitate the readers' understanding of the texts, the name legends have undergone minor processing that does not affect thematic matters concerning the formation of the place-name, which is the main subject of this book. For the original texts, see Dahamshe 2009, 2:4–106.

3. I refer here to the concept of "myth" and its derivatives in its narrow sense—as a kind of historical story of a people or a historical figure of a collective. Over time, these figures have become symbolic and exemplary, because they mark sublime and sacred values in the community's perception. See Sivan 1997, 9–13.

4. Name legends quoted in their entirety in this chapter are in Hebrew alphabetical order of the names in the category under discussion.

5. The companions of the Prophet Muḥammad.

6. Informant: Muḥammad Zuʿabī, 2002.

7. Islamic sources mention Duḥaya as an infidel Arab king who converted to Islam voluntarily. Muḥammad tasked him with spreading Islam in the Greater Syria region (al-Nāzilī 1930, 186).

8. The episode of the female dog appears in nineteenth-century sources in the context of the name ad-Daḥī: Conder and Kitchener 1881, 1:132.

9. Informant: Mūsā Sughayr.

10. The Muslim army (in the first half of the seventh century) moved from south to north. This historical fact contradicts the narrator in the legend of the name Shafāʿamr: "ʿAmr on his way to the liberation of Egypt passed through Shafāʿamr," that is, traveled from north to south.

11. According to the Talmud, the leadership of the Sanhedrin lived in the town of Shefarʿam from the Hellenistic period (b. Rosh Hash. 31a–b).

In the geographical dictionary of Yāqūt al-Ḥamāwī (d. circa 1225), the form Shafaraʿamm (شَفَرَعَمّ) is recorded (al-Ḥamāwī [1906–7] 1990, 3:353).

12. In my meetings with Christian informants, it became clear to me that the presence of the first name ʿAmr alone in the Arabic form challenges the folk imagination, and this is exploited to insert linguistic and content-related elements that obscure the traces of the Muslim commander's rule mentioned in the Muslim version. According to a tradition I heard from a female Christian informant, the phoneme ʿAmr refers to ʿUmar Ẓāhir az-Zaydānī, an Ottoman governor. In history books, az-Zaydānī is portrayed as renowned for his tolerant attitude toward Christians and Europeans (al-Muḥāmī 1996, 297–302).

13. Also: Ṭayyiba, al-Ṭayyiba (in the Jezreel Valley). Ṭayyiba is the name of several localities in Israel and neighboring countries. According to the sources, this name was given to localities whose name had included the phoneme ʿafr, interpreted in Arabic as ʿifrīt, an evil spirit. See *Mappa Encyclopedia* 2000, 3:136. Hartman (cited in Rainey 1982, 22) pointed out the existence of the alternative forms Umm Ṭayyiba (أم طيبة) and especially the form Ṭayyibat al-Ism (طيبة الإسم). The latter is particularly documented in fifteenth-century sources and appears in sixteenth-century Turkish censuses (Hütteroth and Abdulfattah 1977, 116).

14. Informant: Muḥammad Zuʿabī, 2002.

15. Informant: Muḥammad Qāsim, 2001.

16. Al-Ḥamawī uses the one-word name *Kawkab*. According to al-Ḥamawī, the name, which is used to indicate various places in Greater Syria, was given to a fortress overlooking Tiberias that was liberated by Saladin. The component Abū al-Hījā was apparently added later, following historical circumstances related to Abū al-Hījā's participation as a commander in the battle of Hattin (al-Ḥamawī 1990, 4:494).

17. The legend does not mention the battle of Hattin, but this is a fact that is reported in the chronicles and is found in the local tradition about the history of the Abū al-Hījā tribe and its part in the battle of Hattin.

18. The hidden history constituted by name legends is a "hidden transcript" in the sense coined by James Scott. This is a linguistic discourse that serves the subaltern and the subordinate, through which they give expression to their opinions and claims without being exposed to the threatening gaze of the hegemonic group (Scott 1990, ix, 6–10).

19. The "Romans" (the term *ar-Rūm* in Arabic chronicles refers to both the ancient Romans and the later Byzantines) and the Crusaders are seen as infidels and demons whom God has cursed. See Ibn al-Athīr 1956, 2:412, 2:417, 10:105, and elsewhere.

20. The "small" place is the local territory, or the feeling of belonging to a defined place; the "big" place is the territory of the nation or of the people, and at the same time it is an "idea." The "big" place represents history and ideology (Gurevitch and Aran 1991, 11).

21. Informant: Maḥmūd Mrisāt, 2001.

22. Informant: Aḥmad Zuʿabī, 2002.

23. Informant: Khālid Muḥammad Ghanāʾim, 2001.

24. Informant: Muṣṭafā ʿAbbāsī, 2004.

25. Kadmon (2004, 26) notes the al-Jishsh form; Ha-Parḥi (1897, 289) indicates two alternatives: Gush Ḥalav and Jūsh.

26. In a comprehensive essay on the Arab tribes in general and the Palestinian ones in particular, no trace is found of the Jisqāla tribe, whose name is attributed to the village of Jishsh (al-Wāʾilī 2002).

27. In Jewish sources, al-Jishsh is identified with Gush Ḥalav of the Talmudic and Mishnah periods. Josephus called Jishsh by the Greek name Giscala (Vilnai 1977, 2:1276). The name Gush Ḥalav is mentioned in Josephus Flavius's book *The Jewish Wars* (1915, 2.20).

28. *Walī*: a Muslim saint.

29. Informant: Aḥmad Abū Zayd, 2004.

30. It is possible that it was the shaykh's resting near the spring that gave the village of ʿAyn al-Asad, close to Dayr al-Asad, its name. However, the residents of ʿAyn al-Asad have their own explanation that is not related to the story of the shaykh and the lion.

31. Donkey or she-ass. In a similar story the word *donkey* appears. See IFSA, story no. 21.857.

32. Unlike the local explanation of the name, which originates in a local legend transmitted orally, according to written sources the name Dayr al-Asad was established following a historical event and involving figures that existed in reality: the Ottoman sultan Suleiman Kanuni (the Magnificent; r. 1520–66) asked Shaykh al-Asad to settle in the place as a reward for his piety. The shaykh agreed and his name was given to the place (al-Būrīnī 1959–62, 1:178).

33. For Hebraizing of surnames and first names, see Toury 1988, 152–72; Azaryahu 2000, 79–82. On the Judaization of place-names as part of shaping the cultural space of the new identity in Israel/Palestine, see Azaryahu 2000, 82–85.

34. For a binary reading of the map of the names created by Israeli government institutions, see Benvenisti 1997; Laor 1995, 131.

35. Some Galilee Arabs pronounce the form ʿArābya. In nineteenth-century Ottoman censuses, the form ʿArrāba was recorded. See Hütteroth and Abdulfattah 1977, 187.

36. Informant: ʿAlī Kanʿān.

37. A first-generation *tannā* (sage) who lived and worked in the first century CE. On Rabbi Ḥanina's connection to the village of ʿArāb (which is identified with the present-day locality of ʿArrāba, according to the *Mappa Encyclopedia* 2000, 6:106), see y. Ber. 4:1 (7c). This story appears in additional parallel versions in the tannaitic literature. The abbreviations used

for references to rabbinic works follow the list found at the Society for Biblical Literature's blog, accessed July 2, 2025, https://sblhs2.com/2016/11/10/mishnaic-talmudic-related-literature-abbreviations/.

38. This son has no mention in the Jewish tradition, but there is a reference to the daughter of Rabbi Ḥanina ben Dosa.

39. A fourth-generation *amorā* who lived and worked in the third century CE (Margoliouth 1995, 2:190). Many sayings of his are scattered throughout the Talmudic tradition. See Klein 1976, 112.

40. A similar story also exists in the Jewish sources, in which Sama is the name of a place and not the name of a person: t. Hul. 2:22 (Zuckermandel [1881] 1963, 503); y. Avod. Zar. 2:2 (40a); y. Shabb. 12:4 (12d). In some of the parallels of this story in Jewish sources, the name Kfar Sama is replaced by Kfar Saknia (e.g., b. Avod. Zar. 27b; Eccl. Rab. 1, 3 [Vilna print]). Indeed, Kfar Sama is identified with Kfar Saknia. See Klein 1976, 9. Reuven Kimelman believes that these are two places in the Lower Galilee adjacent to each other: Kfar Simai and Kfar Sakhnin, in both of which Jacob of Naburiya was active. See Irshai 1973, 154n9.

41. Informant: Karmila Shaḥāda, 2001.

42. In the twelfth century, Petachiah of Regensburg reports the story of the "cave of Jonah ben Amitai" in the village of Kana, near Mashhad, so-called because it is the cave where Jonah is buried (Petachiah of Regensburg 1967, 10 [introduction 3]).

43. The locality is also known in Arabic as Yāfat al-Nāṣira, "Jaffa of Nazareth," to distinguish it from the city of Jaffa (Yāfā).

44. Informant: Muḥammad Khalayliyya, 2004.

45. It is not inconceivable that the etiological explanation of the name was borrowed from ancient Christian sources, since one of the Christian texts dedicated by the pilgrim Antoninus of Vicenza to Nazareth tells of the particularly beautiful appearance of the Jewish girls of Galilee, who stood out not only in physical beauty but also in their virtue. See Limor 2005, 11.

46. The desire to please Israeli society is also evident in the fact that Palestinians prefer to use the way Hebrew speakers pronounce the names of Arab localities. For example, Buʿayna (Bʿeina), Daburiyya (Daburiyyeh), Kfar Qara (Kufr Qaraʿ), and the like.

47. Scholars interpret the phenomenon of Arab authors writing in Hebrew as expressing a longing to break out of the rejected margins into the canonical literary center and the Israeli political center (Hever 1991, 33–37).

48. Minority attempts to actively participate in the practices of the hegemony have been explored in different cultural spaces. For example, the reggae dances of Black girls in the UK reflect a new hybrid ethnicity, through which Black girls actively participate in the British sexual discourse (McRobie 1996, 35–36).

49. For different kinds and contents of heterotopia, see Foucault 1984; Azoulay 2003, 61–74.

50. Suleiman (2004, 12–13) cites as an example his use of English instead of Arabic whenever he arrives in West Jerusalem and the Israeli army checkpoints.

51. See the multitude of examples in al-Dabbāgh (1967) 2003, 5–93.

52. According to Yehuda Feliks (1997, 131–32), the name is *santal*: *Santalum album*, a fragrant tree that grows in the islands of Malaysia. This is not the Palestinian plant mentioned in the Bible.

53. Informant: Hāshim ʿUmarī, 2003.

54. Ṭamra in the Jezreel Valley.

55. This seems to refer to the land of the Hadassah hospital in Safed.

56. Informant: Kamāl Dhiyāb, 2005.

57. Informant: Munʿim Ḥaddād, 2004.

58. The name also appears in the form Ḥusayniyya (*Mappa Encyclopedia* 2000, 3:55).

59. This is a concept prevalent in the ancient world, according to which holy sites and holy cities form the center of the world, and other objects are arranged around them in ever-expanding circles (Eliade 1954, 18–23).

60. Notice the suffix –*a*, which indicates the feminine form in Arabic.

61. Galit Hasan-Rokem presents a critical view according to which all conquerors of Jerusalem in all generations have treated her as a woman who should be respected and beautified but also has to be penetrated and controlled. The masculine conception attributed a female imagery to Jerusalem and referred to it by the titles of blood relations due to geopolitical motives (Hasan-Rokem 1995).

62. Also: Ṭūbā-ʿArab al-Hayb; see al-Dabbāgh (1967) 2003, 7.2:173. The form Ṭūbā az-Zangariyya also appears—two villages merged in 1988 into one local council. See *Mappa Encyclopedia* 2000, 3:132.

63. Al-Sharīʿa: a nickname for the Jordan River and its surroundings.

64. Informant: Aḥmad Hayb, 2005.

65. Informant: Muḥammad ʿUmarī, 2004.

66. The motif of resuscitating a dead child also appears south of Nīn. According to biblical tradition, in the locality of Shunam (Sulam), on the western slopes of the Givat Hamoreh ridge, Elisha revived the son of the Shunamite woman (2 Kings 4:32–37).

67. Informant: Wahīb Qāsim, 2005.

68. No ethnographic studies and books have been found on place-names that have various explanations for the name of a particular locality.

69. All four versions that explain the origin of the name Tarshīḥā were told to me by Rita Bishāra in 2002.

70. These are the words of the narrator.

71. Al-Dabbāgh (2003, 7.2:421) explains the name in connection with the words Jabal al-Shīḥ—the mountain of the broom plant (*Spartium junceum* L.).

72. The subjects of tests for the lover (and future husband) in their various manifestations appear in the Thompson motif index, H499–H310, especially H310, H335, and O2 (see Thompson 1955–1958, s.v.).

73. See also Patai 1936, 10–11.

74. Honko (1981, 27) notes that folk legends migrate from one cultural environment to others and adapt to the receiving culture. The legend that explains the origin of the name Tarshīḥā in connection with the poet and the girl serving water has a biblical equivalent centered on a meeting between the prophet Elijah, who asks for water and bread, and a poor woman (1 Kings 17:8–16). An identical story is told by the Arabs of the Upper Galilee who tell of the abundance of water in the village of Peqiʿin near Tarshīḥā. This story also concerns a prophet who requests water from a local old woman. The latter story appears in Falah and Shenhar 1978, 24.

75. The form Ṭarshīḥā also exists (Hütteroth and Abdulfattah 1977, 192).

76. Shīḥā is mentioned in the chronicles as a commander who fought in Saladin's ranks in the attack on Acre. In Tarshīḥā, there is evidence for his activity in the area, for example, Jabal al-Mujāhid, the mountain of the warrior (Shīḥā). At the gate of the village mosque, a stone slab with the following sentence engraved on it remained in situ until 1953: "Here [lies] the late Shīḥā Jamāl al-Dīn al-ʿAyyūbī who died in 1111 AH" (ʿArrāf 1993, 1:309).

77. Under the influence of the contextual turn in the study of folk literature, the narrator is no longer perceived as a "messenger" or a "bearer of tradition" but is the original creator of the story. The text is part of the event, which includes the narrator, the audience, and the circumstances of the statement (Alexander-Frizer 2008, 19).

78. For the meaning obtained from linking space to the figures of warriors, see Arieli 1992, 398.

3. THE NARRATIVE OF THE LAND AND NATURAL LANDSCAPE IN PALESTINIAN NAMES

1. According to totemic theory, the names of animals originate in the primordial belief that humans have animal ancestors and that peoples are named after the animal they belong to. This theory, which was accepted by anthropologists for a long time, is not fully applicable to the Arabic geographical names in this book, since only a minority derive from animals' names.

2. The names of Druze men were placed in a separate category.

3. Informant: Khālid Ghanāʿim, 2004.

4. Ṣaʿīdī/Ṣaʿīdiyya is a term for a person from Upper Egypt.

5. This issue is discussed in depth in chapter 4.

6. *Khalāyil*, sing. *khalla*—see chapter 1.

7. Informant: Muḥammad Fuqarā, 2004.

8. On this custom, see Ashkenazi 2000, 69.

9. According to others, the spring is called ʿAyn Sīkh, in reference to Jabal Sīkh, "Mount Sīkh" (the meaning of the word *sikh* is unknown to the locals).

10. Informant: Zarīfa Shālabana, 2005.

11. These are usually plots of land set aside by the community for the benefit of the clergy.

12. *Qārita*: a plot of land for agriculture with an area of approximately twenty to twenty-five dunams.

13. During and after Ottoman rule, much of the Palestinian population was illiterate, to the extent that a resident of a certain village had to wander among the neighboring villages to find someone who could read and write (al-Barghūthī 1990, 222–23).

14. According to the biblical story, during their wanderings in the desert, the Israelites demanded water from Moses. He struck a rock and water gushed out of it: "Then Moses raised his arm and struck the rock twice with his staff. Water gushed out, and the community and their livestock drank" (Numbers 20:11, NIV translation). A similar version of this story is repeated in the Qurʾan: "And when Moses asked for water for his people, We said: Smite with thy staff the rock. And there gushed out therefrom twelve springs (so that) each tribe knew their drinking-place" (Qurʾan 2:60, trans. Pickthall).

15. *Waqf*: The literal meaning is standing, stopping. An *arḍ waqf* is a plot of land owned by an endowment that is prohibited from being transferred, sold, or given as a gift to any other body. Lands of this type originate in the custom of dedicating (the income of) a plot of land to charitable and benevolent purposes.

16. Nabī Sabalān: There is not much information about this character in the literature. Some identify him with Zebulun, the son of Jacob. Maqām Nabī Sabalān, located at the top of Mount Zebul in Ḥurfeish, is the second-holiest place for the Druze in Israel, after Nabī Shuʿayb (Dana 1998, 80–81).

17. Informant: Yūsuf Sawāṭīrī, 2004.

18. The narrative pattern in which the holy man succeeds in affecting cosmic events is reminiscent of the miracle of Ḥoni the Circle Dweller in Jewish folk literature. The name Wādī al-Ḥabīs, whose origin is attributed to the rains that blocked the bandits and surrounded them, also connotes the meaning of Ḥoni the Circle Dweller's name, which is explained in the Mishnah: "It happened, that when Ḥoni the Circle Dweller was told that it had rained, he drew a circle and stood in it and said: Lord . . ." (b. Taʾan. 23:1–2).

19. An example of this are folk songs condemning the British and praising the revolt. Bards recited these songs at wedding ceremonies and other occasions (Sirḥān 1989, 3:777–92).

20. Informant: Nāḍim ʿAlī, 2005.

21. The rebels, *al-thuwwār*, are Palestinian groups that rebelled against the British presence in Palestine. For the villagers' support of the rebels, see Cohen 2004, 99–146.

22. Informant: ʿAdhrā Fāʿūr, 2003.

23. For example, the commemoration of women versus men in Harare, the capital of Zimbabwe, is completely restricted (Zvinashe, Itai, and Davi 2018). The representation of women compared to men in the streets of Israeli cities is also very limited (Edut 2017).

24. Informant: Khalīl Ḥusayn, 2003.

25. On conflicts between stepmothers and stepdaughters and the relationships between brothers and sisters in the Palestinian story, see Muhawi and Kanaana 1994.

26. This brings to mind the term *nīf*, which means loyalty to the honor of the male lineage and its good name. *Nīf* is the loyalty to cleansing a man's ancestors from any stain and insult caused by damage to the family's honor. See Bourdieu 1979, 110–11, 120–21.

27. The song was reported by the informant Zarīfa Shalābina in 2003.

28. It is possible that the owl symbolizes the figure of Lilith. According to Isaiah 34:14–15, Lilith resides at night in the desolate ruins in the desert of Edom, among the goats, owls, jackals, and so on.

29. In other cultures, too, such as the Celtic tradition, the owl is seen as an ominous sign and symbolizes evil and death. See Fischman 2002, 68.

30. Informant: Muḥammad Mazʿal, 2004.

31. Due to concerns about harming the reputation of this woman's family, I had difficulty finding informants who were willing to expand on the matter.

32. Secret love that ends in the murder of the girl who wants to choose a partner for herself is repeated in the name legend of Jabal Banāt, "the Mount of Girls," in the Paran oasis in Sinai. According to the legend, on this mountain, three girls who were destined for the dignitaries of the tribe, even though they wanted to marry shepherds of their own choosing, killed themselves by jumping from a height (Levi 1994, 70–76).

33. Many examples can be found in Patai 1942, 1:68–69. On the comparison of the woman to the field, see Patai 1942, 1:189–205.

34. Informant: Muḥammad Nafāʿ, 2005.

35. Informant: Kuraym Muḥammad, 2003.

36. Lūbiyya: a displaced Palestinian village.

37. In this context, it means the wheat that will be ground to obtain bulgur, wheat that is cracked and boiled (after preparation).

38. *Faranjiyya*: Foreign, in this context, refers to sorghum that is not locally produced.

39. Informant: Ibrāhīm Abū Rās, 2004.

40. *Ruwaysa* (*ruwaysat* in the genitive): a low hill with a not very large area (approximately twenty dunams). This is a diminutive of *ra's/rās*, "head."

41. Such as Kharrūbāt al-ʿArayis, "the carob trees of the brides," in Dayr Ḥanā and Kharrūbat al-ʿUrsān, "the carob tree of the bridegrooms," in Kābūl, among others.

42. In different cultures, men and women are compared to trees. For example, in Finnish riddles deciduous trees are identified with women, and conifers are identified with men. See Köngäs Maranda 1971, 204.

43. The narrator used ironic exaggeration, hyperbole, to say that the bride's demands these days are not as modest as in the past. Informant: Muḥammad Baṣ ūl, 2003.

44. Georg Simmel perceives every border as reflecting a two-way space of entry and exit. See Simmel 1997, 173.

45. Informant: Falīḥ Khawālid, 2003.

46. From the story "The stones as people, between Kafr Samīʿ and Kafr Kasrā" (Falah and Shenhar 1978, 23–24).

47. An echo of this motif already exists in the Bible. There it is said that Lot's wife, who disobeyed God's command, became a pillar of salt, and therefore, she stands motionless to this very day.

48. Although the attempt to explain the origin of the names is central to most of the stories, there are other stories, found in the IFSA database but not discussed in this book, in which the etiological element is aimed at explaining a topographical phenomenon without explaining the name of the place. For example, the stories "The stones as people, between Kafr Samīʿ and Kafr Kasrā" and "Why is Wadi Hammam littered with stones?" (see IFSA a21.034; cf. Falah and Shenhar 1978, 23–24).

49. See the discussion of this in chapter 4.

50. This is the name given to the northern sea passage from the Pacific to the Atlantic Ocean (Room 1977, 3).

51. According to the peasants, it is not impossible that the olive trees are from the time of the Crusaders and even earlier, from the Byzantine period (late antiquity).

52. *ʿĀmūd*: pillar, a nickname for ancient olive trees.

53. Informant: Ṣāliḥ Khayr, 2003.

54. Informant: Aḥmad Khaṭīb, 2003.

55. Informant: ʿUmar Shaykh-Muḥammad, 2005.

56. Currently owned by the Jewish National Fund/Keren Kayemet.

57. Informant: ʿAbd al-Ghānī Qādirī, 2004.

58. Informant: Shafīq Jahshān, 2004.

59. Informant: Muḥammad Nafāʿ, 2004.

60. Informant: Fāris Maghīṣ, 2005.

61. Informant: Fuad Hāshūl, 2004.

62. In medieval Arabic sources, the form is ʿAyn al-Fulūs (عين الفلوس) (Al-Farākih 2003, 31).

63. Al-ʿUzayr: This refers to the residents of al-ʿUzayr who live in the south of al-Baṭūf.

64. Al-Shafā: a fertile plateau. "And al-Shafā is known for its marrying off of bachelors": the bachelors found livelihood and financing for their wedding in the land of al-Shafā.

65. Informant: Aḥmad Kuraym, 2005.

66. Informant: ʿAbbās Fallāh, 2004.

67. The term *bāb*, meaning "gate," is typical of the Arabic names of natural formations. Sometimes it means a narrow natural opening, and sometimes it means a narrow place leading to a very open area of land. Hebrew names in which the term *shaʾar* is present are based on places whose ancient name included the element *bāb*, for example, *shaʾar ha-gai* (the gate to the valley) on the way to Jerusalem, whose Hebrew form is a translation of the Arabic name Bāb al-Wād.

68. The Arabic form *daraj* was absorbed into the Hebrew name Naḥal Deragot.

69. Lewis criticizes the measurement methods that continued to be used by the Arabs long after the invention of Western measurement methods. However, Lewis, whose book is not without orientalist undertones, ignores the fact that measurement of distances was carried out in a much more sophisticated way than he describes.

70. Informant: Ṣāliḥ Khayr, 2004.

71. Informant: Muḥammad Qāsim, 2005.

72. Seven is a typological number that appears in many folktales.

73. Informant: Masʿūd Mazʿal, 2004.

74. The term *belief legend* also includes stories centered on general beliefs, while the term *folk belief* is limited to legends about supernatural beings. On this concept in folklore studies, see Tangherlini 1990, 406–13.

75. Bar-Tzvi 1979, 7.

76. The Arabic name for February.

77. Informant: Rāḍī al-ʿĀṣī, 2004.

78. Informant: Walīd Abū al-Suwayd, 2005.

79. Levy 1976, 417–18.

80. *Khānūq*: a narrow strip of land between two hills.

81. Predators, wild animals, cattle, mammals, birds, fish, insects, reptiles, and vermin are present in large numbers in the Palestinian nomenclature of geographical objects (Al-Dabbāgh 1988, 121–219).

82. Informant: Masʿūd Mazʿal, 2004.

83. Contrary to what is said in the name legend and the local tradition, another source states that the stream got its name from a leopard that killed a shepherd from al-ʿAramsha village in 1965 (*Mappa Encyclopedia* 2000, 5:152). Yehuda Ziv (2005, 37) indicates that it was the governmental naming committee that gave the stream the name Naḥal ha-Namer (Heb: "the spring of the leopard") and that the local Arabs, who used to call it Wādī Dilib, began calling it Wādī al-Nimr following the Hebrew form.

84. See parallel in *Pes. Rab Kah.*, pisqa 11: "When a man's ways please the Lord, He maketh even his enemies eager to give up life for him (Prov. 16:7). By 'enemy' here, according to R. Meir, is meant a (wild) dog; according to R. Joshua ben Levi, a snake. R. Meir, who said a dog is meant, told the story of herdsmen who had just milked a cow. A snake came and drank of the milk, and a dog saw it drinking. When the herdsmen sat down to eat, the dog began to bark warningly at them, but they did not understand what his barking meant. Whereupon the dog sprang forward, drank of the venom-tainted milk, and died. When the herdsmen buried him, they set a monument over him, which to this day is called 'The Dog's Monument'" (Kapstain and Braude 2002, 269).

85. Informant: Ṣāliḥ Khayr, 2004.

86. See also the motifs later in this chapter: 292B, an animal (dog) helps a person and his servant; 529B, an animal (dog) saves a human life; 540B, an animal (dog) redeems and saves (Thompson 1955–58).

87. Cf. the story "the daughter of the crosser, crosses" (Meron, Shehadi, and Masarwi 1997, 260–65).

88. Compare to the Talmudic proverb: "This is what the nations say: The ewe-lamb follows the ewe-lamb. As the actions of the mother so are the actions of the daughter" (b. Ketub. 63a; Yal. on Proverbs, §948).

89. Palm Sunday falls a week before Easter. The holiday marks Jesus's entry into Jerusalem riding a donkey. The crowd welcomed him with palm branches and chants of "Hosanna, son of David."

90. Informant: Jarīs Qasīs, 2005.

91. The small number of people in the village of Judida can perhaps be understood from the meaning of the village's name, "new," which hints at the young age of a small village that has not developed (Grossman 1994, 60).

92. Historical studies have also indicated the local stamp on the Palestinian population's consciousness of identity. Palestinian society has preserved regional, rural, and tribal identities for generations. An example of this is a Palestinian from Hebron, who defines himself first of all as a *Khalīlī* (Hebronite), and see Khalidi 1997, 153, 254.

93. The personal stories that influence the formation of names are part of the general story. However, and in the spirit of the insights of Nurit Gertz and George Khalifi (2006, 69–91), the generality is broken down into different identities—gender, class, and local.

94. A high density of geographical names is typical of a cultural background of peasants, farmers, and shepherds. For example, the economy of the Shetland Islands in northern Scotland relies mainly on sheep and goat farming. These people give identifying names to every corner, mound, cliff, stone, and stream in their living space—to every small place on the border of which animals find shelter. Part of each child's training was learning all the names of the natural features, so that they could function as more effective shepherds (Stewart 1975, 19).

95. The term *insider* indicates an internal observation of geographical entities, cities, and streets by describing the environment and the feelings it creates for those present in it. Being inside a place means identifying with it and experiencing it personally. In contrast, the term *outsider* indicates an external observation of the environment and its phenomena, that is, the examination of settled localities and the environment with the help of maps, aerial photographs, and more (Ley 1983, 132–37; Relph 1976, 49–55).

96. The detailed names used by the Bedouins to identify plants in their environment also suggest a similar conclusion: the plants were not given their names to indicate benefit or harm. These names only reflect the botanical expertise of the desert dwellers (Bailey and Danin 1974, 4–8).

97. On the centrality of place in the construction of Palestinian identity and nationality, see Rubinstein 1990, 9–12, 23–26; Parmenter 1994, 21–24; Swedenburg 1990, 23–24.

98. On the symbolism with which the Palestinian national movement loaded the land and the Palestinian peasant, see Parmenter 1994, 70–77; Swedenburg 1990, 18–24.

99. Physical time is the time measured by objective devices whose accuracy is not in doubt, such as clocks, calendars, and other sophisticated tools. With their help, one determines the occasion and duration of an event.

4. DISTINCTION BETWEEN NAMES OF INHABITED LOCATIONS AND NAMES OF NATURAL FEATURES

1. Zvinashe, Muwati, and Mutasa 2018, dealing with the commemoration of women on nameplates in Harare, should be excluded from this rule. Yoram Bar-Gal (1992) also examined how the names of streets in urban settlements in Israel reflect political struggles within Israeli society.

2. See Blumen 2005 for a critique of the binary approach.

3. As an example of the social division of the space into two contrasting geocultural areas, we can take the pair Jerusalem–Tel Aviv in modern Hebrew literature. See Govrin 1988, 42–64.

4. For the name legends of inhabited localities, see chapter 2.

5. The terms *collective memory* and *autobiographical memory* are borrowed from Halbwachs, who mainly emphasized the role of collective memory

(historical events that happened a long time ago and became mythology) and sometimes the importance of autobiographical memory (things that happened to people acting in the place they call home) in shaping collective identity, determining the historical sequence on which this identity is constructed, and appropriating a casual space and turning it into a place charged with meaning and emotion. See Halbwachs 1992, 18–34.

6. For example, the town of Nazareth ʿIllit ("Upper Nazareth," now called Nof Ha-Galil, "Galilee View") was founded in 1957 on expropriated Palestinian lands in an area overlooking the Arab city of Nazareth. The fact that its name is designed to convey ethnoclass superiority is indicated by the deliberate choice of the adjective. The superiority remains even after the name changed.

7. Etymological legends told by Bedouins in the south of the country provide additional evidence for the converse case, as they tend to explain vertical and protruding natural features such as steep mountains or rock formations, using stories centered on phallic images (Levi 1987, 179–80).

5. ARAB PALESTINIAN TOPONYMY— FROM ARABISM TO HEBRAIZATION

1. The term *space-time* was developed by Torsten Hägerstrand. According to this geographer's conceptualization, time and space are a single structural framework—space-time—in which people move and act. By mapping human movement in time-space, it is possible to locate the system of constraints that affects human activity (Hägerstrand 1970, 7–21).

2. The practice of the same motif for different names is common in traditional regions, for example, among the Indians living in Onodoga County in the United States (Gordon 1984, 221–28).

3. On the motif of the abundant land that is benevolent to the Palestinians, see Shiḥāda 2009, 62–112.

4. And cf. Tilley (1994, 32), on the poetic qualities of narrative and story.

5. Alternatively, in rare cases, the names express a sarcastic attitude to the land, and it suffices to mention the name Jahannum (جهنم) "hell," to indicate the scorching climate that prevails in and around a piece of land located on the borders of Ṭayyiba in the Jezreel Valley.

6. The terms *upper map* and *lower map* are taken from Yigal Schwartz's (2014, 221–88) discussions of the movement of the characters in the story "Nomads and Viper."

7. However, history, memory, and literary texts do not work in isolation, and alongside the dialectic there is mutual dependence between them (Zerubavel 1994, 42, 62; Zemon Davis and Starn 1989, 5). Historians have long used oral sources, and this use expands their field of action. See Thompson 2009, 26, 29.

8. Wright as quoted by Schwartz 2014, 31.

9. For a deeper understanding of these practices, see Dahamshe 2021a.

10. *Ḥomeṭ* is a Hebrew word for chameleon.

11. Government Yearbook 1951, 279.

12. Zochrot (literally, "those who remember" [fem.]) aims to raise awareness about the Nakba and Palestinian historical geography among the Jewish Israeli public. The association has been working for more than a decade to revive the lost Palestinian map (http://www.zochrot.org).

13. After the conquest of East Jerusalem in 1967, within three months Israel changed the name al-Quds, in use since the seventh century CE, to Urūshalim al-Quds.

14. The issue of the acculturation of the subaltern by the colonial government is widely discussed in the postcolonial discourse. An example of this discussion is Frantz Fanon's (1967, 15) famous essay. Israel is not a colonial government in the classical sense, but its policies toward the Palestinians in Israel on demographic, economic, and educational issues is reminiscent of a colonial policy.

15. The quantitative marginality of the Palestinian national political motif in street names is made obvious by the fact that out of sixty-six street names given by the Ṭurʿān local council, an Arab settlement in northern Israel, there is only one with a national symbolic name: Mahmoud Darwish Street (Dahamshe 2017). Palestinian national commemoration through street names is a kind of cautious commemoration, as Tamir Sorek (2017, 125–37) put it in his discussion of Palestinian commemorative monuments in Israel.

16. In rare cases, Arab local authorities have memorialized names of Jewish leaders or donors to places in their localities. For example, Safra Square in Shafr-ʿamr (after the philanthropic Jewish Safra family) and President Chaim Weizmann in Bāqa al-Gharbiyya (Ashkenazi 2005).

17. Dahamshe 2024.

BIBLIOGRAPHY

ʿAbd al-Karīm, Ibrāhīm. 2001. *Tahwīd al-arḍ wa-asmāʾ al-maʿālim al-filasṭīniyya.* Damascus: Ittiḥād al-Kitāb al-ʿArabī.

ʿAbduh, Qāsim. 1993. *Bayn al-tārīkh wal-fulklūr.* Cairo: ʿAyn.

Abu-Lughod, Lila. 1986. *Veiled Sentiments: Honor and Poetry in a Bedouin Society.* Berkeley: University of California Press.

Abū Muṣliḥ, Kamāl. 1989. *Al-Muʿjam al-ʿarabī al-mustʿajam min asmāʾ al-mudun wal-qurā wal-amākin fī jumhūriyyat Lubnān al-kabīra.* Beirut: Al-Dār al-Taqaddumiyya.

Abu-Sitta, Salman. 2004. *Atlas of Palestine 1948.* London: Palestine Land Society.

Abu-Sitta, Salman. 2007. "Istiʿādat jughrāfiyyat Filasṭīn al-mughayyaba." *Al-ʿArabī* 582:30–35.

Alexander-Frizer, Tamar. 2008. *The Heart Is a Mirror: The Sephardic Folktale.* Translated by Jacqueline S. Teitelbaum. Detroit: Wayne State University Press.

Allen, Amy. 2013. *The Politics of Our Selves: Power, Autonomy, and Gender in Contemporary Critical Theory.* New York: Columbia University Press.

Altman, Irwin. 1975. *The Environment and Social Behavior: Privacy, Personal Space, Territory, Crowding.* Monterey, CA: Brooks/Cole.

Amir, Ayala. 2016. "Kimʿat sheloshim shana aḥarei—torat ha-sippur ha-yom." In *Ha-Poetiqa shel ha-sipporet,* edited by Ayala Amir et al., 1:381–404. Raʾanana: Open University.

Anderson, Benedict. 1983. *Imagined Communities: Reflections on the Origin and Spread of Nationalism.* London: Verso.

Arieli, Daniella. 1997. "Havnaya tarbutit shel ṭevaʿ: Ha-miqreh shel ha-ḥevrah le-haganat ha-ṭevaʿ be-Yisraʾel." *Megamot* 38 (2): 189–206.

Arieli, Yehoshua. 1992. *Hisṭoria ve-poliṭiqa.* Tel Aviv: Am Oved.

al-ʿĀrif, ʿĀrif. 1961. *Al-Mufaṣṣil fī tārīkh al-Quds*. Jerusalem: Maṭbaʿat al-Maʿārif.

ʿArrāf, Shukrī. 1993. *Ṭabaqāt al-anbiyāʾ wal-awliyāʾ al-ṣāliḥīn fī al-arḍ al-muqaddasa*. 2 vols. Tarshīḥā: n.p.

ʿArrāf, Shukrī. 1996. *Al-Qarya al-ʿarabiyya al-filasṭīniyya*. Miʿiliyā: Ilā al-ʿAmq.

ʿArrāf, Shukrī. 2004. *Al-Mawāqiʿ al-jughrāfiyya fī Filasṭīn, al-asmāʾ al-ʿarabiyya wal-musammiyyāt al-ʿibriyya*. Beirut: Muʾassasat al-Dirāsāt al-Filasṭīniyya.

Ashkenazi, Elie. 2005. "Ba-yishuvim ha-ʿarviyyim margishim paḥot meḥubarim li-shemot ha-reḥovot Safra u-Weizmann." *Haaretz*, January 21. http://www .haaretz.co.il/misc/1.1495069.

Ashkenazi, Tuvia. 2000. *Ha-Beduwim be-Ereṣ Yisraʾel*. Jerusalem: Ariel.

Azaryahu, Maoz. 1998. "Le-ʿavret ereṣ: Yeṣirat ha-mappa ha-ʿivrit bi-shenot ha-ḥamishim." *Moreshet Derekh* 78:4–7.

Azaryahu, Maoz. 2000. "ʿIvrit ve-ʿivrut: hebeṭim shel yeṣirat zehut tarbutit." *Jewish Studies* 40:77–88.

Azaryahu, Maoz. 2005. *Tel Aviv—The Real City*. Tel Aviv: Machon Ben-Gurion.

Azaryahu, Maoz. 2012. *ʿAl shem: Historia ve-politiqa shel shemot reḥovot be-Yisraʾel*. Jerusalem: Carmel.

Azaryahu, Maoz, and Aharon Kellerman. 1999. "Symbolic Places of National History and Revival: A Study in Zionist Mythical Geography." *Transactions of the Institute of British Geographers* 24:109–23.

Azoulay, Ariela, trans. 2003. "Aḥarit davar: Ṣeʾṣaʾei ha-zeman va-dayyarei ha-merḥav." In *Heteretopy*, by Michel Foucault, 61–74. Tel Aviv: Ressling.

Bachealard, Gaston. (1958) 1964. *The Poetics of Space: The Classic Look at How We Experience Intimate Places*. Translated by Maria Jolas. Boston: Beacon.

Baer, Gabriel. 1973. *ʿArviyyei ha-mizraḥ ha-tikhon: Ukhlusiyya ve-ḥevra*. Tel Aviv: Hakibbutz Hameuchad.

Bailey, Clinton (Yitzhak), and Avinoam Danin. 1974. "Shemot ha-ṣemaḥim eṣel ha-beduwim." *Reshimot be-nosé ha-beduwim* 5:2–48.

Baker, A. 1998. *Voices of Resistance: Oral History of Moroccan Women*. Albany: State University of New York Press.

Baker, Roland F. 1972. "The Role of Folk Legend in Place Names Research." *Journal of American Folklore* 85:367–73.

Bakhtin, Michael M. 1981. "Forms of Time and of the Chronotope in the Novel." In *The Dialogic Imagination*, edited and translated by Caryl Emerson and Michael Holquist, 84–258. Austin: University of Texas Press.

al-Bakrī, ʿAbdallāh b. ʿAbd al-ʿAzīz. 1976. *Muʿjam mā ʾstaʿjam min asmāʾ al-bilād wal-mawāḍiʿ*. Beirut: ʿĀlam al-Kutub.

Bar-Gal, Yoram. 1992. "Hasmala poliṭit ba-merḥav ha-ʿironi: Shemot reḥovot be-Yisraʾel." *Horizons in Geography/Ofaqim be-geografiya* 33–34:119–32.

Bar-Itzhak, Haya. 2001. *Jewish Poland: Legends of Origin. Ethnopoetics and Legendary Chronicles*. Detroit: Wayne State University Press.

Barakāt, Ḥalīm. 1986. *Al-Mujtamaʿ al-ʿarabī al-muʿāṣir.* Beirut: Markaz Dirāsāt al-Waḥda al-ʿArabiyya.

Bar-Tzvi, Sasson. 1979. "Meʾafyenim shel ḥayyei ha-beduwim ba-Negev be-ṭerem hitnaḥalut." In *Ereṣ ha-Negev: Adam u-midbar,* edited by Avshalom Shmueli and Yehudah Gordus, 621–31. Tel Aviv: Ministry of Defense Publishing House.

al-Barghūthī, ʿAbd al-Laṭīf. 1990. "Al-Tarbiya fī ʿahd al-intidāb al-barīṭānī ʿalā Filastīn." In *Al-Mujtamaʿ al-Filasṭīnī: Arbaʿīn ʿāmman ʿalā al-nakba wa-wāḥid wa-ʿishrūn ʿāmman ʿalā iḥtilāl al-ḍaffa al-gharbiyya,* edited by Nawāf ʿAbd al-Ḥasan, 221–62. Taybeh: Markaz Iḥyāʾ al-Turāth al-ʿArabī.

Barthes, Roland. 1977. *Mythologies.* Translated by Annette Lavers. London: Paladin.

Basso, Keith H. 1988a. "'Speaking with Names': Language and the Landscape among the Western Apache." *Cultural Anthropology* 3:99–130.

Basso, Keith H. 1988b. "Stalking with Stories: Names, Places and Moral Narratives among the Western Apache." In *Text, Play and Story: The Construction and Reconstruction of Self and Society,* edited by Edward M. Bruner, 19–55. Washington, DC: Waveland Press.

Basso, Keith H. 1990. *Western Apache Language and Culture: Essays in Linguistic Anthropology.* Tucson: University of Arizona Press.

Basso, Keith H. 1996. *Wisdom Sits in Places.* Albuquerque: University of New Mexico Press.

Ben-Amos, Dan. 1975. "Kategoriyot analiṭiyot ve-zhanerim etniyyim." *Ha-Sifrut* 20:136–49.

Ben-Amos, Dan. 1984. "The Seven Strands of Tradition: Varieties in Its Meaning in American Foklore Studies." *Journal of Folklore Research* 21:31–79.

Ben-Arieh, Yehoshua. 1970. *Ereṣ Yisraʾel ba-meʾa ha-yud-ṭeṭ: giluya me-ḥadash.* Jerusalem: Carta.

Ben-Arieh, Yehoshua. 1974. "Ereṣ Yisraʾel ke-nosé limmud geʾografi hisṭori." *Quarterly for Social Research/Rivʿon le-meḥqar ḥevrati* (Haifa) 9–10:5–26.

Ben-Arieh, Yehoshua. 1991. "Le-ofya shel ha-sifrut ha-geʾografit-hisṭorit shel Ereṣ Yisraʾel mi-ha-meʾa ha-yud-ṭeṭ." In *Meḥqarim be-geʾografiya hisṭorit-yishuvit shel Ereṣ Yisraʾel,* vol. 2, edited by Yossi Ben-Artzi and Haim Goren, 13–27. Jerusalem: Yad Ben-Zvi.

Ben-Artzi, Yossi. 1997. *Early Jewish Settlement Patterns in Palestine, 1882–1914.* Magnes: Jerusalem.

Ben-David, Yosef. 1981. *Jebaliyya, sheveṭ beduwi be-ṣel ha-minzar.* Jerusalem: Cana.

Ben-Gurion, David, and Yizhak Ben-Zvi. 1979. *Ereṣ Yisraʾel ba-ʿavar u-be-hové.* Edited by M. Eliav and Y. Ben Arieh. Jerusalem: Yad Ben Zvi.

Benvenisti, Meron. 1988. *Ha-qelaʿ ve-ha-ala: sheṭaḥim, yehudim, ve-ʿaravim.* Jerusalem: Keter.

Benvenisti, Meron. 1997. "Ha-mappa ha-ʿivrit." *Theory and Criticism/Theoria u-vikoret* 11:7–30.

Benvenisti, Meron. 2000. *Sacred Landscape: The Buried History of the Land Since 1948*. Translated by Maxine Kaufman-Lacusta. Berkeley: University of California Press.

Berg, Lawrence D., and Robin A. Kearns. 1996. "Naming as Norming: 'Race', Gender and the Identity Politics of Naming Places in Aotearoa/New Zealand." *Environment and Planning D: Society and Space* 14:99–122.

Berg, Lawrence D., and Jani Vuolteenaho, eds. 2009. *Critical Toponymies: The Contested Politics of Place Naming*. Farnham: Ashgate.

Berleant-Shiller, Riva. 1991. "Hidden Places and Creole Forms: Naming the Barbudan Landscape." *Professional Geographers* 43 (1): 92–101.

Berry, John W. 1999. "Emic and Etics: A Symbolic Conception." *Culture and Psychology* 5:165–171.

Bhabha, Homi K. 1990. "The Other Question: Difference, Discrimination and the Discourse of Colonialism." In *Out There: Marginalization and Contemporary Cultures*, edited by Russel Ferguson et al., 71–88. Cambridge, MA: MIT Press.

Bhabha, Homi K. (1988) 1995. "Cultural Diversity and Cultural Differences." In *The Post-Colonial Studies Reader*, edited by Bill Ashcroft, Gareth Griffiths, and Hellen Tiffin, 206–9. London: Routledge.

Bigon, Liora. 2016. Introduction to *Place Names in Africa: Colonial Urban Legacies, Entangled Histories*, edited by Liora Bigon, 1–25. Cham: Springer.

Bigon, Liora, and Amer Dahamshe. 2014. "An Anatomy of Symbolic Power: Israeli Road-Sign Policy and the Palestinian Minority." *Environment and Planning D: Society and Space* 32 (4): 606–21.

Bitan, Hana. 1992. "Vaʿadat ha-shemot ha-memshaltit." *Eretz-Yisrael* 23:366–70.

Bitan, Hana. 2013. "Vaʿadat ha-shemot ha-memshaltit: Toldotéha ve-ʿeqronot ʿavodatah." *Horizons in Geography/Ofaqim be-geografiya* 83:67–84.

Blumen, Orna. 2005. "Space and Periphery: The Other Place of Women." In *Space, Periphery and Gender in the Negev*, edited by Henriet Dahan-Kalev, Niza Yanay, and Niza Berkovitch, 17–41. Sede-Boker: Ben-Gurion Research Institute and Xargol Publishers.

Boal, Frederick W. 1989. "Segregation." In *Social Geography, Progress and Prospect*, edited by Michael Pacione, 90–128. New York: Croom Helm.

Bonfil, Robert (Reuven). 1989. "Mitos, reṭoriqa va-hisṭoria be-ʿiyyun be-*Megillat Aḥimaʿaz*." In *Tarbut ve-ḥevra be-toldot Yisraʾel bi-yemei ha-beynayim: qoveṣ maʾamarim le-zikhro shel Haim Hillel Ben-Sasson*, edited by Menahem Ben-Sasson, Robert Bonfil, and Joseph R. Hacker, 99–135. Jerusalem: Zalman Shazar Center.

Borée, Wilhelm. 1968. *Die alten Ortsnames Palästinas*. Hildesheim: G. Olms.

Bourdieu, Pierre. 1979. *Algeria 1960: The Disenchantment of the World: The Sense of Honour: The Kabyle House or the World Reversed: Essays*. Translated by Richard Nice. Cambridge: Cambridge University Press.

Bourdieu, Pierre. 1985. "The Social Space and the Genesis of Group." *Theory and Society* 14:723–44.

Braudel, Fernand. 1980. "History and the Social Sciences: The *Longue Durée*." In *On History*, translated by Sarah Matthews, 25–54. Chicago: University of Chicago Press.

Brockelmann, Carl. 2017. *Geschichte der Arabischen Literatur = Brockelman in English: The History of the Arabic Written Tradition Online*. Translated by Joep Lameer and edited by Jan Just Witkam. Leiden: Brill. https://referenceworks.brillonline.com/browse/brockelmann-in-english.

al-Būrīnī, al-Ḥasan. 1959–62. *Tarājim al-aʿyān min anbāʾ al-zamān*. 2 vols. Damascus: Maṭbūʿāt al-Majmaʿ al-ʿIlmī.

Cajete, Gregory. 2000. *Native Science, Natural Laws of Interdependence*. Santa Fe, NM: Clear Light.

Calvino, Italo. 1974. *Invisible Cities*. Translated by William Weaver. London: Picador.

Cameron, Deborah, and Thomas Markus. 2002. *The Words between the Spaces: Buildings and Language*. London: Routledge.

Canaan, Taufik. 1928. "Plant-Lore in Palestinian Superstition." *Journal of the Palestine Oriental Society* 8:129–68.

Cavallaro, Samantha, and Jing Yi Yom. 2020. "Colonialism and Toponyms in Singapore." *Urban Science* 4 (4): 64. https://doi.org/10.3390/urbansci4040064.

Chamberlin, Edward J. 2004. *If This Is Your Land, Where Are Your Stories: Reimagining Home and Sacred Space*. Cleveland: Pilgrim.

Cirlot, Juan Eduardo. 1978. *A Dictionary of Symbols*. Translated by Jack Sage. London: Routledge.

Clermont-Ganneau, Charles Simon. 1876. *Palestine inconnue*. Paris: Leroux.

Cohen, Hillel. 2004. *Ṣavaʾ ha-ṣelalim: Mashtapim palesṭinim be-sherut ha-ṣiyonut, 1917–1948*. Jerusalem: Ivrit.

Cohen, Soul, and Nurit Kliot. 1992. "Place-Names in Israel's Ideological Struggle over the Administered Territories." *Annals of the Association of American Geographers* 82 (4): 653–80.

Conder, Claude Ringer, and Horatio Herbert Kitchener. 1881. *The Survey of Western Palestine: Arabic and English Names Lists Collected during the Survey*. Transliterated and explained by Edward Henry Palmer. London: Committee of the Palestine Exploration Foundation.

Cosgrove, Denis F. 1984. *Social Formation and Symbolic Landscape*. London: C. Helm.

al-Dabbāgh, Muṣṭafā. (1967) 2003. *Bilādunā Filasṭīn*. 10 vols. Kafr Qarʿ: Dār al-Hudā.

al-Dabbāgh, Muṣṭafā. 1988. *Al-Mamlakatān al-nabātiyya wal-ḥayawāniyya fī buldāniyyat Filasṭīn wa-āthāruhā fī tasmiyyat amkinatihā*. Acre: Dār al-Asrār.

Dahamshe, Amer. 2009. "Shem le-maqom—shemot ha-yishuvim ha-ʿarviyyim ba-galil u-shemot ha-ʿaṣamim min ha-ṭevaʿ ba-sifrut ha-ʿamamit." 2 vols. PhD diss., Hebrew University of Jerusalem.

Dahamshe, Amer. 2010. "Nishul leshoni." *Haaretz*, June 30. https://www.haaretz.co.il/opinions/1.1209564.

Dahamshe, Amer. 2017. "Names under Supervision: Israeli Linguistic Regulation on Arab Streets—Ṭurʿan as Case Study." *Journal of Levantine Studies* 7:9–34.

Dahamshe, Amer. 2018. "Symbolic Distinctions in Traditional Palestinian Toponymy: Class, Gender, and Village Prestige in Palestinian Space in Israel." *Narrative Culture* 5 (1): 95–120.

Dahamshe, Amer. 2021a. "Palestinian Arabic versus Israeli Hebrew Place-Names: Comparative Cultural Reading of Landscape Nomenclature and Israeli Renaming Strategies." *Journal of Holy Land and Palestine Studies* 20 (1): 66–82.

Dahamshe, Amer. 2021b. "Shemot af ʿal pi ken—shemot palesṭinim shel yishuvin ve-nofei tevaʿ ba-siaḥ ha-yisraʾeli." Talk given at the Nineteenth Conference of the Association for Language and Society, Tel Aviv, NYU Tel Aviv.

Dahamshe, Amer. 2024. "Ka-asher ha-yisraʾelim hofkhim le-yelidim: sheʾilat shemot meqomot mi-ʿarvit ba-ḥevra ha-yisraʾelit ve-tefisat ha-aḥer ha-ʿaravi." *Jerusalem Studies in Jewish Folklore* 36:175–209.

Dana, Nissim. 1998. "Ha-druziyut halakha le-maʿaseh." In *Ha-Druzim*, edited by Nissim Dana, 37–49. Ramat Gan: Bar Ilan University.

Darzie, Orly. 1993. "Merḥav u-shemot: Shemot yishuvim, tahalikhim leʾumiyyim ve-yaḥasim ḥevratiyyim." Master's thesis, Tel Aviv University.

Davis, Rochalle A. 2007. "Mapping the Past, Re-creating the Homeland—Memories of Village Places in pre-1948 Palestine." In *Nakba: Palestine, 1948, and the Claims of Memory*, edited by Ahmed H. Saʾdi and Lila Abu-Lughod, 53–75. New York: Columbia University Press.

De Certeau, Michel. 1984. *The Practice of Everyday Life*. Translated by Steven Rendal. Berkeley: University of California Press.

Degani, Rami. 1989–90. "Bekhi ha-almana." *Moreshet Derech* 29:39–41.

Dodge, William A. 2007. *Black Rock: A Zuni Cultural Landscape and the Meaning of Place*. Jackson: University Press of Mississippi.

Duncan, Jim, and Nancy Duncan. 1988. "(Re)reading the Landscape." *Environment and Planning D: Society and Space* 6:117–26.

Edut, Galit. 2017. "Maʾavaq le-hakara: Lama kol kakh meʿaṭ reḥovot ba-areṣ qeruyyim ʿal shem nashim?" *Maʾariv*, March 13. https://www.maariv.co.il/news/israel/Article-577507.

Eliade, Mircea. 1954. *The Myth of the Eternal Return*. New York: Pantheon.

Elitzur, Yoel. 1989. "Shemot meqomot bnei shtei milim ba-nomenklatura ha-ʿaravit shel Ereṣ Yisraʾel u-ba-miqraʾ." *Proceedings of the Tenth World Congress of Jewish Studies* D1:21–28.

Elitzur, Yoel. 1993. "Shemot meqomot ʿatiqim she-nishtamru be-fi ha-ʿaravim ba-areṣ: Ha-beḥina ha-leshonit." PhD diss., Hebrew University of Jerusalem.

Elitzur, Yoel. 2004. *Ancient Place Names in the Holy Land: Preservation and History*. Translated by David Louvish. Jerusalem: Magnes.

Elitzur, Yoel. 2018. "Amer Dahamshe, *Maqom la-dur bo ve-shem lo: Qeriʾa sifrutit ve-tarbutit ba-shemot ha-ʿarviyyim shel ha-areṣ*." *Zion* 83:390–97.

Endres, Danielle, and Samantha Senda-Cook. 2011. "Location Matters: The Rhetoric of Place in Protest." *Quarterly Journal of Speech* 97 (3): 257–82.

Epstein, Eliyahu. 1933. *Habeduwim, ḥayyeihem un-minhageihem*. Tel Aviv: Stiebel.

Eusebius of Caesarea. 2003. *The Onomasticon*. Translated by G. S. P. Freeman-Grenville. Jerusalem: Carta.

Falah, Ghazi. 1996. "The 1948 Israeli-Palestinian War and Its Aftermath: The Transformation and De-Signification of Palestine's Cultural Landscape." *Annals of the Association of American Geographics* 86 (2): 256–85.

Falah, Salman, and Aliza Shenhar. 1978. *Sippurei ʿam druziyyim*. Jerusalem: Center for Folklore Studies.

Fanon, Frantz. 1967. *Black Skin, White Masks*. Translated by Charles Lamm Markmann. New York: Grove.

Feige, Michael. 2002. *One Space, Two Places: Gush Emunim, Peace Now, and the Construction of Israeli Space*. Jerusalem: Magnes.

Feliks, Yehuda. 1997. *ʿAṣei besamin, yaʿar ve-noy*. Jerusalem: Rubin Mass.

Fenster, Tovi. 1998. "Migdar (gender) u-merḥav: hebeṭim shel tikhnun u-pituʾaḥ yishuvei ha-beduwim ba-Negev." *Studies in the Geography of Israel/Meḥqarim ba-geʾografiya shel Ereṣ Yisraʾel* 16:229–54.

Fischman, Ruthie. 2002. *Simbolim*. Hod Hasharon: Astrolog.

Foley, William A. 1977. *Anthropological Linguistics: An Introduction*. Malden, MA: Blackwell.

Foucault, Michel. 1984. "Des espaces autres (conférence au Cercle d'études architecturales, 14 mars 1967)." *Architecture, Mouvement, Continuité* 5:46–49.

Fraser, Nancy. 1989. *Unruly Practices: Power, Discourse and Gender in Contemporary Social Theory*. Minneapolis: University of Minnesota Press.

Garth, Myers. 2009. "Naming and Placing the Other: Power and the Urban Landscape in Zanzibar." In *Critical Toponymies: The Contested Politics of Place Naming*, edited by Lawrence D. Berg and Jani Vuolteenaho, 85–100. Farnham: Ashgate.

Geertz, Clifford. 1973. *The Interpretation of Cultures: Selected Essays*. New York: Basic.

Geertz, Clifford. 1976. "'From the Native's Point of View': On the Nature of Understanding." In *Meaning in Anthropology*, edited by K. Basso and H. Selby, 221–37. Albuquerque: University of New Mexico Press.

Gertz, Nurit, and George Khalifi. 2006. *Nof ba-ʿarafel: ha-merḥav ve-ha-zikaron ba-qolnoʿa ha-palesṭini*. Tel Aviv: Am Oved.

Ginat, Joseph. 2000. *Niqmat dam: niduyi, tivvukh u-kevod ha-mishpaḥa.* Tel Aviv: Zmora Bitan.

Goffman, Erving. 1959. *The Presentation of Self in Everyday Life.* New York: Doubleday.

Golan, Arnon, and Ma'oz Azryahu. 2004. "Le-ʿavret ereṣ: yeṣirat ha-mappa ha-ʿivrit shel Ereṣ Yisra'el (1949–1960)." In *Meḥqarim be-Ereṣ Yisra'el—Sefer Aviel Ron,* edited by Yoram Bar-Gal, Nurit Kliot, and Ammatzia Peled. Haifa: Haifa University Press.

Gordon, Jeffrey J. 1984. "Onodoga Iroquiois Place-Names: An Approach to Historical and Contemporary Indian Landscape Perception." *Names* 32 (3): 218–33.

Gould, Peter, and Rodney White. 2012. *Mental Maps.* New York: Routledge.

Govrin, Nurit. 1988. *Ketivat ha-areṣ: araṣot ve-ʿarim ʿal mappat ha-sifrut ha-ʿivrit.* Jerusalem: Carmel.

Gramsci, Antonio. 1971. *Selections from the Prison Notebooks.* London: Lawrence and Wishart.

Greenzweig, Michael. 2000. "Shemot meqomot be-sifrut ha-tanna'im: Onomasṭiqon be-hebeṭ balshani ve-geʾografi-hisṭori." PhD diss., Hebrew University of Jerusalem.

Gregory, Derek. 1989. "The Crisis of Modernity? Human Geography and Critical Social Theory." In *New Models in Geography—the Political-Economy Perspective,* edited by Peet Richard and Nigel Thrift, 348–85. London: Unwin Hyman.

Gross, Larry. 1988. "Minorities, Majorities and the Media." In *Media, Ritual and Identity,* edited by Tamar Liebes and James Curran, 87–102. London: Routledge.

Grossman, David. 1994. *Ha-kfar ha-ʿaravi u-benotav.* Jerusalem: Yad Ben-Zvi.

Grosz, Elizabeth. 1992. "Bodies-Cites." In *Sexuality and Space,* edited by Beatriz Colomina, 241–54. New York: Princeton Architectural Press.

Guérin, Victor. 1868. *Description géographique, historique et archéologique de la Palestine.* Paris: Imprimérie impériale.

Gurevitch, Zeli, and Gideon Aranne. 1991. "ʿAl ha-maqom." *Alpayim* 4:9–44.

Hägerstrand, Torsten. 1970. "What about People in Regional Science?" *Ninth European Congress of Regional Science Association* 24:7–21.

Hägerstrand, Torsten. 1976. "Geography and the Study of Interaction between Nature and Society." *Geoforum* 7:329–34.

Halbwachs, Maurice. 1992. *On Collective Memory.* Translated and edited by Lewis A. Coser. Chicago: University of Chicago Press.

al-Ḥamāwī, Yāqūt. (1906–7) 1990. *Muʿjam al-buldān.* 6 vols. Beirut: Dār Rāṣid.

Harvey, David. 1973. *Social Justice and the City.* London: Amold.

Hasan-Rokem, Galit. 1995. "Not the Mother of All Cities: A Feminist Perspective of Jerusalem." *Palestine-Israel Journal* 2/3. http://www.pij.org/details.php?id=627.

Hasan-Rokem, Galit. (1995) 2000. "Ha-qol qol aḥoti: demuyot nashim ve-semalim nashiyyim be-midrah Eikha Rabba'." In *Ashnav le-ḥayyeihen shel nashim be-ḥavarot yehudiyot*, edited by Yael Atzmon, 95–111. Jerusalem: Shazar Center.

Hasan-Rokem, Galit. 2000. *Web of Life: Folklore and Midrash in Rabbinic Literature*. Translated by Batya Stein. Stanford: Stanford University Press.

Hasan-Rokem, Galit. 2012. "Nasénu be-ḥodot, nasénu be-tavniyot: ʿAl yesod ha-transformatsiya ba-struqturalizm ke-gesher min ha-moderniyut el ha-post-moderniyut." In *Ot LeTova: Pirqei meḥqar mugashim le-Professor Tova Rosen-Moked*, edited by Eli Yassif, Haviva Ishay, and Uriah Kfir, 273–84. Beersheba: Heksherim Institute for Jewish and Israeli Literature and Culture/Moshe David Gaon Center for Ladino Culture.

Ḥasan, Manār. 2017. *Semuyot min ha-ʿayin: Nashim ve-he-ʿarim ha-palesṭiniyot*. Jerusalem: Van Leer Institute.

Hazan, Haim. 1992. *Ha-si'aḥ ha-anthropologi*. Tel Aviv: Ministry of Defense.

Hever, Hannan. 1991. "ʿIvrit me-ʿeṭ ʿaravi: Shisha peraqim ʿal 'Arabesqot' me'et Anton Shamas." *Theory and Criticism/Theoria u-vikoret* 1:23–38.

Hever, Hannan. 1993. "'Ha-peliṭut la-peliṭim': Emil Habibi ve-qanon ha-sifrut ha-ʿivrit." *Ha-mizraḥ he-ḥadash* 35:102–14.

Hever, Hannan. 2002. *Producing the Modern Hebrew Canon: Nation Building and Minority Discourse*. New York: New York University Press.

Hever, Hannan, and Adi Ophir. 1994. "Homi K. Bhabha: Theoria ʿal ḥevel daq." *Theory and Criticism/Theoria u-vikoret* 5:141–43.

al-Ḥilw, ʿAbdallāh. 1999. *Taḥqīqāt tārīkhiyya lughawiyya fī al-asmā' al-jughrafiyya al-sūriyya*. Beirut: Bīsān.

Hobsbawm, Eric, and Terence Ranger, eds. 1983. *The Invention of Tradition*. London: Verso.

The Holy Bible, New International Version. 2011. Palmer Lake, CO: Biblica.

Honko, Lauri. 1981. "Four Forms of Adaptation of Tradition." *Studia Fennica* 26:19–33.

Hütteroth, Wolf-Deiter, and Kamal Abdulfattah. 1977. *Historical Geography of Palestine, Transjordan and Southern Syria in the Late 16th Century*. Erlangen: Selbstverlag der Frankischen Geographischen Gesellschaft.

Hymes, Dell. 1996. *Ethnography, Linguistics, Narrative Inequality—Toward the Understanding of Voice*. London: Taylor & Francis.

Ibn al-Athīr, ʿIzz al-Dīn. 1956. *Al-Kāmil fī al-tārīkh*. 10 vols. Beirut: Dar Sader.

Ibn al-Farākiḥ, Ibrāhīm. 2003. *Bāʿith al-nufūs ilā ziyārat al-Quds al-maḥrūs*. Edited by ʿAbd al-Ḥamīd Ḥamadān. Cairo: Maktabat Madbūlī.

Ibn Manẓūr, Muḥammad b. Makram. 1988. *Lisān al-ʿarab al-muḥīṭ*. Vol. 1. Beirut: Dār al-Khalīl.

Ibn Munqidh, Usāma. 1999. *An Arab-Syrian Gentleman and Warrior in the Period of the Crusades: Memoirs of Usāmah ibn-Munqidh (Kitāb al-Iʿtibār)*. Translated by Philip K. Hitti. New York: Columbia University Press.

Ibn ʿAbd al-Ḥaqq, Ṣafī al-Dīn. 1954–55. *Marāsid al-iṭṭilāʿ ʿalā asmāʾ al-amkina wal-buqāʿ*. Beirut: Dār al-Maʿrifa.

Irshai, Oded. 1983. "Yaʿqov ish Niburaia—ḥakham she-nikhshal be-minut." *Jerusalem Studies in Jewish Thought/Meḥqarei Yerushalayim be-Maḥshevet Yisraʾel* 2:255–77.

Jason, Heda. 1972. *Genre: An Essay in Oral Literature*. Tel Aviv: Tel Aviv University Press.

Josephus Flavius. 1915. *The Wars of the Jews*. Translated by William Whiston. London: J. M. Dent.

Kadman, Noga. 2015. *Erased from Space and Consciousness: Israel and the Depopulated Palestinian Villages of 1948*. Bloomington: Indiana University Press.

Kadmon, Naftali. 2000. *Toponymy: The Lore, Laws and Language of Geographical Names*. New York: Vintage.

Kadmon, Naftali. 2004. *Ṭoponomastiqon: Sefer ha-shemot ha-geʾografiyyim be-Yisraʾel*. Jerusalem: Carta.

Kampffmeyer, Georg. 1892. "Alte Namen im heutigen Palästina und Syrien." *Zeitschrift des Deutschen Palästina-Vereins* 15:65–116.

Kapstein, Israel J., and William G. Braude, trans. 2002. *Pěsikta Dě-Rab Kahăna: R. Kahana's Compilation of Discourses for Sabbaths and Festal Days*. Philadelphia: Jewish Publication Society.

Katz, Yossi. 1998. "Shemot meqomot u-tafqidam ha-poliṭi: Ha-maʾavaq ha-ṣiyoni le-shemirat shemot ha-meqomot ha-ʿivriyyim be-tequfat ha-Yishuv." *Meḥqarim ba-Geographia shel Ereṣ Yisrael* 15:105–16.

Khalidi, Rashid. 1997. *Palestinian Identity. The Construction of Modern National Consciousness*. New York: Columbia University Press.

Khammār, Constantine. 1980. *Asmāʾ al-amākin wal-mawāqiʿ wal-maʿālim al-ṭabīʿiyya wal-bashariyya wal-jughrāfiyya al-maʿrūfa fī Filasṭīn ḥattā al-ʿām 1948*. Beirut: al-Muʾassasa al-ʿArabiyya lil-Dirāsāt.

Khurshīd, Fārūq. 2002. *Adīb al-asṭūra ʿind al-ʿarab*. Kuwait: ʿĀlam al-Maʿrifa.

Kimmerling, Baruch. 2004. *Mehagrim, mityashvim, yelidim: Ha-medina ve-ha-ḥevra be-Yisraʾel, beyn ribuyi tarbuyot le-milḥemet tarbut*. Tel Aviv: Am Oved.

Klein, Samuel. 1976. *Sefer ha-yishuv le-meqomotav mi-yemei ḥorban bayit sheni ʿad kibush ereṣ Yisraʾel ʿal-yadei ha-ʿaravim*. Jerusalem: Yad Ben-Zvi.

Kliot, Nurit. 1990. "Mashmaʿut shemot ha-yishuvim ha-ʿarviyyim be-ereṣ Yisraʾel ve-hashvaʾatam le-shemot yishuvim ʿivriyyim." *Horizons in Geography/Ofaqim be-geografiya* 30:71–79.

Kliot, Nurit. 1994. "Nofei mishʿar imperiyaliyyim: Simlei Briṭaniya ve-ḥever ha-ʿamim ha-briṭi be-ereṣ Yisraʾel." *Ariel* 100–101:113–22.

Köngäs Maranda, Elli. 1971. "The Logic of Riddles." In *Structural Analysis of Oral Tradition*, edited by Pierre Maranda and Elli Köngäs Maranda, 189–232. Philadelphia: University of Pennsylvania Press.

Krenawi, Alean. 2000. *Ethno-psychiatriya ba-ḥevra ha-beduwit-ʿaravit ba-Negev*. Tel Aviv: Hakibbutz Hameuchad.

Labov, Walter, and Joshua Waletsky. 1967. "Narrative Analysis: Oral Versions of Personal Experience." In *Essays on the Verbal and the Visual Arts*, edited by June Helm, 3–38. Seattle: University of Washington Press.

Landry, Rodrigue, and Richard Y. Bourhis. 1997. "Linguistic Landscape and Ethnolinguistic Vitality: An Empirical Study." *Journal of Language and Social Psychology* 16 (1): 23–49.

Laor, Yitzhak. 1995. *Anu kotvim otakh moledet: Masot ʿal sifrut yisraʾelit*. Tel Aviv: Hakibbutz Hameuchad.

Le Strange, Guy. 1890. *Palestine Under the Moslems: A Description of Syria and the Holy Land from A.D. 650 to 1500, Translated from the Works of the Mediaeval Arab Geographers*. London: A. P. Watt.

Leach, Edmund. 1976. *Culture and Communications, The Logic by Which Symbols Are Connected: An Introduction to the Use of Structuralist Analysis in Social Anthropology*. London: Cambridge University Press.

Lefebvre, Henri. 1991. *The Production of Space*. Translated by Donald Nicholson-Smith. Oxford: Blackwell.

Lévi-Strauss, Claude. 1963a. *Structural Anthropology*. New Haven, CT: Yale University Press.

Lévi-Strauss, Claude. 1963b. "The Structural Study of Myth." In *Structural Anthropology*, 206–31. New York: Basic.

Lévi-Strauss, Claude. 1966. *The Savage Mind (La pensée sauvage)*. Anonymous translation from the French. London: Weidenfeld and Nicolson.

Lévi-Strauss, Claude. 1967. "The Story of Asdiwal." In *The Structural Study of Myth and Totemism*, edited by Edmund Leach, 1–47. London: Routledge.

Lévi-Strauss, Claude. 1969. *Totemism*. Translated by Rodney Needham. Boston: Beacon.

Levi, Shabbetai. 1987. *Ha-beduwim be-midbar sinai*. Tel Aviv: Schocken.

Levi, Shabbetai. 1994. *Mot Saraya ha-yafa*. Tel Aviv: Hakibbutz Hemeuchad.

Levine, Mark, and Gershon Shafir. 2012. "Introduction: Social Biographies in Making Sense of History." In *Struggle and Survival in Palestine/Israel*, edited by Mark Levine and Gershon Shafir, 1–20. Berkeley: University of California Press.

Levy, Zeʾev. 1976. *Struqṭuralizm beyn metoda ve-temunot ʿolam*. Tel Aviv: Sifriyyat Poʿalim.

Lewis, Bernard. 2002. *What Went Wrong? The Clash between Islam and Modernity in the Middle East*. New York: Oxford University Press.

Ley, David. 1983. *A Social Geography of the City*. New York: Harper and Row.

Lieberman, Saul. 1988. *Tosefta ʿal-pi ketav yad Vienna*. New York: JTS.

Limor, Ora. 2005. "Maria ve-ha-yehudim: Shelosha sippurei ʿedut." *Alpayim* 28:129–51.

Lind, Ivan. 1962. "Geography and Place Names." In *Readings in Cultural Geography*, edited by Philip L. Wagner and Marvin Mikesell, 118–28. Chicago: University of Chicago Press.

Lubbānī, Ḥusayn. 2004. *Muʿjam asmāʾ al-mudun wal-qurā al-filasṭīniyya, maʿānīhā lughawiyyan wa-maʿālimuhā tārīkhiyyan wa-jughrāfiyyan*. Beirut: Bāḥith lil-Dirāsāt.

Lubin, Orly. 2013. "The Gaze in Space." In *Where am I Situated? Gender Perspective on Space*, edited by Roni Halpern, 17–75. Herzliya: Friedrich Ebert Stiftung and Beit Berl Academic College.

Lutwack, Leonard. 1984. *The Role of Place in Literature*. Syracuse, NY: Syracuse University Press.

Mappa Encyclopedia. 2000. 9 vols. Tel Aviv: Mappa.

Marchant, Carolyn. 1983. *The Death of Nature: Women, Ecology and the Scientific Revolution*. San Francisco: Harper and Row.

Margoliouth, Mordecai. 1972. *Midrash Vayiqra Rabbah*. Jerusalem: Wahrmann.

Margoliouth, Mordecai. 1995. *Enṣiqlopedya le-ḥakhmei ha-Talmud ve-ha-geʾonim*. Tel Aviv: Yavneh.

Maʿānī, Sulṭān ʿAbdallāh. 1994. *Asmāʾ al-mawāqiʿ fi muḥāfaẓat al-Karak*. Muwatta: Muwatta University Press.

McCarthy, Kevin M. 1975. "Street Names in Beirut." *Names* 23:74–88.

McRobie, Angela. 1996. "Different, Youthful, Subjectivities." In *Post-Colonial Questions*, edited by Iain Chambers and Lidia Curti, 30–46. London: Routledge.

Menicucci, Garay. 1999. "Kulthum Auda, Palestinian Ethnographer: Gendering the Palestinian Landscape." In *The Landscape of Palestine: Equivocal Poetry*, edited by Ibrahim Abu-Lughod, Roger Heacock, and Khaled Nashef, 79–94. Birzeit: Birzeit University Publication.

Meron, Joram, Carmela Shehadi, and Nimr Ahmad Masarwi. 1997. *Garger harimon: Ha-isha be-sippurei ha-ʿam ha-ʿarviyyim*. Givat Haviva: Jewish-Arab Center for Peace.

Miller, Mary Rita. 2000. "In the Land of Pleasant Living in Virginia's Northern Neck." *Names* 48:169–76.

Mitchell, W. J. T. 2002. *Landscape and Power*. Chicago: University of Chicago Press.

Momaday, N. Scott. 1974. "Native American Attitude to the Environment." In *Seeing with a Native Eye: Essays on Native American Religion*, edited by Walter H. Capps, 179–85. New York: Harper and Row.

al-Muḥāmī, Tawfīq Muʿammar. 1996. *Ẓāhir al-ʿUmar*. Nazareth: al-Maʿhad al-ʿĀlī lil-Funūn wa-Bayt al-Kitāb.

Muhawi, Ibrahim, and Sharif Kanaana. 1994. *Speak Bird, Speak Again: Palestinian Arab Folktales*. Austin: University of Texas Press.

al-Nāzilī, Muḥammad. 1930. *Khazīnat al-asrār*. Cairo: n.p.

Nicolaisen, Wilhelm F. H. 1976. "Place Names Legends: An Onomastics Mythology." *Folklore* 87:146–57.

Nicolaisen, Wilhelm F. H. 1979. "Field Collecting in Onomastics." *Names* 37:162–78.

Nicolaisen, Wilhelm F. H. 1990. "Placenames and Politics." *Names* 38 (3): 193–207.

Noy, Dov. 1976. *Sippurei ba'alei ḥayyim be-'edot Yisra'el*. Haifa: Municipality of Haifa, Ethnology and Folklore Museum.

Ohana, David, and Robert S. Wistrich, eds. 1995. *The Shaping of Israeli Identity: Myth, Memory and Trauma*. London: F. Cass.

Olsen, F. Erin. 2012. "The War of the Words." In *Struggle and Survival in Palestine/Israel*, edited by Mark Levine and Gershon Shafir, 399–412. Berkeley: University of California Press.

Ha-Parḥi, Ashtori. 1897. *Kaftor va-Ferach*. Jerusalem: Beit Hamidrash le-Halachah ba-Hityashvut.

Parmenter, Barbara. 1994. *Giving Voice to Stones: Place and Identity in Palestinian Literature*. Austin: University of Texas Press.

Patai, Raphael. 1936. *Ha-mayim: Meḥqar le-yedi'at ha-areṣ u-le-folqlor ereṣyisra'eli be-tequfat ha-miqra' ve-ha-mishna*. Tel Aviv: Dvir.

Patai, Raphael. 1942. *Adam ve-adama: Meḥqar be-minhagim, emunot ve-aggadot eṣel Yisrae'el ve-umot ha-'olam*. 3 vols. Jerusalem: Hebrew University Press.

Petachiah of Regensburg. 1967. *The Travels of R. Jacob bar Nathaniel; The Travels of R. Benjamin of Tudela*. Jerusalem: n.p.

Philo, Chris. 2002. "Michel Foucault." In *Thinkers on Space and Place*, edited by Phil Hubbard, Rob Kitchin, and Gil Valentine, 121–28. London: Sage.

Pickthall, Marmaduke M. 1930. *The Meaning of the Glorious Koran*. London: Alfred A. Knopf.

Pinchevski, Amit, and Efraiem Torgovnik. 2002. "Signifying Passage: The Signs of Change in Israel Street Names." *Media Culture and Society* 24:365–88.

Pinto, Meital. 2011. "Minority Language and Language Policy: The Case of Arabic in Israel." In *The Status of the Arabic Language in Israel*, edited by Uzi Rabi and Arik Rudinski, 3–4. Tel Aviv: Dayan Center.

Portelli, Alessandro. (2006) 2009. "What Makes Oral History Different." In *The Oral History Reader*, edited by Robert Perks and Alistair Thomson, 32–42. London: Routledge.

Portugali, Yuval. 1985. "Ge'ografya qogniṭivit." *Enṣiqlopedya 'Ivrit*. Supplement: 264–65. Tel Aviv: Encyclopaedia Hebraica Publishing Company.

Portugali, Yuval. 1999. *Merḥav, zeman ve-ḥevra be-ereṣ Yisra'el ha-qeduma, ḥeleq A*. Ra'anana: Open University.

Portugali, Yuval. 2000. "1500 mila ve-yoter 'al ha-ge'ografya shel ha-adam: Masa' el tokh ha-diṣiplina." *Theory and Criticism/Theoria u-vikoret* 16:213–22.

Prawer, Joshua. 1971. *Toldot mamlekhet ha-ṣalbanim be-ereṣ Yisra'el*. Jerusalem: Mossad Bialik.

Press, Isaiah. 1955. *Ereṣ Yisraʾel: Enṣiqlopedya ṭopografit-hisṭorit.* 4 vols. Jerusalem: Rubin Mass.

Rabinowitz, Dan. 1998. *Antropologya ve-ha-palesṭinim.* Raʾanana: Institute for Israeli Arab Studies.

Rainey, Anson. 1982. "Shem, shemot meqomot." In *Enṣiqlopedya Miqraʾit,* 8:11–29. Jerusalem: Mossad Bialik.

Randall, Richard R. 2001. *Place Names: How They Define the World—And More.* Lanham, MD: Scarecrow.

Relph, Edward. 1976. *Place and Placelessness.* London: Pion.

Rendell, Jane. 2002. *The Pursuit of Pleasure: Gender, Space and Architecture in Regency London.* New Brunswick, NJ: Rutgers University Press.

Rimmon, Helena. 2007. "Ha-zeman ve-ha-maqom shel Mikhail Bakhtin." In *Ṣurot ha-zeman ve-ha-khronotop ba-roman—masa ʿal poʾetiqa hisṭorit,* by Mikhail Bakhtin, translated from Russian by Dina Markon, 227–334. Or Yehuda: Dvir.

Rimmon-Kenan, Shlomith. 1983. *Narrative Fiction: Contemporary Poetics.* London: Methuen.

Robinson, Edward. (1856) 1970. *Biblical Research in Palestine, Mount Sinai and Arabia Petraea: A Journal of Travels in the Year 1838.* 3 vols. New York: Arno.

Room, Adrian. 1997. *Placenames of the World: Origins and Meanings of the Names for Over 5000 Natural Features, Countries, Capitals, Territories, Cities and Historic Sites.* Jefferson, NC: McFarland.

Rose-Redwood, Reuben, Derek Alderman, and Maoz Azaryahu. 2010. "Geographies of Toponymic Inscription: New Directions in Critical Place-Name Studies." *Progress in Human Geography* 34:453–77.

Roseman, Marina. 1998. "Singers of the Landscape: Songs, History and Property Rights in the Malaysian Rain Forest." *American Anthropologist* 100 (1): 105–21.

Rubinstein, Danny. 1990. *Ḥibuq ha-teʾena: "Zekhhut ha-shiva" shel ha-palesṭinim.* Jerusalem: Keter.

Ryden, Kent C. 1993. *Mapping the Invisible Landscape: Folklore, Writing, and the Sense of Place.* Jackson: University Press of Mississippi.

Saegret, Susan. 1980. "Masculine Cities and Feminine Suburbs: Polarized Idea, Contrasting Realities." *Signs* 5 (3): 96–107.

Said, Edward. 1978. *The Question of Palestine.* New York: Times.

Said, Edward. 1995. *Orientalism.* Harmondsworth: Penguin.

Salamon, Hagar. 2016. "Embroidered Palestine: A Stitched Narrative." *Narrative Culture* 3 (1): 1–31.

Saussure, Ferdinand de. 1974. *Course in General Linguistics.* Translated by Wade Baskin. London: Peter Owen.

Schur, Nathan. 1984. *Masaʿot Napoleon le-ereṣ Yisraʾel.* Tel Aviv: Am Oved.

Schwartz, Yigal. 2014. *The Zionist Paradox. Hebrew Literature and Israeli Identity.* Translated by Michal Sapir. Waltham, MA: Brandeis University Press.

Scott, James C. 1990. *Domination and the Arts of Resistance: Hidden Transcripts.* New Haven, CT: Yale University Press.

Shamai, Shmuel. 1991. "Sense of Place: Towards an Empirical Measurement." *Geoforum* 22 (3): 347–58.

Shammas, Anton. 1988. *Arabesques: A Novel.* Translated by Vivien Eden. New York: Viking.

Shammas, Anton. 2005. "Haqdama le-ḥiburo shel Elias Khoury." In *Bab al-Shams*, by Elias Khoury, translated from Arabic by Moshe Hakham. Tel Aviv: Andalus.

Sharrāb, Muḥammad Muḥammad Ḥasan. 2000. *Muʿjam asmāʾ al-mudun wal-qurā al-filasṭīniyya wa-tafsīr maʿānīhā wa-madlūlātihā al-siyāsiyya wal-ḥaḍāriyya.* Amman: al-Ahliyya lil-Nashr wal-Tawzīʿ.

Shenhar, Aliza. 2001. "Aggadot maqom ereṣyisraʾeliyot be-sippurei ʿam druziyim." *Ariel* 143–44:165–73.

Shenhav, Yehouda 2010. *Be-malkodet ha-qav ha-yaroq: Masa poliṭit yehudit.* Tel Aviv: Am Oved.

Shiḥāda, Rajā. 2009. *Ṭiyulim be-Palesṭin: Reshimot ʿal nof holekh ve-neʿelam.* Tel Aviv: Am Oved.

Shoval, Noam. 2013. "Street-Naming, Tourism Development and Cultural Conflict: The Case of the Old City of Acre/Akko/Akka." *Transactions of the Institute of British Geographers* 38 (4): 612–26.

Simmel, Georg. 1997. *Simmel on Culture: Selected Writings.* Edited by D. Frisby and M. Firestone. London: Sage.

Sims, Martha, and Martine Stephens. 2005. *Living Folklore: An Introduction to the Study of People and Their Traditions.* Logan: Utah State University Press.

Sirḥān, Nimr. 1989. *Mawsūʿat al-fulklūr al-filasṭīnī.* Part 3. Amman: al-Bayādir.

Sivan, Emmanuel. 1997. *Mitosim poliṭiyim ʿarviyyim.* Tel Aviv: Am Oved.

Sivan, Emmanuel. 2005. "Qedushat Yerushalem be-Islam be-tequfat masʿei ha-ṣelav." In *ʿAliya la-regel: Yehudim, noṣrim, muslimim*, edited by Ora Limor, Elchanan Reiner, and Miriam Frenkel, 287–303. Raʾanana: Open University.

Slyomovics, Susan. 1998. *The Object of Memory: Arab and Jew Narrate the Palestinian Village.* Philadelphia: University of Pennsylvania Press.

Smith, George. (1896) 1972. *The Historical Geography of the Holy Land.* 3 vols. London: Hodder and Stoughton.

Smith, William Robertson. 1966. *Kinship and Marriage in Early Arabia.* London: Adam and Charles Black.

Soja, Edward. 1989. *Postmodern Geography.* London: Verso.

Sorek, Tamir. 2017. *Palestinian Commemoration in Israel: Calendars, Monuments and Martyrs.* Stanford, CA: Stanford University Press.

Steinmann, Susanne H. 2005. "Changing Identities and Changing Spaces in Village Landscapes of Settled Pastoralists in Eastern Morocco." In *Geographies of*

Muslim Women: Gender, Religion and Space, edited by Ghazi-Walid Falah and Caroline Nagel, 91–124. New York: Guilford.

Steinsalz, Adin. 1988. *The Jerusalem Talmud.* Jerusalem: Israel Institute for Talmudic Publishing.

Steinsalz, Adin. 1998–2004. *The Babylonian Talmud.* Jerusalem: Israel Institute for Talmudic Publishing.

Stewart, George. 1975. *Names on the Globe.* New York: Oxford University Press.

Stewart, Pamela, and Andrew Strathern. 2003. *Landscape, Memory and History: Anthropological Perspectives.* London: Pluto.

Suleiman, Yasir. 2004. *A War of Words: Language and Conflict in the Middle East.* Cambridge: Cambridge University Press.

Swedenburg, Ted. 1990. "The Palestinian Peasant as National Signifier." *Anthropological Quarterly* 63:18–30.

Talmon-Heller, Daniella. 2002. "The Cited Tales of the Wondrous Doings of the Shaykhs of the Holy Land by Diya al-Din Abu Abd Allah Muhammad b. Abd al-Wahid al-Maqdisi (569/1173–643/1245): Text, Translation and Commentary." *Crusades* 1:111–54.

Tamari, Salim. 1999. "The Palestinian Society: Continuity and Change." In *The Palestinians in the Twentieth Century: A View from Within,* edited by Adel Manaa and Maya Sela, 31–61. Jerusalem: Van Leer Jerusalem Institute.

Tangherlini, Timothy R. 1990. "'It Happened Not Too Far from Here . . .': A Survey of Legend Theory and Characterization." *Western Folklore* 49 (4): 371–90.

Thompson, John B. 1987. "Language and Ideology: A Framework for Analysis." *Sociological Review* 35:516–35.

Thompson, Paul. 2009. "The Voice of the Past: Oral History." In *The Oral History Reader,* edited by Robert Perks and Alistair Thomson, 25–31. London: Routledge.

Thompson, Stith. 1955–1958. *Motif-Index of Folk Literature.* Bloomington: Indiana University Press.

Thornton, Thomas F. 1997. "Anthropological Studies of Native Place Naming." *American Indian Quarterly* 21 (2): 209–28.

Tilley, Christopher Y. 1994. *A Phenomenology of Landscape: Places, Paths and Monuments.* Oxford: Berg.

Toelken, Barre. 1979. *The Dynamics of Folklore.* Logan: Utah State University Press.

Toury, Gideon. 1988. "'Ivrut shemot mishpaḥa be-ereṣ Yisrae'el ke-targum sifruti.' Targil shildi be-misgeret ha-semiyoṭiqa shel ha-tarbut." In *Nequdat taṣpit: Tarbut ve-ḥevra be-ereṣ Yisrae'el,* edited by Nurit Graetz, 152–72. Tel Aviv: Open University.

Tuan, Yi-fu. 1974. *Topophilia: A Study of Environmental Perception Attitudes and Values.* Englewood Cliffs: Prentice-Hall.

Tuan, Yi-fu. 1991. "Language and the Making of Place: A Narrative Descriptive Approach." *Annals of the Association of American Geographers* 81 (4): 684–96.

Turner, Victor, and Edith L. B. Turner. 1978. *Image and Pilgrimage in Christian Culture, Dreams, Fields, and Metaphors—Symbolic Action in Human Society*. New York: Columbia University Press.

Twain, Mark. 1871. *The Innocents Abroad*. Hartford, CT: American Publishing Company.

Vico, Giambattista. 1968. *The New Science of Giambattista Vico*. Edited and translated by Thomas Goddard Bergin and Max Harold Fisch. Ithaca, NY: Cornell University Press.

Vilnai, Zeev, ed. 1977. *Ariel: Enṣiqlopedya le-yediʿat ha-areṣ*. 8 vols. Tel Aviv: Am Oved.

Vilnai, Zeev. 1955. *Shemot yishuveinu: Meqoroteihem ba-sifrut, ba-nof, ba-ʿavoda, ba-masoret u-be-qommemiyut Yisraʾel*. Tel Aviv: Masada.

Vilnai, Zeev. 1982a. "Shemot yishuvim ʿarviyyim." In *Ariel: Enṣiqlopedya le-yediʿat ha-areṣ*, edited by Zeev Vilnai, 9 (Supplement): 667–76. Tel Aviv: Am Oved.

Vilnai, Zeev. 1982b. "Shemot yishuvim ʿivriyyim." In *Ariel: Enṣiqlopedya le-yediʿat ha-areṣ*, edited by Zeev Vilnai, 9 (Supplement): 683–67. Tel Aviv: Am Oved.

al-Wāʾilī, ʿAbd al-Raḥmān. 2002. *Mawṣūʿat qabāʾil al-ʿarab*. Amman: Dār Usāma.

Whitelam, Keith W. 1996. *The Invention of Ancient Israel: The Silencing of Palestinian History*. London: Routledge.

Whorf, Benjamin Lee. 1964. *Language, Thought, and Reality: Selected Writings*. Cambridge, MA: MIT Press.

Wild, Stefan. 1988. "Palestinian Place-Names." In *Study in the History and Archaeology of Palestine, Proceedings of the First International Symposium on Palestine Antiquities*, vol. 3, 103–12. Aleppo: Aleppo University.

Yacobi, Haiem. 2004. "Whose Order, Whose Planning? Introduction." In *Constructing a Sense of Place: Architecture and the Zionist Discourse*, edited by Haiem Yacobi, 3–15. Aldershot: Ashgate.

Yalqut Shimoni. (1876–78) 1968. Edited by Simon of Frankfort. Jerusalem: n.p.

Yassif, Eli. 1999a. "Aggada ve-hisṭoria: Hisṭoryonim qorʾim be-aggadot ʿivriyot mi-yemei ha-beynayim." *Zion* 82:187–220.

Yassif, Eli. 1999b. *The Hebrew Folk Tale: History, Genre, Meaning*. Translated by Jacqueline S. Teitelbaum. Bloomington: Indiana University Press.

Yassif, Eli. 2005. "ʿAl maqom ve-zikaron: Aggadot maqom ba-tarbut ha-ʿaravit be-Yisraʾel." In *Aggada shel kfar*, edited by Yoram Meron, Riyad Kabha, and Rafiʿ Abu Riya, v–xv. Givat Haviva: Jewish-Arab Center for Peace.

Yassif, Eli. 2011. *Aggadot Ṣefat: Hayyim ve-fantasiya be-ʿir ha-mequbbalim*. Haifa: University of Haifa Press.

Yeoh, Brenda. 1996. "Street Naming and Nation-Building: Toponymic Inscriptions of Nationhood in Singapore." *Area* 28 (3): 298–307.

Young, Robert J. C. 2003. *Postcolonialism: A Very Short Introduction*. New York: Oxford University Press.

Zemon Davis, Natalie, and Randolph Starn. 1989. "Introduction to a Special Issue on Collective Memory and Counter-Memory." *Representations* 26:1–6.

Zerubavel, Yael. 1994. "Mot ha-zikaron ve-zikaron ha-mavet: Meṣada ve-ha-shoʾa ke-meṭaforot hisṭoriyot." *Alpayim* 10:42–67.

Zerubavel, Yael. 1995. *Recovered Roots: Collective Memory and the Making of Israeli National Tradition*. Chicago: University of Chicago Press.

Zerubavel, Yael. 2008. "Desert and Settlement—Space Metaphors and Symbolic Landscapes in the Yishuv and Early Israeli Culture." In *Jewish Topographies—Visions of Space, Traditions of Place*, edited by Julia Baruch, Anna Lipphardt, and Alexander Nocke, 201–22. Aldershot: Ashgate.

Zinkin, Vivian. 1984. "The Generic Component in West Jersey Place Names." *Names* 32 (3): 252–66.

Ziv, Yehuda. 2005. *Regaʿ shel maqom: Sippurim meʾaḥorei shemot meqomot*. Jerusalem: Tzivʾonim.

Zuckermandel, Simon, ed. (1881) 1963. *Tosefta ʿal Masekhet Ḥullin*. Jerusalem: Wahrmann.

al-Zuḥaylī, Wahba. 1985. *al-Fiqh al-islāmī wa-adillatuhu*. Vol. 1. Damascus: Dār al-Fikr.

Zvinashe, Mamvura, Itai Muwati, and Davi E. Mutasa. 2018. "'Toponymic Commemoration Is Not for One Sex': The Gender Politics of Place Renaming in Harare." *African Identities* 16 (4): 429–43.

AMER DAHAMSHE currently teaches at the Arab Academic College of Education in Israel-Haifa and is a research fellow at the University of Haifa. His first book, *A Local Habitation and a Name: A New Literary and Cultural Reading of the Arabic Geographical Names of the Land*, was published in Hebrew, and he is editor (with Yossef Schwartz) of *Place-Names and Spatial Identity in Israel-Palestine Majority-Minority Relation, Oblivion, and Memory*. Amer currently resides in Kafr Kannā.

For Indiana University Press

Sabrina Black, Editorial Assistant

Lesley Bolton, Project Manager/Editor

Anna Francis, Assistant Acquisitions Editor

Anna Garnai, Production Coordinator

Samantha Heffner, Marketing Production Manager

Katie Huggins, Production Manager

Alyssa Nicole Lucas, Marketing and Publicity Manager

Annie L. Martin, Editorial Director

Dan Pyle, Online Publishing Manager

Jennifer L. Wilder, Senior Artist and Book Designer